L

DISCARD

A Brief History of Germany

A BRIEF HISTORY OF GERMANY

JASON P. COY

Facts On File
An imprint of Infobase Publishing

A Brief History of Germany

Facts On File, Inc.
An imprint of Infobase Publishing
132 West 31st Street
New York NY 10001

Library of Congress Cataloging-in-Publication Data

Coy, Jason Philip, 1970–
  A brief history of Germany / Jason Philip Coy.
      p. cm.
  Includes bibliographical references and index.
  ISBN 978-0-8160-8142-4
  1. Germany—History. 2. Germany. I. Title.
  DD17.C69 2011
  943—dc22   2010023139

Text design by Joan M. McEvoy
Maps by Dale Williams
Composition by Hermitage Publishing Services
Cover printed by Art Print, Taylor, PA
Book printed and bound by Maple Press, York, PA
Date printed: December 2010
Printed in the United States of America

10 9 8 7 6 5 4 3 2 1

This book is printed on acid-free paper.

*To my parents for inspiring my love of history
and to my wife, Amy, for her tireless support of my research.*

CONTENTS

LIST OF ILLUSTRATIONS

LIST OF MAPS

LIST OF ABBREVIATIONS

ADAV	General German Workers' Association (Allgemeiner deutscher Arbeiterverein)
BDF	Federation of German Womens' Associations (Bund deutscher Frauenvereine)
BRD	Federal Republic of Germany (Bundesrepublik Deutschland)
CDU	Christian Democratic Union
CSU	Christian Social Union
DNVP	German National People's Party (Deutschnationale Volkspartei)
DVP	German People's Party (Deutsche Volkspartei)
EC	European Community
EEC	European Economic Community
EU	European Union
FDJ	Free German Youth (Freie Deutsche Jugend)
FDP	Free Democratic Party
GDR	German Democratic Republic
IMF	International Monetary Fund
ISAF	International Security Assistance Force
KPD	Communist Party of Germany (Kommunistische Partei Deutschlands)
NATO	North Atlantic Treaty Organization
NSDAP	National Socialist German Workers' Party or Nazi Party (Nationalsozialistische Deutsche Arbeiterpartei)
RAF	Red Army Faction (Rote Armee Fraktion, or Baader-Meinhof Gruppe)
SA	Assault Division (Sturmabteilung)
SAPD	Socialist Workers' Party of Germany (Sozialistische Arbeiterpartei Deutschlands)
SDAP	Social Democratic Workers' Party of Germany (Sozialdemokratische Arbeiterpartei Deutschlands)
SED	Socialist Unity Party (Sozialistische Einheitspartei Deutschlands)
SPD	Social Democratic Party of Germany (Sozialdemokratische Partei Deutschlands)

SS	Protection Squadron (Schutzstaffel)
UN	United Nations
USPD	Independent Social Democratic Party of Germany (Unabhängige Sozialdemokratische Partei Deutschlands)
WTO	Warsaw Treaty Organization

ACKNOWLEDGMENTS

This project owes scholarly debts to a trio of friends and mentors. First, I would like to take the opportunity to thank Mary Lindemann for encouraging me to take on this project and for her ongoing support of my research endeavors. I would also like to thank David Sabean for training me as a historian and for inspiring my interest in the history and culture of Germany, including the rustic pleasures of Swabian cuisine. Finally, I owe a debt of gratitude to Rich Bodek, my colleague at the College of Charleston, who read every word of my manuscript and provided me with invaluable advice and guidance.

I would also like to thank three members of the editorial staff at Facts On File, Claudia Schaab, Melissa Cullen-DuPont, and Alexandra Lo Re, for their continual encouragement and support. Their careful editorial attention to the project has improved this work considerably.

Finally, I would like to thank three institutions for their permission to reproduce the images that appear in the book: Art Resource (New York), the Bildarchiv Preussischer Kulturbesitz (Berlin), and the Bundesarchiv (Germany).

INTRODUCTION

While Germany has a history that stretches back to antiquity, it is important to remember that it was first unified as a nation-state only in 1871, making it in a sense even younger than the United States. Located in the heart of Europe, without natural boundaries, Germany has experienced centuries of immigration, confrontation, and negotiation. Consequently, the arrangement of its constituent parts has changed repeatedly, with individual territories joining together or breaking apart. Thus, Germany's boundaries, and what it means to be German, have always been unstable and have evolved continually throughout the region's long and troubled history.

Situated along ancient migration routes, the area known today as Germany has become home to an endless stream of migrants since prehistoric times. In fact, paleontologists have recovered traces of early hominid habitation in Germany going back almost 50 million years, as distant ancestors of modern humans migrated there from Africa. During the last ice age, extinct relatives of humans called Neanderthals, named after the German valley where their remains were first discovered, followed these earliest migrants into the region. They were joined around 40,000 years ago by another group of migrants, early humans known as Cro-Magnons, who lived alongside them in the area that comprises modern Germany. Remarkably, some of the most important archaeological finds relating to these prehistoric peoples have been made in Germany within the last few years. These recent discoveries have even prompted some archaeologists to think that an area on the Swabian Alb in southern Germany may have been where early humans first discovered music, and perhaps even art itself, around 35,000 years ago.

During the Bronze Age, beginning in the third millennium B.C.E., Celtic peoples migrated into the area and built their own sprawling civilization in central Europe, one that lasted centuries. The actual historical record, however, does not begin in Germany until the so-called Migration Period, when Greek and Roman writers first described the inhabitants of the region. During this turbulent time, from roughly 300 to 500 C.E., nomadic peoples speaking Germanic languages—including the tongues that would one day develop into modern German and

English—migrated into the area now known as Germany from the east, encountering the Celtic peoples already living there. In the centuries that followed, these warlike Germanic tribes gradually supplanted the Celts and encroached upon the Roman Empire along its Rhine and Danube frontiers. For the Romans, the fierce peoples across their borders, inhabitants of a shadowy land they called Germania, were frightening barbarians bent on destruction. However, modern scholarship presents a different picture of the Germanic tribes, accentuating the role they played in creating the hybrid civilization that prevailed in medieval Europe after the collapse of Roman imperial administration.

After the collapse of Roman authority in the western provinces in the late 400s C.E., one of these Germanic peoples, the Franks, gradually brought the various Germanic tribes under their authority and Christianized the remaining pagans in the region. Frankish rulers, including the famous Charlemagne, portrayed themselves as heirs of the Roman emperors and, in the 800s C.E., established the foundations of the Holy Roman Empire. The empire, a decentralized imperial institution that bound the individual Germanic duchies into a loose confederation, would dominate political life in central Europe until modern times. After Charlemagne, the Carolingian Empire dissolved, fragmenting into several diverse kingdoms. The eastern portion of the Frankish realm, where a Germanic language was spoken, became a distinct kingdom under a Carolingian ruler known as Louis the German. The creation of a Germanic state in central Europe, whose rulers would inherit the crown of the Holy Roman Empire, was an important milestone in the development of German identity, as language and political allegiance fused.

During the medieval and early modern eras, the imperial structure provided the fragmented German territories with an administrative and legal framework, while preserving the liberty of hundreds of individual German princes and towns. The unity of the Holy Roman Empire was shattered, however, during the 16th century, with Martin Luther's protest against the Catholic Church. This dramatic event, a turning point in German and global history, split Germany and eventually all of Europe into rival confessional camps, Protestant and Catholic. The nadir of this religious strife was reached in the 17th century, when the Thirty Years' War plunged central Europe into decades of warfare and misery. In the wake of this ruinous struggle, one that saw the territorial monarchies of Europe wage their wars on German soil, plaguing her with rapacious mercenary armies, the empire was left devastated, with large areas depopulated. The Thirty Years' War greatly diminished the power and prestige of the Holy Roman Emperor and destroyed the delicate balance within the empire between imperial authority and territorial autonomy. Thus, the empire no longer functioned as a confederation of principalities, but rather became the arena for a struggle for dominance by a few powerful princes. In this competition, the centralized, militarized state of Prussia emerged as the dominant power in northern Germany, with Austria, the ancestral home of the Habsburg emperors, the most powerful principality in the south. These developments would have dire consequences for Germany in the modern era, as German nationalism took on autocratic and militaristic overtones.

The modern period was ushered into Germany by Napoléon's revolutionary armies, who helped facilitate the collapse of the venerable Holy Roman Empire and the foundation of an ambitious German nation-state in its place. In 1806, during the Napoleonic Wars, the French dissolved the Holy Roman Empire and spread revolutionary, nationalist ideals within Germany. After the defeat of Napoléon, the German states were joined in the Austrian-led German Confederation, a loose alliance established in 1815 by the Congress of Vienna in a futile attempt to restore the old political order in central Europe. The rise of Prussia, an aggressive military powerhouse, led to the declaration of a German empire in 1871, a unified Germany ruled by a Prussian monarch. Under Prussian leadership, Germany underwent rapid industrialization, and militant German nationalism flourished in the late 19th century. The reckless ambition of the Prussian ruling house and Germany's delayed unification prompted the new German nation to demand inclusion among the major powers of Europe, pressures that contributed to the outbreak of World War I. World War I proved a disaster for Germany, and the peace afterward, a disaster for the world. According to the punitive Treaty of Versailles, Germany was forced to accept a series of crushing and humiliating terms. The trauma of war ending in defeat fostered a combination of political discontent and economic depression in the country that crippled the fledgling postwar regime, the ill-fated Weimar Republic, Germany's first democratic government.

Germany's first experiment with democratic government proved abortive, ending in tragedy in 1933. Amid political and economic chaos, the National Socialist German Workers' Party, a radical fascist group, took control in Germany after their fanatical leader, Adolf Hitler, was appointed chancellor. Under autocratic Nazi leadership, Germany descended into a nightmare of totalitarian dictatorship and racist oppression of its Jewish citizens. In the end, Hitler's "Thousand Year Reich" lasted only a decade but brought the Germans catastrophic defeat in World War II and the genocidal madness of the Holocaust. After the war, the victorious Allies partitioned the smoldering wreckage of Germany, a division that was ossified during the cold war. The U.S., British, and French zones of occupation were combined to establish the Federal Republic of Germany, or West Germany, in 1949, with the German Democratic Republic (East Germany) forming in the Soviet zone. While West Germany returned to democratic government and joined the North Atlantic Treaty Organization (NATO) and the European Union, East Germany was part of the Soviet-controlled Warsaw Pact, its isolation from the West symbolized by the Berlin Wall. In 1989, in the course of the peaceful Wende revolution, the East German government collapsed and the wall came down. In 1990, East Germany was reunited with West Germany, forming today's unified, federal democracy.

Having emerged from the trauma of its past, today's Germany is a federal parliamentary republic, with its capital and largest city in Berlin. Having experienced mass immigration from Eastern Europe and the Mediterranean region, Germany is a multicultural society, and in 1999, the German Parliament passed a new citizenship law that made it easier for long-term, foreign-born residents to acquire German citizenship. Having taken its place among the leading nations of the world, a confident, reunified Germany is a prominent member of the United Nations, NATO, and the G8 an economic powerhouse boasting the world's third-largest economy. Germany's growing economic might is increasingly matched by its diplomatic importance, and this modern democracy maintains a key position in European affairs and supports a multitude of close partnerships on a global level. After centuries of autocratic rule, imperial and totalitarian, the new Germany has embraced liberal democracy. Its history marred by episodes of shameful oppression of racial and ethnic minorities, the country has now reformed, and its citizens live under the rule of law. Finally, having experienced centuries of disunity, dissension, and division, the German people have come together to found a new Germany based upon a shared identity as citizens, unified not by purity of blood but by a shared set of civic values. In the chapters that follow, we will trace this remarkable historical journey in greater detail, exploring 2,000 years of tragedies and triumphs, experiences that created today's Germany.

1

PREHISTORIC GERMANY

In June 2009, German archaeologists working at the Hohle Fels site near the south German city of Ulm announced an astonishing discovery. They had excavated three flutes crafted by early humans during the last ice age. Radiocarbon dating indicates that these fragile instruments were fashioned between 35,000 and 40,000 years ago. One carved from bird bone and two from mammoth ivory, these artifacts provide the earliest evidence of music in human history. The Hohle Fels Cave, a fascinating source of information about humankind's earliest ancestors, has also yielded traces of the first figurative sculpture yet uncovered, including carvings of humans, horses, and fantastic beasts. Thus, the caves of southwestern Germany may have been the first place on Earth to resonate with the sound of music, the first where humans crafted representations of people and animals.

Having emerged in Africa and gradually moved into Eurasia, the early humans who fashioned these artifacts were recent migrants to the area around Hohle Fels Cave, where they seem to have invented both art and music—distinctive aspects of human culture—soon after their arrival. These early humans settled alongside the original inhabitants of the region, their genetic cousins the Neanderthals, and eventually supplanted them. The *Homo sapiens* who inhabited the Hohle Fels Cave were just the first of a long line of peoples who migrated into the area known today as Germany during its tumultuous history.

Land and Water

Located in the heart of central Europe, crossed by a trio of great rivers, the Rhine, Danube, and Elbe, and lacking natural barriers to migration or invasion, the region now known as Germany has been home to a great variety of peoples. For most of its history, Germany was a fragmented land with fluid borders, open to the movement of peoples, and subject to centuries of unremitting warfare and political instability.

Accordingly, through the centuries, Germany's constituent parts have come together or pulled apart repeatedly, and its linguistic, cultural, and political boundaries have expanded or contracted accordingly. Thus, Germany's boundaries, and German identity itself, have always been in flux, and both have been constructed differently in different eras.

The area that now makes up Germany covers 137,847 square miles in central Europe. This is an area slightly smaller than that of the state of Montana in the United States of America. Southern Germany has a mountainous elevation, which gradually slopes to the marshy flatlands along the country's northern coast. Accordingly, Germany's highest elevation is in the mountainous alpine region in the south, where the country's tallest peak, the Zugspitze, towers at 9,718 feet. Its lowest elevations are along the shores of the North Sea in the northwest and the Baltic Sea in the northeast. Between the Alps and the coast lie the forested uplands of central Germany and the low-lying marshlands of northern Germany. These areas are watered by some of the greatest rivers of Europe, most notably the Rhine, Danube, and Elbe.

Germany's landscape changes quite dramatically from the northern coastline to the alpine areas in the south. The northern third of the country is a broad, flat plain. A series of mighty rivers, including the Elbe, Ems, Weser, and Oder, crosses this fertile region. Along the northwestern coast, near the Dutch border, lie many rich wetlands marked by significant biodiversity. Central Germany, on the other hand, is drier than the north and marked by a rough, hilly countryside. The landscape here is cut by the Rhine River valley in the west and punctuated throughout by a series of upland regions. West of the Rhine, these include mountainous regions known as the Eifel and the Hunsrück, as well as the densely forested and mountainous areas of the Palatinate region. Other mountainous areas in central Germany include the Taunus hills north of Frankfurt, the Vogelsberg Massif, the Rhön Mountains, and the Thüringer Wald, a hilly, forested region. The eastern part of central Germany, including the Spreewald, features areas with sandy soil and river wetlands. Finally, southern Germany is dominated by mountain ranges, including the Swabian and Franconian Alb and the alpine territory that ranges along the country's southern border. On the southwestern border with France, the Black Forest separates the Rhine from the headwaters of the Danube.

Germany's moderate climate is determined by its northern latitude, which is roughly parallel to southern Canada but is ameliorated by the effects of the Atlantic Gulf Stream. Thus, in the northern, coastal regions of Germany, a mild maritime climate predominates, caused by

Topographic Map of Germany

warm westerly winds off the North Sea. To the south, a continental climate prevails throughout most of Germany, with greater seasonal change marked by warmer summers and colder winters. In the southern, alpine areas, a mountain climate is present, with the altitude causing colder temperatures and increased precipitation. Germany's annual mean temperature is around 48 degrees Fahrenheit, about the same as the state of Iowa in the United States. Germany's maritime region in the north experiences fewer weather extremes, with more diurnal and seasonal variation in the southern part of the country than in the north. Thus, in the coldest month, January, the average temperature is around 35 degrees Fahrenheit in the north of Germany and only about 28 degrees in the southern parts. Likewise, in July, the warmest month, the average temperature in northern Germany is a moderate 63 degrees, whereas in the south it averages around 66 degrees. Germany receives ample rainfall, with annual precipitation averaging between 23 and 31 inches, about the same amount as the U.S. state of Minnesota.

The Earliest Inhabitants
The Neanderthals

Throughout its history, the fertile region situated at the heart of central Europe, known today as Germany, has attracted repeated waves of migrants. Located at the crossroads of ancient migration routes with few natural barriers to the movement of peoples, it has been home to a variety of cultures. The first of these migrants were the Neanderthals, cousins of modern-day humans who found the land in the grip of the Ice Age.

As Ice Age glaciers retreated from Europe, about 130,000 years ago, bands of Neanderthals, hominid cousins of anatomically modern humans who likely emerged in Africa half a million years ago, began to wander into the Continent, eventually making their way to central Europe. The Neanderthals were a hardy, robust species closely related to modern humans, well adapted to survive amid the harsh conditions of a glacial environment. The Neanderthals are named after the Neander Valley in Germany, near Düsseldorf, where their remains were first discovered in 1856. Neanderthals spread throughout Eurasia, ranging from western Europe to central Asia and from the Low Countries to the shores of the Mediterranean. They died out in Europe, perhaps on Gibraltar, around 30,000 years ago, most likely falling victim to a changing environment and competition from more recent arrivals on the Continent, the more adaptable early humans.

Analysis of Neanderthal sites located in Germany that were discovered in the last century has given scholars a fascinating view into their culture. With a cranial capacity similar to anatomically modern humans, Neanderthals crafted sophisticated stone tools for bringing down game and butchering meat. They also made use of fire in their cave-dwellings. Paleontologists who have examined the Neanderthal

THE NEANDER VALLEY DISCOVERY AND THE ORIGINS OF MODERN PALEOANTHROPOLOGY

The discovery of the first Neanderthal remains in a quarry in 1856 not only changed 19th-century humans' understanding of their origins but also helped spawn a new field of science. In August 1856, miners working in a limestone quarry in the Neander Valley near Düsseldorf found a collection of strange bones in a cave. The laborers took the heavy bones, including a skull cap, several ribs, fragments of a pelvis, a shoulder blade, and various pieces of arm and leg bones, to a local teacher and naturalist, Johann Carl Fuhlrott (1803–77), thinking they were the remains of a bear. Fuhlrott had studied the natural sciences as an undergraduate and soon recognized the potential significance of the find. Having identified the remains as human bones, but of an unusual type, Fuhlrott delivered them to an anatomist at the University of Bonn, Hermann Schaafhausen (1816–93). Positing that the bones were those of an ancient strain of humans, distinct from modern man, Fuhlrott and Schaafhausen announced the discovery of the remains a year later, but the find, seemingly contradicting Scripture, only spawned controversy. By 1864, however, with the dissemination of Charles Darwin's (1809–82) theory of evolution, the remains fostered the recognition among scientists that a new species of prehistoric human had been discovered. An Irish geologist proposed the name *Homo neanderthalensis* for the new species, in recognition of the site of the discovery of "Neanderthal 1" in Germany's Neander Valley.

While earlier finds of Neanderthal remains were subsequently identified, it was the 1856 discovery in the Neander Valley that prompted the identification of this new species of human. The workmen's discovery outside Düsseldorf in 1856, three years before the publication of Charles Darwin's pathbreaking work, *On the Origin of Species,* also helped give birth to the science of paleoanthropology, which studies the fossil remains of prehistoric humans. Since the original discovery in the Neander Valley, paleoanthropologists have identified the remains of several hundred other Neanderthals, greatly expanding current knowledge of the species.

In 1999, paleoanthropology returned to its roots when scientists rediscovered the original site where Neanderthal 1 was found in 1856. At the site, they found new bone fragments. Incredibly, one of these bone fragments fit together perfectly with one of the bones found in 1856, helping to complete the Neanderthal 1 skeleton 140 years after the original discovery.

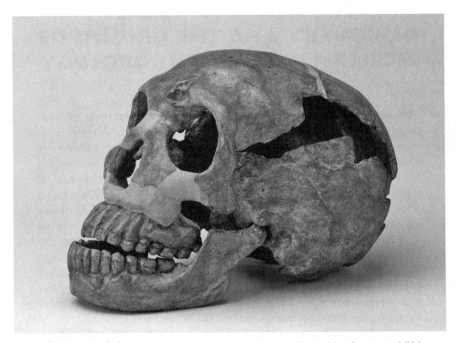

Skull of a Neanderthal (Bildarchiv Preussischer Kulturbesitz, Berlin / Art Resource, NY / Museum für Vor- und Frühgeschichte, Staatliche Museen zu Berlin / Klaus Göken)

remains suggest that these hominids probably had a spoken language, facilitating cooperation within their small hunting parties and the development of complex cultural forms. It seems, for example, that they practiced ritual burials involving grave goods, suggesting some sort of concept of an afterlife.

In 2006, on the 150th anniversary of the discovery of the first Neanderthal fossil, the Max Planck Institute for Evolutionary Anthropology in Leipzig, Germany, announced an exciting new endeavor that will shed new light on these prehistoric Europeans. In collaboration with the 454 Life Sciences Corporation of Branford, Connecticut, scientists from the Max Planck Institute for Evolutionary Anthropology are working to extract Neanderthal DNA and to sequence the species' entire genome, made up of about 3 billion base pairs. Preliminary results suggest that the DNA of Neanderthals and modern humans is more than 99 percent identical, and thus the project promises to shed new light on the development of modern humans and to uncover whether Neanderthals interbred with *Homo sapiens* before disappearing as a distinct species.

Arrival of *Homo sapiens* in Germany

Anatomically modern *Homo sapiens* migrated into the area that is now Europe during the last ice age and began living alongside their Neanderthal cousins in Germany. Paleontologists now use the term "early modern humans" to describe these ancestors of contemporary humans. However, they were once commonly referred to as Cro-Magnons, after the site in France where their fossils were first discovered in 1868. Early modern humans first appeared in Africa sometime around 200,000 years ago and began to migrate out of Africa about 100,000 years ago, gradually spreading throughout the Middle East and from there into Europe.

These early humans were quite similar to Neanderthals anatomically, although more slightly built, but exhibited a richer material culture than their burly hominid relatives. *Homo sapiens* fashioned more sophisticated flaked tools than the Neanderthals and created art, including beautiful cave paintings and sculptures of both humans and animals. The most famous of these carvings have been discovered in Austria and Germany, rich depositories of early human culture. Thought to have been part of fertility rites, the most prominent of these sculptures depict women with exaggerated sexual features and thus are often called Venus figurines. The first of these to be discovered was the so-called Venus of Willendorf, a small limestone sculpture dating from around 23,000 B.C.E. that was found in Austria in 1908.

More recently, in September 2008, another Venus figurine was discovered in Hohle Fels, the cave where the prehistoric flutes carved from bird bone and mammoth ivory were found. At this fascinating site, archaeologists from Tübingen University uncovered a stylized sculpture of a woman

The Venus of Willendorf (Bildarchiv Preussischer Kulturbesitz, Berlin / Art Resource, NY / Naturhistorisches Museum, Vienna / Lutz Braun)

that is recognized as the oldest known example of representational art. This figurine, known as the Venus of Hohle Fels or, alternatively, as the Venus of Schelklingen, dates from the earliest appearance of *Homo sapiens* in Europe, between 35,000 and 40,000 years ago. The region where this mammoth-ivory sculpture was discovered, the Swabian Alb, has yielded other figurines—and several musical instruments—from the same period. This has prompted some scholars to suggest that this area may have been the first to exhibit several characteristic human behaviors, including fully articulated figurative art, instrumental music, and perhaps even religion itself, given the purported ritualistic function of the fertility fetishes found at the site.

The Neolithic Revolution

The last ice age ended around 10,000 years ago, and the Mesolithic period began, a time when small groups of *Homo sapiens* roamed through central Europe, hunting and gathering in order to procure their food. These Mesolithic hunter-gatherers practiced this nomadic way of life for several millennia, until agriculture began to transform human life in the area that is now called Germany. During the Neolithic period, which lasted from around 5000 to 3500 B.C.E., people living in prehistoric Germany gradually developed the ability to raise crops and animals, revolutionizing their relationship with their environment. As Neolithic humans turned from finding food to producing it through farming and herding animals, they eventually stopped roving in search of game and edible plants and established settled societies in northern central Europe. The transition to agriculture was gradual, and the start of the Neolithic period varies by area. Despite such regional variation, it appears that by the sixth millennium B.C.E., groups of foragers in many areas of north-central Europe had begun to settle seasonally along lakes and rivers, including the wetlands along the Rhine in Germany, where they relied upon rudimentary farming along with traditional forms of hunting and fishing.

Between 5400 and 5000 B.C.E., one of these prehistoric peoples, known as the Linear Pottery culture after the distinctive decoration of its ceramic ware, settled in central Europe and then gradually began producing its own food through herding and farming. Important archaeological sites in Germany, including several along the Danube, Elbe, and Rhine, have greatly increased current knowledge about this period, yielding ceramics, stone implements, and flint tools produced by both Mesolithic and Neolithic peoples.

One important archaeological site on the shores of a glacial lake in lower Saxony known as the Dümmer has given a unique view into life in prehistoric Germany. Along the shores of this lake, a series of archaeological strata demonstrate the gradual transition from foraging to food production, known as the Neolithic Revolution, crucial to the advent of human civilization. Three separate sites, occupied between 4900 and 3600 B.C.E., have been uncovered on the Dümmersee. The first shows no signs of either herding or farming, while the second and third, associated with the so-called Funnel Beaker culture, also named for the people's distinctive ceramics, provide ample evidence of these activities. By around 3900 B.C.E., these Funnel Beaker peoples had introduced agriculture throughout northern Germany, most notably along the Baltic coast and lake basins near Mecklenburg.

The Beaker culture persisted into the Bronze Age, which succeeded the Neolithic period in the late third millennium B.C.E. and lasted north of the Alps until around 600 B.C.E. A diverse period, the Bronze Age was marked by a variety of different cultures in the area and the development of more stratified societies that worked metal. One important site of the Unetice culture, which flourished between about 1800 and 1600 B.C.E., located at Sömmerda, near Erfurt, Germany, has afforded scholars an interesting look at life in early Bronze Age Germany. At the Sömmerda excavation, archaeologists have uncovered a rich burial site that included grave goods fashioned from gold, protected by a massive stone cairn, a demonstration of the sophistication of the people who erected it.

Celtic Germany

The most widespread and advanced culture that called Germany home during the prehistoric period was the Celts, a remarkable people who came to the region at some point during the Bronze Age and remained there until the classical period, when Greek and Roman writers described their civilization. Linguistic and archaeological evidence indicates that at their peak Celtic peoples, dominant in central Europe throughout this period, were spread throughout Europe from Spain to Hungary, and from Ireland to the Mediterranean. While their origins are obscure, some scholars argue that a people known as the Urnfeld culture, because they cremated their dead and buried them in urns, may have been the ancestors of the Celts who lived in central Europe.

The Urnfeld culture was dominant in northern Germany and the Low Countries during the late Bronze Age, from around 1200 to 700 B.C.E. While there are no written records or linguistic evidence to conclusively determine the ethnic origins of the Urnfeld peoples, many

9

scholars speculate that this culture in fact gave rise to the Celts. In any case, by around 500 B.C.E., the Urnfeld culture gave way to several other civilizations in central Europe that were almost certainly Celtic. The first of these is an early Iron Age civilization known as the Hallstatt culture. The Hallstatt flourished from around 800 to 450 B.C.E. and are named after one of their sites discovered in modern Austria. The Hallstatt culture died out around 450 B.C.E., during the late Iron Age, giving way to the La Tène culture, a vibrant civilization that spread as far as Ireland and Anatolia. The Celts likely stemmed from these powerful Iron Age peoples, forging their own dynamic civilization in turn.

The Celts were a tribal society geared toward war. Celtic warriors, led by a bellicose military aristocracy, were feared throughout the classical world for the ferocity of their attacks and frequency of their raids. In 390 B.C.E., a Celtic tribe, the Gauls, even sacked the mighty city of Rome, extorting a staggering ransom from its humbled citizens. Their society was tribal and clan-based, founded upon a rigid hierarchy of warrior aristocrats, druids (practitioners of a mysterious animist religion), and commoners. Interestingly, Celtic women enjoyed more autonomy than either their Roman or Greek contemporaries, serving as warriors and even as rulers in some cases. The Celts were pastoralists, with herds of cattle as the primary form of wealth and source of sustenance within a tribal gift economy.

Celtic bronze helmet from the La Tène period
(Bildarchiv Preussischer Kulturbesitz, Berlin / Art Resource, NY / Keltenmuseum, Hallein / Herbert Kraft)

While Celtic culture persisted into historical times in much of northern and central Europe, the Celts have left few inscriptions. Thus, the best sources for understanding their culture remain the biased, often negative descriptions written by classical authors from Greece and Rome. The most detailed account available today is the *Commentarii de bello Gallico (Commentaries on the Gallic War)*, written by Julius Caesar (100–44 B.C.E.) in the first century B.C.E. In this famous, and self-aggrandizing, description of his conquest of the region the Romans called Gaul (modern-day France, Luxembourg, and Belgium), the future emperor provides interesting ethnographic descriptions of Celtic society in areas of what is today German-speaking Europe.

Caesar's expedition into Gaul, and his conquest of the Celtic peoples there, was prompted by growing disruption along the Roman frontier, caused in part by the arrival of the Germanic tribes in central Europe. A Celtic tribe allied with Rome, the Aedui, had been defeated by its tribal enemies and called upon the Romans for help. A warlike Germanic people known as the Suebi, who had recently migrated into the region, had joined in the attack on the Aedui, further angering the Romans. Meanwhile, the Helvetii, a Celtic people whose homeland was on the Swiss plateau, had begun their own mass migration to live among allied tribes, pressured by the incursions of Germanic tribes from the northeast who were migrating into their territory. All of these events instigated instability, threatening the Roman frontier in Cisalpine Gaul and prompting a military expedition under Caesar's command in 58 B.C.E. to crush the Helvetii and the Suebi. Over the next several years, Caesar waged a series of brutal campaigns against the Celtic and Germanic tribes of the region. These campaigns eventually extended the Roman Empire to the North Sea coast, with the conquest of the Belgae. Caesar even invaded Celtic Britain in 55 B.C.E. After this invasion, Caesar returned to Gaul, where he put down a pair of revolts in occupied territory, the first led by the Celtic chieftain Ambiorix of the Eburones. The second, larger revolt, in 52 B.C.E., was led by Vercingetorix of the Arverni, who had managed to unite many of the Celtic tribes in Gaul against the Romans. Having countered these grave threats, the conquest of Gaul was complete.

In *Commentaries on the Gallic War,* Caesar provides an account of these campaigns, waged between 58 and 50 B.C.E., as well as a unique view into the mysterious Celtic societies that dominated northern Europe, including the area that is today Germany. According to Caesar, the fiercest Celts were those farthest removed from the civilizing influence of the Romans and closest to their dangerous, ancestral enemies, the Germanic tribes who "dwelt beyond the Rhine." Caesar maintained that the Celtic bands that had the least contact with the Roman merchants who traded in the area and engaged instead in constant tribal warfare with the Germans were the fiercest:

> *All Gaul is divided into three parts, one of which the Belgae inhabit, the Aquitani another, those who in their own language are called Celts, in ours, Gauls, the third. All these differ from*

> each other in language, customs and laws. The river Garonne
> separates the Gauls from the Aquitani; the Marne and the
> Seine separate them from the Belgae. Of all these, the Belgae
> are the bravest, because they are furthest from the civilization
> and refinement of [our] Province, and merchants least fre-
> quently resort to them, and import those things which tend to
> effeminate the mind; and they are the nearest to the Germans,
> who dwell beyond the Rhine, with whom they are continually
> waging war; for which reason the Helvetii also surpass the
> rest of the Gauls in valor, as they contend with the Germans
> in almost daily battles, when they either repel them from their
> own territories, or themselves wage war on their frontiers.
> (Caesar in M'Devitta 1853: 1–2)

In his account of his campaigns in Gaul, Caesar provides a sort of proto-ethnographic analysis of the Celts who inhabited the region, detailing their political, social, and religious customs. His account is heavily biased and often distorted by negative portrayals of his Celtic enemies. However, it provides modern readers with an invaluable view on Roman attitudes toward this shadowy people, and affords a few priceless insights into their customs. For example, Caesar remarks on the clan-based social organization practiced by the Gallic Celts. He describes the egalitarian nature of their tribal society, marked by loose war-bands governed by chieftains who distinguished themselves in battle and cemented the loyalty of their tribe through lavish gifts and ritual feasting, impressions confirmed by recent excavations of Celtic burial sites. Archaeologists have discovered the remains of Celtic chieftains buried with hoards of weapons, war chariots strewn with valuables, and stacks of massive drinking horns, equipped for fighting and feasting in the afterlife.

The religion of the Celts has proven more elusive than their social organization, and Caesar was mystified by Celtic religiosity, controlled by a mysterious priestly class, the druids. Druidic religion was preserved orally, handed down through the centuries, and scholars can say little conclusively about its nature. Roman accounts, however, give some ideas about its essential features. The privileges and religious functions of the druids were of particular interest to Caesar. For this Roman military commander, it is the druids' utility in encouraging Gallic warriors to display valor on the battlefield that is of the most importance:

> The druids do not go to war, nor pay tribute together with
> the rest; they have an exemption from military service and a
> dispensation in all matters. Induced by such great advantages,
> many embrace this profession of their own accord, and [many]
> are sent to it by their parents and relations. They are said there

to learn by heart a great number of verses; accordingly some remain in the course of training twenty years. Nor do they regard it lawful to commit these to writing, though in almost all other matters, in their public and private transactions, they use Greek characters. That practice they seem to me to have adopted for two reasons; because they neither desire their doctrines to be divulged among the mass of the people, nor those who learn, to devote themselves the less to the efforts of memory, relying on writing; since it generally occurs to most men, that, in their dependence on writing, they relax their diligence in learning thoroughly, and their employment of the memory.

They wish to inculcate as one of their leading tenets that souls do not become extinct, but pass after death from one body to another, and they think that men by this tenet are in a great degree excited to valor, the fear of death being disregarded. They likewise discuss and impart to the youth many things respecting the stars and their motion, respecting the extent of the world and of our earth, respecting the nature of things, respecting the power and the majesty of the immortal gods. (Caesar in M'Devitta 1853: 147–148)

According to Roman authorities such as Pliny the Elder (ca. 23 C.E.–79 C.E.), it appears that the druids functioned as both priests and monks, presiding over religious rites and preserving Celtic religious lore by memorizing hundreds of sacred verses. The druids likely practiced animism, the worship of nature spirits, worshipping in sacred oak groves strewn with mistletoe. Apparently, the druids preached a belief in a form of reincarnation, which Caesar viewed mainly in its role in inciting Celtic warriors to battlefield valor. The Romans also described the druids as soothsayers, who foretold the future by observing the flight of birds and through the ritual sacrifice of animals and enjoyed tremendous prestige within Celtic society. According to many Roman observers, the druids also practiced human sacrifice. While archaeological finds have not provided conclusive evidence of such practices, Roman authorities suppressed the druidic religion in the second century B.C.E. on the basis of their revulsion of supposed human sacrifice. The ancient faith of the Celts died out in the following century, and not a single written record of this oral religion survives.

Caesar's campaigns in Gaul scattered the once mighty Celtic tribes who had dominated the region since the Bronze Age. Subjugated by the Romans, the Celts were left vulnerable to the incursions of a new wave of migrants into central Europe. These warlike newcomers, the Germanic tribes, were to play a dominant role in the history of the region and gave Germany its language and its modern name.

2

GERMANIA: BARBARIAN GERMANY

While Julius Caesar and his legions humbled the Celts during his Gallic campaign, a warlike people who migrated into the region from the east during the first century B.C.E. proved more difficult for the Romans to bring to heel. Across the Roman frontier that ran along the Rhine and the Danube, these peoples, known as the Germanic tribes, built a society marked by its egalitarian nature and martial power. Fearing the military threat posed by these belligerent tribes, the Romans invaded their homeland in 12 B.C.E., in an attempt to conquer and pacify the region. Despite committing thousands of troops to the campaign, the Roman armies spent decades battling the Germanic tribes without gaining the upper hand. Finally, in 9 C.E., a decisive battle took place deep in the Teutoburg Forest.

Unfortunately for the Romans, the battle proved to be the worst defeat they ever suffered in centuries of imperial expansion. The fierce Germanic warriors they encountered were drawn from a number of tribes and commanded by a Cheruscan chieftain known to the Romans as Arminius (ca. 18 B.C.E.–19 C.E.), who had fought as a mercenary for the Romans and understood their tactics. Ambushed and attacked from all sides in a woodland glade, three Roman legions under the command of Publius Quinctilius Varus (d. 9 C.E.), the cream of the Roman military, were butchered. The attack was the culmination of a revolt against Roman occupation by the Germanic tribes, and the heavy losses that the Romans suffered in the Teutoburg Forest convinced Emperor Augustus (63 B.C.E.–14 C.E.) to abandon the costly conquest of Germany. In the 19th century, Arminius, known to modern Germans as Hermann, became a potent symbol of nationalistic pride and German military might, celebrated in scores of patriotic songs and nationalistic books.

The Hermannsdenkmal, a monument constructed near the Teutoburg Forest in honor of the Cheruscan chieftain Arminius. The monument, completed in 1875, became a rallying point for German nationalists and a popular site for tourists, such as this group that visited the site in 1925. (Bundesarchiv, Bild 118-30)

The Germanic Tribes

In the first century B.C.E., life in central Europe was transformed when the Germanic peoples, newcomers to the region, migrated into the area of modern-day Germany. Defined by their shared language, a cluster of Indo-European tongues classified as Germanic by linguists, this ethno-linguistic group seems to have originated in northern Europe. These various tribes did not form a cohesive group, waging constant warfare among themselves and living alongside and intermingling with other peoples during their extensive migrations. The most important of these interactions was with the Celts, who had dominated the region before the appearance of the Germanic tribes.

While sources are hazy for the ancient period, and archaeology has not been able to provide conclusive information, it appears that the migrating Germanic tribes moved from the area that is today southern Scandinavia and northern Germany. In the course of their migrations, they moved to the south, east, and west, coming into contact with Celtic tribes in Gaul and Iranian, Baltic, and Slavic peoples in eastern Europe. During this period, Germanic languages became dominant along the Roman frontier in the area of modern Germany, as well as Austria, the Netherlands, and England. In the western provinces of the Roman Empire, namely, in the Roman province of Gaul, situated in modern-day France and Belgium, the Germanic immigrants were influenced deeply by Roman culture and adopted Latin dialects. The descendants of the Germanic-speaking peoples became the ethnic groups of northwestern Europe, not only including the Germans, but also the Danes, Swedes, Norwegians, and Dutch.

Roman sources are often confused and contradictory in their attempts to identify the menacing Germanic "barbarians" they encountered along their borders. Thus, Roman authors such as Julius Caesar used vague terms such as *Germani* to describe the various Germanic tribes that settled in the area. While scholars are unsure about the extent to which these diverse peoples represent distinct ethnic groups or cohesive cultures, Roman sources mention a range of Germanic tribes including the Alemanni, Cimbri, Franks, Frisians, Saxons, and Suebi.

Caesar marched against the latter of these tribes, the fearsome Suebi, in his conquest of Gaul. In his account of this campaign, he describes these Germanic warriors, whom he compares explicitly with the Celts. According to Caesar, the Germanic tribes he encountered gave primacy to war, rather than to religion or domestic life. Their religion apparently

Known as the Warrior of Hornhausen, this Frankish funerary stele from the seventh century depicts a mounted Germanic warrior. (Bildarchiv Preussischer Kulturbesitz, Berlin / Art Resource, NY / Foto Marburg)

lacked an organized priesthood and centered upon the veneration of nature, and Caesar suggested that the Germanic tribesmen devoted all of their energies to gaining renown in battle.

Caesar also describes the pastoral economy of the seminomadic Germanic tribes that he encountered across the Danubian frontier. Again, he highlighted the Germanic tribes' single-minded focus on warfare, recording that—unlike the Romans—they eschewed both wealth and luxury, living off conquest and raiding. For Caesar, this warrior ethos made the Germanic tribes into formidable enemies, and he contrasted the military vigor of the Germanic tribes with that of the more civilized Celts. Accentuating the bellicosity of the Germanic peoples, he found the once formidable Celts, seduced by Roman luxury, lacking by comparison:

> There was formerly a time when the Gauls excelled the Germans in prowess, and waged war on them offensively, and, on account of the great number of their people and the insufficiency of their land, sent colonies over the Rhine . . . but their proximity to the Province [the Roman province of Gaul] and knowledge of commodities from countries beyond the sea supplies to the Gauls many things tending to luxury as well as civilization. Accustomed by degrees to be overmatched and worsted in many engagements, they do not even compare themselves to the Germans in prowess. (Caesar in M'Devitta 1853: 153)

Tacitus's *Germania*

Julius Caesar was not the only Roman to describe the Germanic tribes who migrated into central Europe and threatened the Roman Empire's Rhine-Danube frontier. Another was Gaius Cornelius Tacitus (ca. 55 C.E.–120 C.E.). Tacitus was a Roman aristocrat born 150 years after Caesar, in Gaul, the province that the emperor had won. He enjoyed a successful political career, becoming senator, consul, and eventually governor of the Roman province of Asia, shortly before his death. In a work known as *Germania*, written in 98 C.E., Tacitus described the Germanic tribes, providing a detailed ethnographic account. Despite its polemical intent—it was written in order to contrast the virtue and vigor of the "barbarians" with the decadence and debility of the Romans—and its reliance on secondhand accounts of the Germanic tribes' customs, his work provides an interesting picture of the Romans' views of their "barbaric" northern neighbors. Scholars doubt whether Tacitus was ever stationed on the Roman frontier, but he made use of learned sources, including Caesar's and Pliny's earlier accounts of the Germanic peoples, in crafting his work. He may have even consulted with Roman soldiers or merchants who had been in direct contact with the Germanic tribes.

In one unfortunate passage, one that would have dire consequences when rediscovered by rabid German nationalists in the 19th century, Tacitus describes the physical power of the Germanic warriors, explaining it as a function of their "racial purity." Marveling at the imposing stature of the Germans, the Roman author maintains that the Germanic tribesmen were "untainted by inter-marriage with other races, a peculiar people and pure like no one but themselves" (Tacitus 1914: 269). Given what is known today of the contact and intermingling between Celts and Germanic peoples in antiquity, and the fluid tribal allegiances among the Germanic peoples themselves, Tacitus's characterization of the Germans' racial purity is doubtful.

He seems more reliable when describing the formidable military might of the Germanic tribes and the source of their remarkable cohesion on the field of battle. According to Tacitus, the Germanic tribes chose their war chieftains according to their merit as military leaders and their feats of valor on the battlefield. Furthermore, these chieftains did not exercise arbitrary authority and ruled only so long as they led their people to victory. In *Germania*, he writes, "They take their kings on the ground of birth, their generals on the basis of courage. These kings have not unlimited or arbitrary authority, and the generals do more by example than by command. If they are energetic, if they are conspicuous, if they fight in the front, they lead because they are admired" (Tacitus 1914: 275).

For Tacitus, the secret to the Germanic tribes' formidable military might was the cohesion of tribal society. The Roman author maintained that unlike the imperial legions of Rome, the Germanic war-bands were composed of clans and families, and their warriors fought alongside their own kinsmen, vying for their respect. In this warrior society, individuals sought the esteem of their peers through conspicuous displays of valor, each seeking to outdo the other in feats of bravery. Young warriors sought to gain the respect of their kinsmen and the recognition of the chieftain, who doled out gifts of plunder to the bravest warriors. Likewise, according to Tacitus, the Germanic tribesmen brought their women and children to the battlefield. Consequently, the Germanic warriors gained remarkable strength from the exhortations of their women, and ferocity from the knowledge that they were defending their families from slaughter and enslavement: "The strongest incentive to courage is that neither chance nor casual grouping makes the squadron or the wedge, but family and kinship. Close by them, too, are those dearest to them, so that they hear the wailing of women and the child's cry. Here are the witnesses who are in each man's eyes most precious, here the praise he covets most" (Tacitus 1914: 275).

Continuing his examination of the tribal war-band, Tacitus also discusses the egalitarian nature of political life within the Germanic tribes, for him in stark contrast to the autocratic domination he endured under the Roman emperors. According to Tacitus, the Germanic tribes assembled periodically to deliberate over important matters. While chieftains spoke first, each warrior enjoyed the right to address the assembly before decisions were reached through mutual assent. The cohesion of the Germanic war-band was also maintained through lavish, drunken feasts, where tribesmen enjoyed the fruits of plunder and the largesse of their chieftain. While Tacitus's treatment of the religious rites of the Germanic peoples, based upon earlier distorted Roman accounts, sheds little light on their beliefs, his account

A view of Germany's Black Forest region (Bildarchiv Preussischer Kulturbesitz, Berlin / Art Resource, NY / Herbert Kraft)

of their marriage customs praises their homespun morality: "the marriage tie with them is strict: You will find nothing in their character to praise more highly" (Tacitus 1914: 289). For Tacitus, the praiseworthy marital fidelity of the Germanic peoples stands in stark contrast to the decadence he perceived within the households of imperial Rome. According to the Roman aristocrat, the Germanic tribes were monogamous and punished adultery harshly. Even the dowry shared by the young couple reflected the martial spirit Tacitus discerned among the tribes, as the groom gives his bride "oxen, a horse and bridle, a shield, and spear or sword" as marriage gifts and "she herself in her turn brings some armor to her husband." Considered their "strongest bond of union," these gifts remind them of the primacy of war in Germanic culture (Tacitus 1914: 289).

Germania Barbara: **Tribal Germany**

As the accounts provided by Caesar and Tacitus suggest, the Romans were hungry for information regarding the Germanic tribes, frightening newcomers encroaching on their northern frontier. Describing these territories beyond their northern border, the Romans used the designation *Germania romana* to describe the Germanic areas that they had pacified, which encompassed part of today's southwestern Germany, Belgium, northwestern Switzerland, and northern and eastern France. Across the Rhine-Danube frontier was *Germania barbara,* a shadowy region the Romans tried to conquer between 12 B.C.E. and 16 C.E. During one of these campaigns, in 9 C.E., three legions under the Roman commander Publius Quinctilius Varus were ambushed by Germanic warriors in the Teutoburg Forest, near Osnabrück. Led by a brilliant Cheruscan war chieftain who had served as an auxiliary in the Roman army, a man the Romans called Arminius, the Germans massacred the Romans, inflicting a costly defeat.

The attack was part of a larger Germanic uprising against the invading Romans, one that succeeded in convincing the aging emperor Augustus that pacifying the Germanic territories east of the Rhine would be too costly. As a result, the Romans established a fortified frontier along the Rhine and Danube that would hold for centuries, bringing an uneasy peace maintained through military excursions, diplomacy, and payments to Germanic chieftains. The battle in the Teutoburg Forest and its role in establishing a static Roman border along the Rhine, the Limes Germanicus, was instrumental in the later development of Germany. This military and cultural boundary forever divided the Germanic tribes west of the Rhine, who lived under Roman dominion in the province of Gaul and adopted Roman language and culture, from those east of it, in Germania, who retained Germanic tongues and customs.

By around 100 C.E., the time of Tacitus's *Germania,* numerous Germanic tribes had settled along the Rhine and the Danube, along the Roman frontier, occupying most of the area of modern Germany. The Roman-Germanic frontier, known as the Limes Germanicus, thus became a site of vibrant cultural exchange, as the Germanic tribes encamped along it bartered for Roman goods and absorbed elements of Roman culture. Roman garrison towns such as Moguntiacum (Mainz), Augusta Treverorum (Trier), and Augusta Vindelicorum (Augsburg) sprang up in pacified areas, fostering further assimilation and providing the foundations for Germany's rich urban life of the Middle Ages. Meanwhile, as the might of Rome began to falter in the late 300s C.E., and Roman troops were pulled from the border defenses, Germanic peoples began raiding the Roman provinces along the frontier. Some Germanic tribes even migrated across the frontier and settled in Roman territory, providing military service in exchange for land grants. After the Goths routed the Roman army in Thracia in 378 C.E., killing Emperor Valens (328–378), his successor, Theodosius (ca. 347–395), was forced to accommodate the invaders, granting them generous land concessions, in an attempt to forestall further depredation and to build a buffer against the incursions of other Germanic tribes.

By the fifth century C.E., Roman central authority was crumbling, and several powerful Germanic tribes, pressured by population growth and the attacks of the Huns (nomadic invaders from Central Asia) began pouring into the old Roman heartland. The Visigoths, pushed across the Danube by the onslaught of the Huns, moved into Greece, and under their ambitious leader, Alaric (ca. 370–410), even sacked Rome in 410 C.E. before settling in Spain. Likewise, the Vandals crossed the Rhine in 406 C.E. and ransacked Gaul before making their way into Spain and ultimately conquering North Africa. In this chaotic period, Germanic chieftains carved out homelands for their peoples, replacing the old imperial administration and subjecting the local Roman population to their domination. These Germanic warrior-kings also waged war with one another, assimilating defeated tribes as they consolidated their hold over their newly won kingdoms. During this chaotic period, Arian Christianity began to spread among these Germanic invaders. This heterodox sect, which denied the divinity of Christ and was declared heretical by the Church of Rome at the Council of Nicaea in 325 C.E., made inroads among the Germanic tribes as they swept into the crumbling empire.

Since the 18th century, historians have often portrayed the Germanic tribes as marauding invaders who caused the collapse of Rome's glittering civilization. However, recent scholarship has amended this view. Today most scholars view the Germanic migrations of the late fifth century not as a cause of Roman political collapse but rather as a response to it. Thus, scholars increasingly understand that the Germanic peoples who migrated into the Roman world during this tumultuous period were incorporated into the fabric of the faltering empire to defend provinces that the imperial authorities could no longer effectively administer. Germanic peoples had long been recruited into the Roman army, and in the waning days of the empire, entire tribes had defended the Roman frontier fighting under their own chieftains. Once Roman centralized authority broke down, these defensive functions gradually shifted to administration and then outright rule, as Roman government passed into the hands of Germanic leaders.

By the sixth century C.E., the Roman Empire had been transformed into a patchwork of Germanic kingdoms, the homelands of Christianized Germanic tribes that dominated and eventually assimilated with the masses of Romans they controlled. Even in Italy, the very heart of the old Roman world, Theodoric the Great (454–526), king of a Germanic tribe known as the Ostrogoths, held sway over a hybrid kingdom made up of the descendants of former Roman citizens and of Germanic warriors. North of the Alps, another of these Germanic kingdoms, the kingdom of the Franks, built upon the crumbling foundations of the former Roman province of Gaul, would shape the future of Germany and the course of European history.

The Franks

Amid the chaos of the late 400s C.E., a Germanic tribe known as the Franks, a people ruled by a dynasty of kings founded by the war chieftain Chlodovocar (ca. 466–511), conquered the old Roman province of Gaul. Known as Clovis, Chlodovocar defeated Syagrius (430–486 or 487), the last Roman official in northern Gaul, at the Battle of Soissons in 486 C.E. and seized the former Roman province. Suddenly the ruler of a sprawling kingdom peopled by Romans, Romanized Gauls, and Germanic Franks, Clovis made a momentous decision that would alter the history of Germany.

23

The Zugspitze in southern Germany (Bildarchiv Preussischer Kulturbesitz, Berlin / Art Resource, NY / C. Lohmann)

On the heels of a hard-won victory over the Alemanni, Clovis converted to Roman Catholicism on the urging of his wife, the Burgundian princess Clotilda (475–545), who was already an adherent of the Latin faith. An account of the famous baptism of Clovis at Rheims in 496 C.E. is preserved in *The Chronicle of St. Denis. The Chronicle* presents the Frankish king's conversion from "idolatry" as a holy miracle, accomplished through divine intervention in order to facilitate the conversion of his subjects to Christianity.

While this account, written by a pious Catholic monk, suggests that divine inspiration and the faith of Clovis's devoted wife swayed the Frankish king, he no doubt also had more worldly motivations. By converting to Latin Christianity, and forcing his Frankish subjects to abandon pagan religiosity as well, Clovis united Romans and Germans under his leadership. This gave the Frankish kingdom its cohesion and vitality, something lacking in the other Germanic kingdoms where the Roman population saw their pagan, or heretical, Arian Christian overlords as foreign tyrants. In any case, Clovis became an effective champion of the Catholic faith. In a series of successful campaigns, he gradually subdued neighboring Germanic tribes, including the Thuringians, who dwelt near the Harz Mountains in central Germany, and the Alemanni, whose lands were located near the shores of Lake Constance in southern Germany and Switzerland, facilitating their subsequent conversion to Christianity.

Clovis founded a dynasty known as the Merovingians, after their mythical progenitor, Merovech. During the fifth and sixth centuries, the Merovingian kings conquered several other Germanic tribes, gradually absorbing these conquered peoples into a growing Frankish kingdom that sprawled across central Europe. Ardent champions of Latin Christianity, the Merovingians compelled conquered Germanic tribes, many of whom still clung to pagan or heterodox religious traditions, to convert to the Roman Catholic faith. Thus, the Merovingians conquered the Alemanni in 496, transforming their homeland in southwestern Germany into a duchy of their growing empire and bastion of Catholic religiosity. By the reign of the Merovingian king Chlothar I (ca. 497–561), who succeeded his father Clovis in 511, the Franks held sway over most of the territory that constitutes modern Germany and had begun incursions into the territory of the pagan Germanic tribe known as the Saxons, whose homeland was in northern Germany near modern Holstein.

In building their kingdom in central Europe, the Merovingians waged constant wars of conquest against other Germanic peoples. Powerful deputies known as mayors of the palace led these campaigns for the Merovingian kings, gradually amassing their own military and political clout. By the 700s C.E., this position had become the hereditary

THE BAPTISM OF CLOVIS

*T*he Chronicle of St. Denis, a history compiled by French clerics during the Middle Ages, provides an account of the famous baptism of Clovis at Rheims in 496 C.E. This event, interpreted by the pious chroniclers as a miraculous occurrence, would help shape German history by linking the Germanic Frankish rulers with the Roman Catholic Church:

> At this time the king was yet in the errors of his idolatry and went to war with the Alemanni, since he wished to render them tributary. Long was the battle, many were slain on one side or the other, for the Franks fought to win glory and renown, the Alemanni to save life and freedom. When the king at length saw the slaughter of his people and the boldness of his foes, he had greater expectation of disaster than of victory. He looked up to heaven humbly, and spoke thus, "Most mighty God, whom my queen Clothilde worships and adores with heart and soul, I pledge thee perpetual service unto thy faith, if only thou givest me now the victory over mine enemies."
>
> Instantly when he had said this, his men were filled with burning valor, and a great fear smote his enemies, so that they turned their backs and fled the battle; and victory remained with the king and with the Franks. The king of the Alemanni was slain; and as for the Alemanni, seeing themselves discomfited, and that their king had fallen, they yielded themselves to Chlodovocar and his Franks and became his tributaries.
>
> The king returned after this victory into Frankland. He went to Rheims, and told the queen what had befallen; and they together gave thanks unto Our Lord. The king made his confession of faith from his heart, and with right good will. The queen, who was wondrously overjoyed at the conversion of her lord, went at once to St. Remi, at that time archbishop of the city. Straightway he hastened to the palace to teach the king the way by which he could come unto God, for his mind was still in doubt about it. He presented himself boldly before his face, although a little while before he had not dared to come before him.

possession of a dynasty founded by the able military commander Charles Martel (ca. 688–741), who invaded the lands of the Saxons and fought Muslim enemies in the Pyrenees in the name of the Merovingians. In 751, his son, Pépin III (Pépin the Short) (714–768), serving as mayor of the palace under the Merovingians, usurped the Frankish throne with

When St. Remi had preached to the king the Christian faith and taught him the way of the Cross, and when the king had known what the faith was, Chlodovocar promised fervently that he would henceforth never serve any save the all-powerful God. After that he said he would put to the test and try the hearts and wills of his chieftains and lesser people: for he would convert them more easily if they were converted by pleasant means and by mild words, than if they were driven to it by force; and this method seemed best to St. Remi. The folk and the chieftains were assembled by the command of the king. He arose in the midst of them, and spoke to this effect: "Lords of the Franks, it seems to me highly profitable that you should know first of all what are those gods that you worship. For we are certain of their falsity: and we come right freely into the knowledge of Him who is the true God. Know of a surety that this same God that I preach to you has given victory over your enemies in the recent battle against the Alemanni. Lift, therefore, your hearts in just hope; and ask the Sovereign Defender, that He give to you all, that which he desire—that He save our souls and give us victory over our enemies." When the king full of faith had thus preached to and admonished his people, one and all banished from their hearts all unbelief, and recognized their Creator.

When shortly afterward Chlodovocar set out for the church for baptism, St. Remi prepared a great procession. . . . When in the church, in the act of bestowing baptism the holy pontiff lifted his eyes to heaven in silent prayer and wept. Straightway a dove, white as snow, descended bearing in his beak a vial of holy oil. A delicious odor exhaled from it: which intoxicated those near by with an inexpressible delight. The holy bishop took the vial, and suddenly the dove vanished. Transported with joy at the sight of this notable miracle, the king renounced Satan, his pomps and his works; and demanded with earnestness the baptism; at the moment when he bent his head over the fountain of life, the eloquent pontiff cried, "Bow down thine head, fierce Sicambrian! Adore that which once thou hast burned: burn that which thou hast adored!"

Source: Davis, William Stearns, ed. *Readings in Ancient History: Illustrative Extracts from the Sources* (Boston: Allyn and Bacon, 1913), pp. 331–334.

the blessing of the bishop of Rome, Pope Zacharius (d. 752). This bold move established the Carolingian dynasty and forged a symbiotic relationship between these rulers and the papacy, with the new Frankish kings offering protection to the church in exchange for ecclesiastical legitimation.

The Carolingian Empire

The greatest of the Carolingian rulers, Charlemagne (742–814), styled himself the successor to the legendary emperors of Rome. Charlemagne, known to the Germans as Karl der Grosse, carved out a Germanic empire that eventually stretched across much of the European continent. His empire blended elements of Roman administration, Christian religiosity, and Germanic military organization, laying the foundations for medieval Europe and for German society. A devout Christian, Charlemagne resumed the Franks' struggle against the pagan tribes on the borders of their sprawling empire, including the Slavs, the Avars, and the Saxons, a Germanic tribe that had stubbornly refused conversion to Christianity.

Charlemagne's adviser and confidant, Einhard (ca. 770–840), wrote a reverent biography of his master, known as *The Life of Charlemagne,* one that records the Carolingian ruler's bitter struggle with the Saxons. According to Einhard, Charlemagne campaigned against the pagan Germanic tribe, which he describes as "a ferocious folk, given over to devil-worship, hostile to our Faith," for 30 years. Finally crushing the Saxons in 804 C.E., Charlemagne ordered their forcible conversion to Christianity and the destruction of their pagan religious sites. The Saxon homeland, a region in northern Germany near modern Holstein, was absorbed into Charlemagne's realm, reduced to tributary status. During his long and active reign, Charlemagne eventually conquered all of the West Germanic peoples, including not only the Saxons but also the Bajuwari, a people who would come to be known as Bavarians, bringing the Germanic tribes under Carolingian authority. In the 770s, Charlemagne extended the Carolingian Empire into northern Italy as well, liberating the papacy from the Germanic occupiers of the region, the Lombards. The Frankish ruler came to the aid of the papacy again in 799 C.E., when he marched on Rome to restore Pope Leo III (750–816) after a revolt.

In return for his support of the Roman Catholic Church, Charlemagne's imperial authority in western Europe was confirmed by his coronation as emperor by Pope Leo in Rome. Historians have traditionally viewed this dramatic event, which took place on Christmas Day in 800 C.E., as the foundation of the Holy Roman Empire, an institution that would dominate Germany for a millennium. Recent scholarship has revised this view somewhat, however. These recent studies highlight instead the discontinuities between Charlemagne's empire and the later medieval Holy Roman Empire. Despite this change in interpretation, no one disputes the significance of Charlemagne's alliance with the papacy or the importance of his reign in shaping medieval Europe.

The throne of Charlemagne, fashioned about 800, is located in the Palatinate Chapel in Aachen Cathedral. (Credits: Bildarchiv Preussischer Kulturbesitz, Berlin / Art Resource, NY / Stefan Diller)

Charlemagne ruled his vast domain by appointing regional governors, known as counts, to administer far-flung parts of the Frankish kingdom, by establishing tributary marches to defend its distant borders, and charging imperial officials, called *missi dominici* to travel throughout the realm, enforcing royal decrees. Thus, he brought the tribal dukes to heel by appointing royal officials to nonhereditary positions that rivaled the power of these war chieftains within the tribes. Monks and priests also served the Carolingian ruler as royal officials, since literacy was confined mostly to the church during this period.

Charlemagne spent a peripatetic reign on the battlefield or holding court at various imperial residences, the most important of which was his royal court at Aachen, which became a center of Latin Christian scholarship and culture.

After Charlemagne's death in 814, the Frankish kingdom experienced a destructive series of wars between his successors, internecine strife that ended with the fragmentation of the Carolingian Empire. The Franks practiced partible inheritance, meaning that all surviving heirs were given a share of the patrimony. Accordingly, in 806 C.E., the aging Charlemagne decreed that after his death his three sons should each receive a portion of the Carolingian Empire to rule. However, only one of these sons, Louis the Pious (774–840), outlived him, becoming emperor in 814 C.E.

Louis's reign was marred by civil war between his own sons, Charles the Bald (823–877), Louis the German (ca. 804–876), and Lothair (795–855), a dispute only quelled by the partitioning of the empire according to the Treaty of Verdun, signed in 843 C.E. Charles the Bald received the western part of the Carolingian kingdom, roughly analogous to modern France and Belgium, and Lothair, who also inherited the imperial title, was granted the central portion, known as Lotharingia or Lorraine, running from the North Sea to central Italy. Louis the German inherited the eastern portion, a kingdom that included all Carolingian lands to the east of the Rhine and to the north and east of Italy, which was known as East Francia. In 870, after a brief interregnum, Charles the Bald and Louis the German partitioned Lotharingia. A decade later, after the death of Charles the Bald, the rulers of East Francia conquered the region and incorporated Lotharingia into their realm as a duchy. For the next 1,000 years, the regions that eventually became France and Germany would continue to fight tenaciously over the territory between them, Lorraine.

Unlike the western portion of the old Carolingian Empire, where a language based upon Latin, the ancestor of modern French, was spoken, in East Francia the inhabitants spoke a Germanic language that would develop into modern German. During the Middle Ages, the descendents of Louis the German gained the imperial title, ruling as the heirs of Charlemagne. The German-speaking confederation they governed, known as the Holy Roman Empire and located in the heart of central Europe, would form the basis of German identity in the centuries to come.

3

MEDIEVAL GERMANY

In 962, in Rome, the pope crowned a Saxon king, Otto I the Great (912–973), as Holy Roman Emperor. A formidable ruler, Otto I had been crowned King of the Germans in Aachen in 936, mounting Charlemagne's throne at Aachen, and had immediately begun building a powerful kingdom in central Europe. Otto demonstrated his prowess on the battlefield by defeating the dreaded Magyar horsemen at Lechfeld in 955 and through his conquest of the Slavic peoples across the Elbe River. He also proved to be a shrewd ruler, shoring up his political might within Germany by gradually bringing its haughty nobility to heel and using powerful bishops as trusted royal administrators.

The imperial throne that Otto ascended in 962 had been vacant for decades, and Otto's coronation enhanced the prestige and sanctity of the German kings by evoking memories of Charlemagne and rebuilding the old Frankish alliance with the papacy. Otto I began a thousand-year tradition of German rulers holding the imperial title, a conjunction that would help to forge German identity in the centuries to come. The Holy Roman Empire encompassed the area known today as Germany, uniting the rulers of the various Germanic tribes, including the Eastern Franks, Alemanni, Bajuwari, Saxons, and Thuringians, under the overlordship of the emperor and providing the foundation of modern Germany.

Ottonian Germany

With the fragmentation of the Carolingian Empire, its successor states were hard-pressed to defend their borders. The Treaty of Verdun created a new German-speaking kingdom in central Europe known as East Francia, comprising several stem duchies, including Saxony, Franconia, Bavaria, and Swabia, derived from the tribal lands of ancient Germanic war-bands. East Francia was overrun by outside invaders attacking the kingdom from all directions: Viking sea raiders from the north and

An ivory carving of Emperor Otto I presenting a model of Magdeburg Cathedral to Christ in the presence of several saints, circa 960 (Credits: Art Resource, NY / Metropolitan Museum of Art, NY / Hermann Buresch)

Magyar horsemen from the east. In 911, amid the growing instability, the eastern branch of the Carolingians died out, and the East Frankish dukes elected a series of ineffectual replacements from among the leading families of the realm. Ironically, the magnates turned to the Saxons, who a century before had been the pagan enemies of the Carolingian emperor. Forcibly converted to Christianity by Charlemagne, the House of Saxony had grown in strength within the Frankish empire, and the dukes elected Henry I (1068–1135), "the Fowler," as King of the Germans in 919. This inaugurated the rise of the Ottonian dynasty, which would dominate the history of medieval Germany. Beset by outside invaders, Henry bound the powerful Bavarian, Franconian, Lotharingian, Saxon, and Swabian nobles to him through feudal allegiance but allowed them to retain their tribal authority over their respective peoples.

Having consolidated his power, Henry took the opportunity to prove his mettle and test these feudal loyalties on the battlefield. In 933, he massed an army drawn from among the various Germanic tribes of East Francia and marched against the Magyars, nomadic raiders from the east. Henry won a great victory over the Magyars, checking their incursions into the German lands, and also campaigned against the Danes in Frisia. These victories earned considerable support for his rule among the German nobles. Throughout his reign, Henry allowed the powerful dukes who ruled the five tribal stem duchies, Bavaria, Franconia, Lotharingia, Saxony, and Swabia, to function as semiautonomous rulers, setting the stage for the decentralized political structure that would mark the Holy Roman Empire in the centuries to come. Henry died suddenly in 936. While his reign was short, his willingness to delegate power to the dukes and his military successes gained support for the election of his son, Otto, as King of the Germans.

In 936, Henry's son, Otto I the Great was crowned at Aachen, ascending the throne of Charlemagne. Otto was an ambitious king and immediately set about building on the successes of his father, forging a mighty Germanic kingdom in central Europe and shoring up royal authority. In documents of the period, he was referred to as Otto I Theutonicorum rex, or "Otto the First, King of the Germans," signaling the identifiably German character of the Ottonian dynasty. The new German ruler soon demonstrated his prowess on the battlefield. His forces crushed the Magyars at the Battle of Lechfeld in 955, securing the borders of his kingdom and initiating the conquest of the Slavic peoples between the Elbe and the Oder. On the heels of subsequent military victories in the east, Otto forcibly converted defeated pagan rulers and appointed bishops to facilitate the conversion of their peoples, gradually bringing Slavs, Bohemians, and Danes into the Roman Catholic fold. Within his realm, he also strengthened the foundations of Ottonian power by asserting more effective royal control over the German magnates, investing powerful bishops whom he incorporated into his government, and by bringing new crown lands under his direct control.

In 962, at the height of his power, Otto I revived the imperial title when he was crowned Holy Roman Emperor in Saint Peter's Basilica in Rome. Otto had come to the papacy's aid during a dispute in Lombardy, and in return Pope John XII (ca. 937–964) offered him the imperial dignity, which had been vacant for nearly 40 years. Otto's ascension augmented the status of the German kings by evoking memories of Charlemagne and rebuilding the old Frankish alliance with the papacy. Under Otto I, the Ottonian emperors began a thousand-year tradition of German rulers holding the imperial title, a relationship that would help to forge German identity in the centuries to come. However, it is important to remember that despite Otto's new imperial pretensions and his attempts to assert more direct control over the stem duchies, East Francia was not a unified "Germany" during this period. Rather, Otto's realm was a confederation of Germanic peoples, including the Eastern Franks, Alemanni, Bajuwari, Saxons, and Thuringians, peoples whose rulers each owed an individual feudal allegiance to their Ottonian overlord. By the time Otto died in 973, he had managed to bring these fractious elements under a tenable royal control through shrewd calculation and the force of his will. After Otto the Great's demise, however, the centrifugal forces at work within Germany again came to the fore, and his Ottonian descendants weathered a series of rebellions involving their own nobles and attacks from external enemies.

Salian Germany

After a century of remarkable rule, the Ottonian dynasty finally died out in 1024 with the death of the able but heirless Henry II (1519–59), creating a power vacuum within the empire. After some wrangling, the tribal leaders elected Conrad II (990–1039) of Franconia as Holy Roman Emperor, founding the Salian dynasty. The Salians held the imperial title for a century, until 1125, and the four emperors who ruled during that period gradually managed to establish the Holy Roman Empire as one of the leading powers of Europe. The Salian emperors managed this by following many of the successful policies pioneered by the Ottonians, steadily building up institutions of centralized imperial administration and by subduing rebellious dukes.

Like the Carolingians and Ottonians before them, the Salians relied upon their alliance with the papacy to buttress their prestige and their power. The first of the Salian emperors, Conrad II, was crowned by Pope John XIX (d. 1032) in Saint Peter's Basilica on Easter in 1027, after a successful campaign in Italy that cemented the allegiance of the papacy. In 1075, however, this symbiosis broke down over the investiture of bishops, as the German lands became the arena for a titanic struggle between the emperor and the pope over supremacy. The Ottonian kings, as Holy Roman Emperors, were titular heads of Christendom. In

Medieval Germany: The Holy Roman Empire, 1200

North Sea

Baltic Sea

Lübeck

Holstein

Pomerania

Bremen

Brandenburg

Brandenburg

Frisia

Saxony

Lusatia

KINGDOM OF POLAND

Cologne

Goslar

Lower Lorraine

Mainz

Thuringia

Meissen

Aix-la-Chapelle

Worms

Prague

Trier

Upper Lorraine

Verdun

Franconia

Bohemia

Moravia

Toul

Augsburg

Swabia

Bavaria

Austria

Salzburg

Besançon

Burgundy-Arles

Carinthia

Styria

KINGDOM OF FRANCE

Milan

Pavia

Lombardy

Roncaglia

Verona

Carniola

KINGDOM OF HUNGARY

Avignon

Arles

Marseilles

Florence

Tuscany

Papal States

REPUBLIC OF VENICE

Adriatic Sea

SERBIA

Corsica

Rome

Apulia

BYZANTINE EMPIRE

N

Sardinia

KINGDOM OF SICILY

Mediterranean Sea

0   150 miles

0   150 km

Sicily

© Infobase Publishing

this capacity, as protectors of the church, they had long held sway in religious issues, but a vibrant reform movement welling up within the clergy in the 11th century sought to free the church from secular influence. During the Investiture Controversy, an ambitious pope, Gregory VII (1020–85), demanded that the Salian emperor Henry IV renounce his right to invest, or appoint, bishops.

Thus, Gregory issued a decree that forbade church officials from accepting ecclesiastical appointments made by secular rulers:

> *Inasmuch as we have learned that, contrary to the establishments of the holy fathers, the investiture with churches is, in many places, performed by lay persons; and that from this case many disturbances arise in the church by which the Christian religion is trodden under foot: we decree that no one of the clergy shall receive the investiture with a bishopric or abbey or church from the hand of an emperor or king or of any lay person, male or female. But if he shall presume to do so he shall clearly know that such investiture is bereft of apostolic authority, and that he himself shall lie under excommunication until fitting satisfaction shall have been rendered. (Synod in Miller 2005: 105)*

The investiture of bishops was a crucial dimension of imperial rule, since bishops often served not only as religious officials but also as major landholders and imperial administrators. Consequently, Henry IV was quick to defend his traditional right to make these ecclesiastical appointments and responded harshly to Pope Gregory in a letter from January 1076, casting him as a power-hungry usurper.

Understandably, Henry's condescending letter did not please Gregory, and as the conflict escalated, he excommunicated Henry, forbidding both church officials and feudal vassals from obeying the emperor. This drastic move fostered a revolt by the German nobility, eager to free themselves from imperial control, against the crown. To defuse the situation, Henry traveled to the Italian Alps in 1077, waiting for days on his knees in the snow for the pope to receive him. Henry's appearing as a humble penitent forced the pope to grant him absolution, but Henry quickly began investing bishops again and even arranged the election of a rival pope to challenge Gregory.

Within the empire, Henry IV's struggle with the pope unleashed a long and bloody rebellion that lasted until a temporary compromise was reached with the Concordat of Worms in 1122. This agreement granted the pope the right to appoint bishops but reserved veto power for the emperor. While these religious concessions were important, the Investiture Controversy also had lingering political effects. The conflict enhanced feudal decentralization in Germany and weakened the emperor's direct control over the empire. The growing tension between central and territorial rulers, and between imperial centralization and regional autonomy, would mark political affairs in the Holy Roman Empire until its dissolution in 1806.

HENRY IV'S RESPONSE TO POPE GREGORY

King Henry IV's scathing letter to Pope Gregory reveals the intense power struggle at the heart of the Investiture Controversy, one that pitted temporal and ecclesiastical authorities against one another:

> *Henry, king not through usurpation but through the holy ordination of God, to Hildebrand, at present not pope but false monk,*
>
> *Such greeting as this hast thou merited through thy disturbances, inasmuch as there is no grade in the church which thou hast omitted to make a partaker not of honor but of confusion, not of benediction but of malediction. For, to mention few and especial cases out of many, not only hast thou not feared to lay hands upon the rulers of the holy church, the anointed of the Lord—the archbishops, namely, bishops and priests—but thou hast trodden them under foot like slaves ignorant of what their master is doing. Thou hast won favor from the common herd by crushing them; thou hast looked upon all of them as knowing nothing, upon thy sole self, moreover, as knowing all things. This knowledge, however, thou hast used not for edification but for destruction; so that with reason we believe that St. Gregory, whose name thou has usurped for thyself, was prophesying concerning thee when he said: "The pride of him who is in power increases the more, the greater the number of those subject to him; and he thinks that he himself can do more than all." And we, indeed, have endured all this, being eager to guard the honor of the apostolic see; thou, however, has understood our humility to be fear, and hast not, accordingly, shunned to rise up against the royal power conferred upon us by God, daring to threaten to divest us of it. As if we had received our kingdom from thee! As if the kingdom and the empire were in thine and not in God's hand! And this although our Lord Jesus Christ did call us to the kingdom, did not, however, call thee to the priesthood. For thou has ascended by the following steps. By wiles, namely, which the profession of monk abhors, thou has achieved money; by money, favor; by the sword, the throne of peace. And from the throne of peace thou hast disturbed peace, inasmuch as thou hast armed subjects against those in authority over them; inasmuch as thou, who wert not called, hast taught that our bishops called of God are to be despised; inasmuch as thou hast usurped for laymen and the*

(continues)

HENRY IV'S RESPONSE *(continued)*

ministry over their priests, allowing them to depose or condemn those whom they themselves had received as teachers from the hand of God through the laying on of hands of the bishops. On me also who, although unworthy to be among the anointed, have nevertheless been anointed to the kingdom, thou hast lain thy hand; me who as the tradition of the holy Fathers teaches, declaring that I am not to be deposed for any crime unless, which God forbid, I should have strayed from the faith—am subject to the judgment of God alone. For the wisdom of the holy fathers committed even Julian the apostate not to themselves, but to God alone, to be judged and to be deposed. For himself the true pope, Peter, also exclaims: "Fear God, honor the king." But thou who does not fear God, dost dishonor in me his appointed one. Wherefore St. Paul, when he has not spared an angel of Heaven if he shall have preached otherwise, has not excepted thee also who dost teach otherwise upon earth. For he says: "If any one, either I or an angel from Heaven, should preach a gospel other than that which has been preached to you, he shall be damned." Thou, therefore, damned by this curse and by the judgment of all our bishops and by our own, descend and relinquish the apostolic chair that thou has usurped. Let another ascend the throne of St. Peter, who shall not practice violence under the cloak of religion, but shall teach the sound doctrine of St. Peter. I Henry, king by the grace of God, do say unto thee, together with all our bishops: Descend, descend, to be damned throughout the ages.

Source: Emperor Henry IV. "Response to Gregory's Admonition." In *Power and the Holy in the Age of the Investiture Conflict: A Brief History with Documents,* edited by Maureen C. Miller (New York: Bedford/ St. Martins, 2005), pp. 87–88.

As these religious and political controversies raged at the highest rungs of the medieval social order, during the 11th and 12th centuries, the common people living in the German lands also experienced dramatic change. The most visible of the changes was rapid urbanization, sparked in part by the economic stimulus provided by the revitalization of long-distance trade precipitated by the Crusades. Chartered by the emperor or by regional nobles or bishops, towns gradually won municipal rights, becoming islands of republican liberty in a sea of feudal serfdom and enjoying status as "free cities" owing allegiance only to the emperor. Wealthy merchants' and craftsmen's associations, known

ℛ exro gat Abbatem! Mathildim Supplicat Atq;

Medieval illumination of Emperor Henry IV appealing to Matilda of Canossa, countess of Tuscany, to intercede on his behalf with Pope Gregory VII during the Investiture Controversy, circa 1114 (Bildarchiv Preussischer Kulturbesitz, Berlin / Art Resource, NY / Dietmar Katz)

as guilds, ruled the towns, regional marketplaces that rapidly became engines of economic development and intellectual activity. Long-distance trade by land and by sea increased during the High Middle Ages (1000–1300), prompting the creation of a powerful trading alliance known as the Hanseatic League, a confederation of cities that dominated trade in northern Germany and the region around the Baltic and North Seas. Finally, this era saw the expansion of German settlement in the Slavic areas east of the Elbe, in Bohemia, Silesia, Pomerania, and Livonia, during the so-called Ostsiedlung, a wave of migration that would have tragic consequences in the 20th century.

Hohenstaufen Germany

In 1125, the Salian dynasty, like the Ottonians before them, died out. This time, however, the imperial succession was not concluded peacefully. Heated controversies arising from the election led to sustained warfare between rival claimants. Ultimately, in 1152, Frederick I of Swabia (ca. 1123–90) emerged victorious, founding a new dynasty known as the Hohenstaufen. Frederick, known as Frederick Barbarossa for his reddish beard, ruled from 1152 to 1190, and spent his long reign in an attempt to restore the power of the imperial crown. The power of the German emperors had declined precipitously since the time of Otto the Great, and the imperial title had become little more than a ceremonial pretension. Within the empire, the German princes ruled their territories like kings and deprived the emperors of both support and money, forcing them to rely upon their own ancestral lands for revenue. In order to rectify this dismal situation, Frederick Barbarossa had to shore up his position in Italy, hoping to use the wealth of the northern Italian cities to finance his efforts in Germany. In the course of his reign, Frederick I undertook six campaigns south of the Alps. During the first of these, in 1155, Pope Adrian IV (1100–59) rewarded Frederick for helping to quell a revolt in Rome by personally crowning him Holy Roman Emperor. These Italian adventures were not Frederick's only distraction, and he was also diverted from the situation in Germany by the lure of the Crusades.

Determined to retake land previously lost to Christian crusaders, the Kurdish general Saladin (Salah a-Din Yusuf ibd Ayyub) (1137–43), head of an Islamic army, ultimately brought about the fall of Jerusalem in 1188. At the Diet of Mainz, a meeting of the Estates General of the Holy Roman Empire held in 1188, Frederick vowed to take up the crusader's cross, which he did the following year. In 1189, Frederick Barbarossa joined the French king Philip Augustus (1165–1223) and the English king Richard the Lionheart (1157–99) on the Third Crusade, also known as the Kings' Crusade, in an attempt to regain the Holy City. In June, despite their smaller numbers, Frederick's force took Jerusalem. On June 10, 1190, however, campaigning outside of Antioch (one of the crusader states created in the First Crusade, including parts of modern-day Turkey and Syria), Frederick drowned in the Saleph River, swept away by the current while trying to cross the river on horseback. Without their leader, the imperial army fell into disarray and was butchered by the Turks: Only a handful of survivors made it to safety in Acre, a city near the eastern shore of the Mediterranean Sea. Despite his rather quixotic reign and the dismal failure of his final campaign, legends surrounding Frederick Barbarossa circulated in Germany for centuries after his death. The most prominent legend promises that the Hohenstaufen ruler is not dead at all but rather sleeps in a chamber under Kyffhäuser Mountain in Thuringia, waiting to awake and return Germany to its ancient greatness in its hour of greatest need.

Regardless of these enduring tales, the chivalrous but ill-fated Frederick Barbarossa was buried in the Holy Land, leaving the problems of imperial rule in Germany to his son, Henry IV (r. 1190–97). Like his father, Henry IV soon became embroiled in a series of fruitless campaigns in Italy. Once again, the German princes took advantage of the absence of their imperial overlord by shoring up their own territorial authority within their domains. After the death of Henry IV, a period of dynastic instability followed, until another Hohenstaufen emperor, Frederick II (r. 1215–50), managed to resume imperial control.

Like his forebears, Frederick I Barbarossa and Henry IV, Frederick II spent most of his time campaigning in Italy, waging costly wars against the pope and his Italian allies. Once again, a Hohenstaufen emperor was forced to bribe the discordant German princes with concessions to preclude them from rebelling against him while he campaigned in Italy, trading authority for security. To gain their allegiance, Frederick II made the German magnates virtually autonomous in their own territories. After the death of Frederick's son, Conrad IV (1228–54), the most powerful German dukes elected multiple claimants to the imperial throne, leading to another chaotic period known as the Great Interregnum that lasted from 1256 to 1273. In the absence of strong central authority, centrifugal forces within the empire accelerated, as the German princes consolidated their control over their own territories, wresting even more authority from the emperor.

The Crisis of the Fourteenth Century

In 1312, Henry VII (1275–1313) of Luxembourg was elected Holy Roman Emperor, enjoying the first uncontested election since the death of Frederick II in 1250. Henry's successors, most notably Charles IV (1316–78), sought to restore imperial authority but were hampered not only by the jealousy of the German territorial princes but also by the appearance of a terrifying crisis within Europe. The Black Death, a pandemic outbreak of bubonic plague that would claim the lives of one-third of Europe's population, appeared in Italy in 1347 and spread throughout Germany by 1350. Fearing the wrath of God, a radical sect of penitents known as the Flagellants appeared in the empire, wandering from town to town scourging their flesh in atonement.

THE BLACK DEATH

The Black Death that ravaged Europe proved to be the most deadly outbreak of epidemic disease in human history. The epidemic, which came to Europe in 1347, killed about one-third of Europe's total population in its initial onslaught and returned periodically to claim new victims during the next 300 years. The Black Death was a product of the economic expansion of Europe in the late Middle Ages, which brought the Continent into closer contact with Asia and the Middle East, as Italian merchants traded for exotic luxury goods on the Black Sea coast, at the terminus of the Silk Road established by the Mongol rulers of China. While archival records are inconclusive, it appears that the disease had ravaged China in the 1330s and gradually infected the Central Asian cities along the Silk Road until it appeared in the trading posts of the Black Sea coast. Italian traders likely contracted the disease there in 1347, bringing it back with their cargoes to the prosperous commercial cities of Italy. From there, the disease spread along the trade routes that moved people and goods northward across Europe, reaching Germany and England in 1348 and striking Scotland and Scandinavia the following year.

The Black Death appeared in Europe during an economic depression and on the heels of a series of famines that spread poverty and hunger throughout many parts of Europe, leaving the malnourished populace vulnerable to infection. The epidemic was likely caused by the microscopic organism known as *Yersinia pestis*, or bubonic plague, a bacilli first identified during plague outbreak in China in 1894. During the Black Death, the plague bacilli was harbored in the bloodstream of fleas, who in turn infested the black rats that occupied the squalid houses and granaries of medieval Europe. Once the plague had killed off the rats, the fleas' preferred host, the insects turned to nearby

The apocalyptic fervor of this sect sparked pogroms against the Jews. Small Jewish communities lived as persecuted minorities in ghettos in many medieval German cities, permitted to reside there by local magistrates or bishops who benefited from their financial activities and medical expertise. Despite this elite protection, the Jews of medieval Germany lived a precarious existence, surrounded by the hatred of the common folk, who seethed with religious prejudice, ethnic hatred, and economic jealousy. As the Flagellants spread anxiety throughout the empire, this despised religious minority was blamed for spreading the

humans. During feeding, fleas regurgitate their stomach contents into the bloodstream of their hosts, and thus their bites served to transmit the plague bacilli to the human population. Horrible dark colored pustules, known as buboes, erupted in victims' armpits and groins as the infection festered in their lymphatic system, giving the disease its name. Some evidence suggests that once this bubonic form of the disease became established among humans it mutated into the more virulent pneumonic form, a deadly infection spread directly from person to person through coughing.

As the Black Death spread through Europe's towns and villages, the death toll mounted, and survivors began stacking corpses in mass graves. Few accurate mortality records survive from the period of the Black Death, but scholars estimate that approximately 60 percent of those infected with the disease died. The horror of the Black Death caused a breakdown in social ties, and accounts of the period speak of family members and friends abandoning their loved ones once they became infected. Thus, many who might have survived if given adequate care likely died of dehydration during bouts of fever associated with the disease. Physicians, relying upon astrological and humoral understandings of disease, proved powerless to stop the epidemic or to help those infected. In fact, their treatments—carried out with dirty instruments—probably did more harm than good. As science proved inept in the face of the Black Death, most people turned to apocalyptic explanations for the epidemic, believing that they were living in the dark times before the Last Judgment. After claiming a third of Europe's population, and spreading disorder and anxiety throughout the continent, the Black Death eventually burned itself out. Another outbreak of bubonic plague appeared in 1361, and the disease reappeared periodically for the next three centuries but never with the same virulence as its initial onslaught.

plague by poisoning Christian wells, despite the obvious fact that Jews died alongside Christians from the epidemic. These irrational fears sparked massacres and the destruction of many Jewish communities in the Rhineland during the plague years. Unfortunately, this shameful episode was not an isolated incident in medieval Germany, as the Jews had suffered similar atrocities during the Crusades of the 11th century, when armies on their way to the Holy Land to kill Muslim "infidels" stopped to slaughter ones closer to home. Even in times of peace in medieval Germany, Jews were forced to wear distinctive clothing and markers, often including a yellow Star of David, presaging the horrors of 20th-century persecutions to come.

The activities of the Flagellants, who also preached that the plague was a punishment from God prompted by the corruption of the clergy and the worldliness of the Vatican, also caused the terrified masses to challenge both religious and secular authority. Although the papacy quickly branded the Flagellants a heretical sect, the church's reaction was hampered by a deepening crisis within the ecclesiastical hierarchy. The Catholic Church had fallen under the sway of the French crown during the so-called Babylonian Captivity (1305–77), a phrase adopted to describe a period when the papacy resided at Avignon, in southern France, instead of Rome. In the absence of effective ecclesiastical leadership, and apparently powerless before the Black Death, a mysterious killer viewed as an instrument of God's wrath, the church suffered in both power and prestige.

In the wake of the conflicts and chaos that accompanied the Black Death, a series of reform initiatives within the Holy Roman Empire sought to bring order to imperial succession. These reform initiatives, prompted by the disruption that had often plagued the election of the Holy Roman Emperor, eventually led to alterations that redefined the very meaning of the empire. The first outcome of these efforts was the Golden Bull of 1356, which mandated set procedures for imperial elections. Henceforth, seven electors, known as the Kurfürsten, would elect the emperor: four secular electors (the King of Bohemia, the Count Palatine of the Rhine, the Duke of Saxony, and the Margrave of Brandenburg) and three spiritual electors (the Archbishops of Mainz, Trier, and Cologne).

Despite these measures, the political situation in the empire remained highly volatile throughout the Middle Ages, and without effective central control, rival dukes frequently waged war with each other, spreading disorder throughout the countryside. Even after the papacy returned to Rome, and the Papal Schism of 1378–1417 (a division in the Western

Church over the question of who was the rightful pope) was finally resolved at the Council of Constance, the medieval vision of a unified Christendom, a Corpus Christianum led by pope and emperor, had faded by the 15th century. With the coronation of Frederick III (1415–93) of the House of Habsburg as Holy Roman Emperor in 1452, efforts to reform the empire and its institutions began in earnest.

Imperial Reform under the Habsburg Emperors

Frederick III spent his reign in a series of fruitless wars and had little inclination for Imperial reform. However, his son and eventual successor, Maximilian I (1459–1519), agreed to attend an assembly of electors and other powerful dukes to discuss potential reforms. In 1495, Maximilian met with the German nobles at the Diet of Worms (a general assembly of the estates of the Holy Roman Empire held at Worms, a small town on the Rhine River in what is now Germany), asking their military and financial support for his wars against the French and the Ottoman Turks, in return for a number of concessions. Among the most important of these reforms was the establishment of an imperial high court, known as the Reichskammergericht, which would adjudicate disputes within the empire. Maximilian, in an attempt to counter the influence of this body, created his own rival imperial court, known as the Aulic Court, or Reichshofrat, in 1497. Another key reform was the creation of six *Reichskreise,* or Imperial Circles, regional organizations used to administer the empire. These circles were finally instituted in 1512, the same year that the empire came to be known as the Holy Roman Empire of the German Nation (Heiliges Römisches Reich Deutscher Nation), perhaps a sign of an emerging

Albrecht Dürer's 1519 portrait of Emperor Maximilian I (Bildarchiv Preussischer Kulturbesitz, Berlin /Art Resource, NY / Kunsthistorisches Museum, Vienna / Eduard Meyer)

45

German identity. Finally, the Diet of Worms achieved the proclamation of an *ewiger Landfriede,* or permanent peace, meant to end the violent cycle of feuds among the German nobility. While Maximilian appeared reluctant to accept many of these reforms, the measures taken in 1495 did in fact create a stable compromise between the emperor and the estates, one that endured (albeit with substantial modifications) until the dissolution of the empire in the 19th century.

4

REFORMATION GERMANY

In 1521, in the Rhineland city of Worms, a Saxon reformer named Martin Luther (1483–1546) faced charges of heresy before the new Holy Roman Emperor, Charles V (1500–58). Luther, once a devoted monk, had challenged the Catholic Church over the issue of indulgences, the sale of spiritual benefits for money. In the wake of this conflict over indulgences, Luther's rift with the church had widened as he came to doubt the efficacy of the Catholic sacraments and the authority of the papacy. His writings had spread throughout Germany, with the help of the recently invented printing press, causing increasing agitation and scandal. Charles V, at 19, had recently been elected emperor and, along with his German possessions, ruled Spain and its New World conquests, the Netherlands, and much of Italy, making him the most powerful ruler since Charlemagne. Threatened with excommunication by Pope Leo X (1475–1521) and with arrest by the emperor, Luther had been summoned to the Imperial Diet at Worms to recant his heretical beliefs and submit to the authority of his ecclesiastical and secular superiors. Standing before the emperor and the assembled German princes, Johann Eck (1486–1543), a prominent Catholic theologian, commanded Luther in the name of the emperor to renounce his writings. Undaunted, the lone reformer answered:

> *Since Your Imperial Majesty and Your Highnesses insist upon a simple reply, I shall give you one—brief and simple but deprived neither of teeth nor horns. Unless I am convicted of error by the testimony of Scripture (for I place no faith in the mere authority of the Pope, or of councils, which have often erred, and which have often contradicted one another, recognizing, as I do, no other guide but the Bible, the Word of God), I cannot and will not retract, for we must never act contrary to our conscience. Such is my profession of faith. Expect none other from me. I am done: God help me. Amen. (Snyder 1958: 77–78)*

Martin Luther's defiant words at the Diet, and the swift imperial and papal response, helped spark the Protestant Reformation, a religious, political, and social revolution that tore Germany asunder and changed the course of European history.

Precursors of the Reformation

The roots of the Reformation, the religious revolution that transformed politics and society in the Holy Roman Empire during the 16th century, extend back into the turmoil of the late Middle Ages. The lingering crisis of faith and disheartening absence of leadership produced by the Babylonian Captivity of the church (1305–77), the Black Death (1347–50), and the Great Schism of Western Christianity (1378–1416) caused Europeans to rethink their religious life and their relationship to the Catholic Church. Thus, John Wycliffe (1330–84) in England (ca. 1325–84) and Jan Hus in Bohemia (ca. 1372–1415) both challenged the authority of the church to interpret Scripture and the privileges of the Catholic clergy. In the absence of a means of propagating their views, however, both paid with their lives. At the Council of Constance (1414–17), for example, church authorities condemned the Bohemian reformer Hus to burn at the stake for heresy. Hus was executed at Constance in 1415 even though he had traveled to the church council from Prague under the protection of an imperial promise of safe conduct. The treachery of this execution sparked a dangerous revolt in Bohemia, one that raged from 1420 to 1434. Hus and Wycliffe were products of the atmosphere of religious foment that gripped Europe in the wake of the Black Death. While the Catholic Church could silence individual malcontents like these, it could not stem the tide of popular calls for reform. In Germany in the following century, these calls, grounded in critiques of the corruption and venality of the clergy and the hunger for a more authentic and interior religious experience for the laity, would overwhelm the ecclesiastical authorities and tear Christendom apart.

The Print Revolution

A series of technological and intellectual changes also helped to pave the way for the coming Protestant Reformation. In Renaissance-era Mainz, a new invention appeared that would change world history. In that German city, in the early 1400s, a goldsmith named Johannes Gensfleisch zum Gutenberg (ca. 1398–1468) developed the first European printing press using movable type. Little accurate information exists about Gutenberg's life, but it seems that he was born in the Rhineland city of Mainz and moved to Strasbourg around 1434. Having worked producing polished metal mirrors for religious pilgrims, Gutenberg returned to his native city sometime between 1444 and 1448 but disappears from the historical record until 1455. In that year, his business partner sued him, trying to recover a large sum, presumably invested in the development of Gutenberg's press and the production of his famous Bible, which first appeared around 1455. Gutenberg's later life is obscure, but it is known that he was rewarded with a pension from the archbishop of Mainz and died in 1468.

Before Gutenberg, European books were copied by hand, often introducing errors and always taking months—or even years—to complete. Woodblock printing was also used in his day, a laborious process that entailed carving an entire page of images and short texts and pressing it onto a single page. After painstakingly casting hundreds of individual pieces of metal type, and developing a wooden frame to hold them that could be pressed against sheets of paper with a machine, likely based upon the winepresses in the vineyards clustered around Mainz, Gutenberg began printing single sheets and small booklets. Having perfected his process, around 1450 he began working on the great work that bears his name: the Gutenberg Bible. According to sources from the period, Gutenberg's printed Bible was finally available in March 1455. Because producing a copy was exceedingly expensive, Gutenberg probably made fewer than 200 of his Bibles, and most of these went to wealthy monasteries and cathedrals. Despite these rather meager beginnings, Gutenberg revolutionized intellectual life in Europe by allowing printers to produce multiple copies of a given work rapidly, facilitating the spread of ideas. The technology quickly spread throughout the cities of Germany, Italy, France, England, and beyond, and by the end of the century, presses throughout Europe were producing hundreds of different titles each year. This flood of printed material, much of it religious, would play an important role in the development of northern—also known as Christian—humanism, as well as in the coming Reformation.

Humanism North of the Alps

The printing revolution helped foster the spread of humanism in Germany, a movement that emphasized the recovery and analysis of texts from the ancient world and that eventually encouraged educated Europeans to challenge the Catholic Church's monopoly on interpreting Scripture. Spreading at the end of the 15th century from Italy, where it had a more civic and secular flavor, humanism adopted a more religious outlook north of the Alps. In fact, the entire humanist enterprise in Germany would eventually be subsumed in the 1520s by the spread of the Reformation controversy in the empire. Unlike Italian humanism, which drew its support from the courts of powerful princes and patricians, the leaders of the German variant were usually affiliated with the universities, which during this period were organs of the church. Thus, during the period that humanism was spreading through the empire, older German universities, such as Vienna (1365), Heidelberg (1386), Cologne (1388), Erfurt (1392), and Würzburg (1402), were joined by Greifswald and Freiburg in 1457, Trier in 1457, Basel in 1459, Ingolstadt in 1472, Tübingen and Mainz in 1477, and Wittenberg 1502. In addition, northern humanism had a more populist character than its Italian progenitor, spreading its ideas and ideals to a broader public through printed works and the establishment of schools such as those founded by the Brothers of the Common Life, a society of lay brothers devoted to communal asceticism and the education of Christian youth.

While both Italian and northern humanists sought to reform society by applying the wisdom of classical antiquity to contemporary problems, they gave primacy to different sorts of texts. Whereas the Italians, ever since the time of Petrarch (1304–74), the so-called father of humanism in the 1330s, had recovered and studied the texts of great Roman orators and statesmen (above all, Cicero, and later, in the early 16th century, Greek philosophers such as Plato), their German counterparts focused on religious texts: Scripture and the writings of the church fathers. Seeking to reform Christian society and to purify the church, northern humanists pored over ancient biblical and early Christian sources in Latin, Greek, and Hebrew to recover the practices and teachings of the primitive church.

The leading pre-Reformation humanists in the Holy Roman Empire included the classicist Rudolph Agricola (1443–85), the professor Jacob Wimpheling (1450–1528), the scholar Johannes Reuchlin (1455–1522), the hermeticist Johannes Trithemius (1462–1505), and, the so-called prince of humanists, Erasmus of Rotterdam (ca. 1466–1536). Most of these prominent northern humanists were affiliated with the church and shared a deep piety and reform-minded sensibilities. Even Agricola, for example, who sparked the spread of humanism in the empire by popularizing the works of Petrarch and through his mastery of classical Latin and Greek, spent the last years of his life studying Hebrew and reportedly completed an original translation of the Psalms. Trithemius, despite a reputation as an occultist, was even more closely affiliated with the church. Abbot of a Benedictine monastery near Sponheim, he transformed it into a center of humanistic learning, amassing a library of more than 2,000 volumes in Latin and Greek that drew scholars from across Germany.

Johannes Reuchlin, born in Pforzheim, was the most prominent German humanist and perhaps the greatest scholar of classical languages in his native land during his lifetime. Having lectured on classical Latin and Greek at Basel for a time, Reuchlin served as a translator and diplomat for the duke of Württemberg. In this capacity, he learned Hebrew from a Jewish physician at court and traveled to Italy, where he visited the Platonic Academy founded by the powerful Medici family in Florence and in 1490 even met with the famous cabbalist and hermeticist Pico della Mirandola (1463–94). This sparked a passion for cabbalistic mysticism, which would lead Reuchlin not only to publish important works on the Cabbala, including 1494's *De verbo mirifico* and 1517's *De arte cabbalistica,* but also prompted him to study and to defend the study of Hebrew. A strident critic of the abuses of the Catholic clergy, he prefigured the Reformation by publishing scathing satirical works that lampooned greedy monks peddling fraudulent relics. Reuchlin's humanist training and knowledge of Hebrew also inspired him to seek a purer translation of the Scriptures, closer to the original sources than the Latin Vulgate edition sanctioned by the church, and in 1512, he printed an original annotated translation of the Penitential Psalms. The impulse to return to the biblical sources of Christian religiosity and to disseminate these purer translations through print would continue with the greatest of the northern humanists, Erasmus, and eventually help to spark the Protestant Reformation in Germany.

Born in Rotterdam around 1466, Desiderius Erasmus was the most famous Christian humanist in Europe. Despite the fact that he never left the Catholic fold, he helped pave the way for the Reformation in Germany through the popularity of his witty critiques of clerical abuses and the printing of his Greek New Testament. Erasmus was the illegitimate son of a physician's daughter and a man who later became a monk. Assailed by poverty, the young Erasmus also entered a monastery, but his dismal experiences there caused him to rail against monasticism in his later writings. He escaped the monastery as soon as he could and enrolled at the University of Paris, where he studied Latin and theology, and later traveled to Italy and England, where he accepted a teaching position at Cambridge. After his time in England, Erasmus worked diligently for three years to master Greek and began a career as an independent scholar, living off the sale of his prolific printed output. Erasmus found a wide audience for his learned and eloquent treatises calling for a renewal of Christian life and of the church, based upon reason and the example set by Christ and the apostles, and became an early print celebrity. Despite Erasmus's personal obedience to the Vatican, these popular writings helped pave the way for the Reformation by drawing attention to the need to reform the church and its practices.

On the eve of the Reformation, in 1516, Erasmus published the first New Testament in Greek, based upon several Greek manuscripts he had collected. The second edition, of 1519, served as the basis of Martin Luther's German Bible, another indication of Erasmus's inadvertent influence on the Reformation. Ironically, he dedicated his Greek New Testament to Pope Leo X, the pontiff who helped instigate the Reformation in Germany. Erasmus considered this work to be his most important contribution to the Catholic faith, but his efforts to purify the church and to rely upon authoritative texts for religious authority would ultimately help spark the Reformation, tearing the Roman Church apart.

Luther and the Protestant Reformation

While historical treatment of the German Reformation in the last 20 years has focused on social and cultural history, the reception of theological ideas among the masses, and how the religious strife of the era affected society, the towering figure of Martin Luther and his impact on German history is impossible to ignore. A devout, even zealous, young man who had risen quickly through the church hierarchy, in 1517 Luther made a very unlikely reformer. Likewise, the issue that precipitated his split with the church, the sale of indulgences, was also improbable. By examining the formative experiences and spiritual crisis that beset Luther in his youth, these events, events that split Germany and eventually all of Europe along confessional lines, will become clearer.

Luther was born in 1483, in Eisenach, a Saxon mining town, the son of a former miner who had become wealthy through a lucrative copper smelting business. At the time of Luther's birth, the Catholic Church was perhaps the most pervasive, powerful, and affluent institution in all of Europe. The church had a presence in every city, town, and village in Germany and a sophisticated bureaucracy in Rome controlled by the pope, at once Vicar of Christ and one of the most powerful princes on the Continent. At the root of the church's power was the authority the pope exercised as supreme arbiter in all religious matters and the monopoly the clergy held over the seven sacraments; without the church one could not reach salvation. The church offered the opportunity of advancement for a bright and ambitious young man like Martin Luther, but his father chose another path for his son, enrolling him at the nearby University of Erfurt to study law in preparation for a career serving at the court of a German prince or magistrate.

Luther lived a typical student's life at the university, studying and carousing, but on July 2, 1505, Luther's life changed forever when he was overcome by a terrifying thunderstorm while returning from a visit with his parents. Afraid that he would be struck by lightning, perhaps even that the storm was diabolical, Luther called out to St. Anne, the patron saint of miners, "Help, St. Anne, [and] I will become a monk!" When he recounted the story to his school companions upon his return to Erfurt, they thought he was joking about his promise to join a monastery, but Luther regarded his utterance during the storm as a solemn promise to the saint. Against his father's strident objections, and even his threats to disown his headstrong son, Luther joined the Observant Augustinian Order in Erfurt. The Observant Augustinians were considered to be the strictest in the city, but their monastery was located near the university, so Luther could later return to his studies, changing his major to theology.

Luther progressed rapidly as a novice and proved to be an exemplary monk. In later life, reflecting on this period, he wrote:

> I was a good monk, and I kept the rule of my order so strictly that I may say that if ever a monk got to heaven through his monkery, surely that would have been I. All my brothers in the monastery who knew me will bear me out. If I had kept on any longer, I would have killed myself with vigils, prayers, reading, and other work. (Bainton 1950: 45)

In fact, the head of the monastery, Johannes von Staupitz (1460–1524), remembered that Luther's confessions, despite the extreme asceticism that regulated the life of the young monk, often lasted six hours.

These wrenching confessions of sins real and imagined were a symptom of a growing despair that gripped Luther during his years as a monk. While Luther devoted himself with ever more intense piety to the monastic life, he was stalked with the terrible uncertainty of his own salvation. Judged by a perfect God, Luther feared that he would ultimately fall short and suffer eternal damnation. Once Luther was ordained as a priest, his uncertainty grew, and when called to perform his first Mass in the monastery's chapel, he was filled with a horrific sense of dread. The church taught that if an unworthy officiant performed the Mass, it was still efficacious for the parishioners but placed the soul of the wayward priest in dire jeopardy.

Afflicted by intense self-doubt, Luther threw himself into his monastic observances and his studies. The head of his order, von Staupitz, recognized the young man's intellect—and the spiritual crisis that was plaguing him—and encouraged Luther to begin intensive theological study at the nearby University of Erfurt. Luther made rapid progress: In 1509, he received a bachelor's degree in biblical studies, and in 1512, he earned a doctorate in theology. Once he had finished these studies, Luther was recruited for a post as lecturer at the University of Wittenberg, which had been founded only a decade before by Frederick the Wise (1463–1525), the powerful elector of Saxony.

Luther was hired to lecture on the Bible and began a series of detailed lectures on the Scriptures, despite the fact that he was still plagued by the crippling fear of damnation, the realization of his own sinful nature, and increasingly by feelings of being abandoned by a vengeful God. During his studies, in 1510, the Observant Augustinians had sent him on a mission to represent the order in Rome, which only seems to have added to Luther's uncertainty. The pious young monk found the trip to Rome, supposedly the holiest city in Christendom and the resting place of countless saints and martyrs, highly discouraging. Shocked by the cynical worldliness, corruption, and venality of the Renaissance Vatican, Luther later recalled a shocking Mass that he attended in the Eternal City. According to the reformer, as the Eucharist was raised by the priest he snickered in Latin "Bread thou art; Bread shall thou remain," blaspheming the central mystery of the Catholic religion (Bainton 1950: 50).

At the University of Wittenberg, the young professor intensified his study of the Bible, as he provided exegesis on its chapters and verses from cover to cover. At some time during this period, from 1513 to 1518, Luther arrived at a series of theological conclusions that gradually resolved his spiritual dilemma and eventually changed the world. The culmination of these insights was the central theological tenet of the Protestant Reformation: *sola fide,* or justification by faith alone, the belief that salvation was not earned through performing good works or by partaking in the sacraments of the Catholic Church, but rather the grace of God was imputed to the believer through the gift of faith. Ironically, however, it was not this paradigm-shattering theological challenge, one that threatened the central tenants of Medieval Catholicism, the centrality of the Sacraments, and the role of the Catholic clergy, that brought Luther into conflict with the church, but rather his involvement in a minor local squabble over indulgences in 1517.

1517: The "Luther Affair"

By the early 16th century, the Renaissance papacy was more remarkable for its lavish patronage of leading artists than its moral rectitude or pastoral activities. Renaissance-era popes were major princes in their own right, who ruled the Papal States in central Italy as secular lords. For example, Pope Alexander VI (1431–1503) was the father of the notorious warlord Cesare Borgia (1475–1507), ruthless hero of Niccolò Machiavelli's (1469–1527) unflinching political manual, *The Prince,* and Pope Julius II (1443–1513), one of Renaissance Italy's most lavish artistic patrons, having commissioned the Sistine Chapel, and also known as the "warrior pope" for the wars he waged on the peninsula during his pontificate. As popes such as Alexander and Julius focused on amassing worldly wealth and power, the ship of the church

A lithograph from the 1870s, celebrating dramatic events from the life of Martin Luther, including his public burning of the papal bull excommunicating him in 1520 (Library of Congress)

55

foundered on the rocks of scandal and abuse. The sexual incontinence of the clergy was scandalous, portrayed in the bawdy works of Giovanni Boccaccio (1313–75) and Geoffrey Chaucer (ca. 1340–1400) for all of Christendom to ridicule. While most Europeans recognized papal corruption and clerical abuses, on the eve of the Reformation, the laity remained deeply religious and hungered for an authentic religious experience. This was a period of growing piety and devout lay religiosity, raising the people's expectations for clerical behavior and feeding anticlerical and antipapal sentiment in Germany.

The sale of indulgences, certificates that could be earned or purchased from the church that spared the bearer temporal punishment, often a specified allotment of time in purgatory, for sins that had already been forgiven, was particularly controversial. Popular with the masses and an increasingly lucrative stream of revenue for the church, indulgences raised the ire of concerned Christian humanists such as Erasmus. In his wildly popular work *The Praise of Folly* (1509), he not only poked fun at the laziness and greed of slovenly monks and worldly priests but also dared to criticize the cynicism of indulgence peddling:

> Or what should I say of them that hug themselves with their counterfeit pardons, have measured purgatory by an hourglass, and can without the least mistake demonstrate its ages, years, months, days, hours, minutes, and seconds, as it were in a mathematical table?
>
> ... And now suppose some merchant, soldier, or judge, out of so many rapines, parts with some small piece of money. He straight away conceives that sink of his whole life quite cleansed; so many perjuries, so many lusts, so many debaucheries, so many contentions, so many murders, so many deceits, so many breaches of trusts, so many treacheries bought off, as it were by compact; and so bought off that they may begin upon a new score. (Erasmus in Allen 1913: 81–82)

For pious intellectuals like Erasmus, and for observant clerics like Luther, the notion that purchasing an indulgence could erase sin without sincere contrition and the required penance was outrageous.

On the eve of the Reformation, Pope Leo X (r. 1513–21) ruled the church. He was a member of the powerful Medici family of Florence, son of Lorenzo the Magnificent (1449–92), and sought to distinguish himself and the papal court through lavish patronage of the arts, humanist scholarship, and above all through the costly rebuilding of St. Peter's Basilica in Rome. To raise the enormous sums required for this project, in 1515 Leo authorized a plenary indulgence, a special papal indulgence that freed souls trapped in purgatory, even those of relatives who were already dead. Indulgences were quite common in Germany, and this plenary indulgence was to be sold there by a Dominican friar named Johan Tetzel (1465–1519) on behalf of the powerful archbishop of Mainz and Magdeburg, Albert of Brandenburg (1490–1545). Like Leo, the archbishop needed money: He owed a massive debt to south German bankers who had financed his purchase of his election to this lucrative position within the church hierarchy and was set to receive half the proceeds from the indulgences sold in his territory.

Luther, lecturing at the University of Wittenberg and also serving as a parish priest in the town, was increasingly alarmed by the stories of his parishioners regarding the indulgences and Tetzel's sales techniques. Apparently, Tetzel was drumming up sales by convincing his customers that buying one of these special certificates was automatically efficacious, freeing them from earthly confession and penance required by the church for the absolution of sins. It is reported that Tetzel, a very successful salesman, had even composed a jingle that gave this impression, promising that: "As soon as the coin in the coffer rings, a soul from purgatory springs!" (Snyder 1958: 64). Hearing of the Dominican's tactics, and fearing that they might lead ignorant Christians into error and damnation, Luther was outraged. In a 1517 letter to the archbishop of Mainz, Luther clearly stated his objections to the tactics of the archbishop's indulgence sellers and the false impressions they created among the ignorant laity.

After his passionate appeal to the archbishop of Mainz fell on deaf ears, Luther penned a series of theological arguments against indulgences in Latin, a typical way for churchmen to initiate an internal debate over controversies. Luther sent these so-called Ninety-five Theses to the archbishop of Mainz and posted them on the church door in Wittenberg, challenging the indulgence peddlers to debate him on his objections to their practices. In any case, the Ninety-five Theses soon tore Germany, and all of Christendom, asunder.

That the Ninety-five Theses set off a firestorm is surprising for several reasons. In the form of a series of rather dry scholarly arguments, they were composed in Latin for a learned, clerical audience. Furthermore, Luther was not the first theologian to question the validity of indulgences, they had been criticized in a much more public way by Erasmus just a decade before. Finally, and most significantly, Luther was exceedingly careful not to attack indulgences per se. Nor did he dare to argue against the pope's authority to dispense indulgences from the church's

LUTHER'S LETTER TO THE ARCHBISHOP OF MAINZ

In this frank letter from 1517 to the archbishop of Mainz, Martin Luther voiced his scathing objections to the sale of the plenary indulgence in Germany, decrying the grave danger he felt it posed for the souls of the laity:

> Papal indulgences for the building of St. Peter's are circulating under your most distinguished name, and . . . I grieve over the wholly false impressions which the people have conceived from them; to wit,—the unhappy souls believe that if they have purchased letters of indulgence they are sure of their salvation; again, that so soon as they cast their contributions into the money-box, souls fly out of purgatory; furthermore, that these graces are so great that there is no sin too great to be absolved, even, as they say—though the thing is impossible—if one had violated the Mother of God; again, that a man is free, through these indulgences, from all penalty and guilt.
>
> O God, most good! Thus souls committed to your care, good Father, are taught to their death, and the strict account, which you must render for all such, grows and increases. For this reason I have no longer been able to keep quiet about this matter, for it is by no gift of a bishop that man becomes sure of salvation, since he gains this certainty not even by the "inpoured grace" of God, but the Apostle bids us always "work out our own salvation in fear and trembling," and Peter says, "the righteous scarcely shall be saved." . . . Why, then, do the preachers of pardons, by these false fables and promises, make the people careless and fearless? Whereas indulgences confer on us no good gift, either for salvation or for sanctity, but only take away the external penalty, which it was formerly the custom to impose according to the canons. . . .
>
> Finally, works of piety and love are infinitely better than indulgences, and yet these are not preached with such ceremony or such zeal; nay, for the sake of preaching the indulgences they are kept quiet, though it is the first and the sole duty of all bishops that the people should learn the Gospel and the love of Christ, for Christ never taught that indulgences should be preached. . . .

Source: Jacobs, Henry Eyster, ed. Works of Martin Luther with Introductions and Notes. Vol. I (Philadelphia: A. J. Holmes Company, 1915), pp. 25–27.

treasury of merit. Rather, he merely criticized what he perceived as the deceptive way these spiritual instruments were being sold in Germany.

Accordingly, Luther argued, on the basis of church dogma, that indulgences only removed temporal punishments, including purgatory, and did not absolve guilt or replace penance. In other words, his contention was that forgiveness could not be bought. In the 15th thesis, for example, he argued that:

> *Christians should be taught that if the Pope knew the greedy crookedness of indulgence preachers, he would prefer to let St. Peter's Basilica be burned to ashes than have it erected with the skin, body, and bones of his flock. (Snyder 1958: 64–65)*

While Luther did not explicitly attack the pope or the church, the power of the printing press would soon make him notorious throughout the empire and shake the mighty Catholic Church to its core.

Soon after he composed the Ninety-five Theses, Luther circulated his theses among his associates, and someone translated them into German and printed them in Nuremberg, Leipzig, and Basel, apparently without Luther's knowledge or permission. Thus, the controversy quickly left the realm of controlled, scholarly debate between trained theologians and became a cause célèbre argued in the workshops and taverns of German cities and towns by humanists, minor clergy, and townsfolk fed up with the Roman church. Within a month, Martin Luther, an obscure Saxon monk, had become a household name throughout Germany. After the archbishop of Mainz sent a copy of his letter to Rome, he was a topic of discussion in the papal household as well.

Initially, the papacy's response was measured, and Pope Leo attempted to use his authority to take care of the matter internally by ordering the Augustinian Order to silence the troublesome monk. When Luther gave a rousing defense of his views, however, at the Order's Heidelberg convocation in April 1518, he dazzled his brothers with his insights and erudition, convincing many to take his side in the dispute. Since the issue was not resolved, the Dominicans, eager inquisitors of suspected heretics and bitter rivals of the Augustinians, took up the defense of their brother, Tetzel. With the controversy escalating, in August 1518 Luther received an official order to appear in Rome within 60 days to recant his statements or he would be charged with heresy.

Martin Luther was unwilling to go against his conscience and knew that if he appeared in Rome he faced excommunication and might even die at the stake like the heretic Jan Hus before him. Thus, he turned to his powerful patron, Elector Frederick the Wise of Saxony, for protection. Frederick was a devoutly Catholic German ruler and even issued his own indulgences for pilgrims who venerated the collection of more than 19,000 relics he had amassed in Wittenberg. Eager to promote his brand-new university, however, Frederick did not want to lose his star professor who had placed the fledgling institution's name on everyone's lips. More important, Frederick was also a shrewd and ambitious ruler, who had no intention of handing over Luther, a valuable bargaining chip in political wrangling with pope and emperor.

In the early years of the Reformation, the political implications of the "Luther Affair" were just as important as the theological ones. The church had to tread lightly in dealing with this bothersome monk for several reasons. On the one hand, there was growing resentment of Rome within Germany, and Leo could not afford to be too heavy-handed in his initial response. Proto-nationalist German writers, such as the imperial knight and humanist Ulrich von Hütten (1488–1523), complained bitterly about the money that flowed from Germany into Italy in the form of tithes and fees to the church, with little pastoral care in return. On the other hand, there was an important imperial election looming, and the pope was anxious to secure his own candidate's election as Holy Roman Emperor.

By 1518, the ailing Emperor Maximilian was trying to ensure that his grandson Charles would be elected emperor after his death. The pope, fearing Habsburg power, sought to block this by persuading powerful German princes, and above all electors like Frederick who would cast votes in the imperial election, to elect his candidate, King Francis I (1494–1547) of France. Given the importance of courting Frederick for the upcoming election, both pope and emperor had to indulge Frederick, and the wily elector was able to arrange a hearing for Luther on German soil. The confrontation was scheduled for October 1518 at the Diet of Augsburg.

The Imperial Diet at Augsburg was dominated by pressing political considerations, including the upcoming imperial election and a planned crusade against the Turks, but Luther also faced the papal legate, the Italian Dominican, Cardinal Cajetan, who was entrusted with examining the supposed heretic's ideas. The stubborn Luther refused to recant, although commanded to do so by Cajetan, and the cardinal later helped write Luther's bill of excommunication. The confrontation prompted Luther to deny the sole authority of the pope to interpret Scripture, which he increasingly considered the ultimate authority in matters of religion. This assertion, *sola scriptura*, that the Bible is the font of all Christian truth, was to become the second major hallmark of Protestant theology, along with justification by faith alone (*sola fide*).

Martin Luther, under the protection of Frederick the Wise, returned to Saxony and spent 1520 writing a triad of seminal works that would lay out his new theological insights and help to launch the Protestant Reformation. These three treatises, printed and reprinted in thousands of copies in the vernacular, enunciated the three major aspects of Lutheran theology. The first, *Address to the Christian Nobility of the German Nation*, served primarily as a political, rather than a theological, appeal to the German princes to oppose the will of the pope, an argument based upon Luther's notion of the "priesthood of all believers," which attacked the primacy and privileges of the Catholic clergy. Appealing to long-standing anticlerical feeling in Germany, the work was enormously popular, and an initial print run of 4,000 copies sold out in two weeks. The second 1520 treatise, *On the Babylonian Captivity of the Church,* was perhaps Luther's most radical work, arguing that the church was being held captive by clerical domination of the sacraments. Here Luther offered a thorough redefinition of the nature and significance of the sacraments. Thus, for the reformer, the Eucharist was not a "good work" that led to salvation but a means of examining and strengthening individual faith, which for Luther was the key to salvation. Finally, *On the Freedom of a Christian* was a powerful statement of the centrality of faith in salvation, as opposed to the official sacraments and good works cited by Catholic dogma.

Together, these works laid out the three theological hallmarks of the German Reformation: the denigration of the Catholic clergy, known as the "priesthood of all believers;" the primacy of Scripture in religious matters, an expression of Luther's notion of *sola scriptura;* and finally, his conception of *sola fide,* justification by faith alone. Given the theological and political implications of his writings, Luther's message appealed not only to common people concerned with church abuses and their own salvation but also to princes and magistrates resentful of the prominent role the Catholic Church played in German cities and princely states. These tracts, along with the Ninety-five Theses, were printed and reprinted in Latin and in German, using the exciting new communications technology of printing. There was a wide and enthusiastic audience for Luther's powerful writings, as well as the scathing polemical literature and pro-Luther propaganda written by his followers, and these works sold briskly in Germany in the 1520s and 1530s. Scholars estimate that around 10,000 pamphlet editions of Luther's works were printed in the pivotal years between 1520 and

1530, as the fragile Protestant movement struggled to survive. Three-quarters of these editions appeared between 1520 and 1526, drowning out Catholic authors' counterattacks.

The papal response to the rising tide of Lutheran printed output was swift and unequivocal. On June 15, 1520, Leo X issued the papal bull Exsurge Domine, named after its opening phrase, "Arise, O Lord." This carefully crafted document commanded Luther to retract 41 specific "errors" that he had expressed in writing or speech within 60 days of receiving it or else he faced excommunication from the church. Once this deadline expired, on December 10, 1520, Luther collected his followers in Wittenberg and burned his copy of the bull. This dramatic event signaled Martin Luther's formal rejection of papal authority. Another papal bull soon followed: Decet Romanum Pontificem, of January 3, 1521, excommunicated Luther from the Roman Catholic Church and ordered ecclesiastical and secular authorities to confiscate and burn all of his printed works. As his followers rallied around him, it was clear that the Protestant Reformation had split the empire and the Catholic world.

Cast from the church, Luther was ordered to appear at the Diet of Worms that convened in late January 1521 by the newly elected, 19-year-old Emperor Charles V. The imperial election of June 1519 had made Charles, grandson of Maximilian and already ruler of Spain with its lucrative overseas colonies, as well as Burgundy, Luxembourg, and the Habsburg Crown Lands in the empire, the most powerful ruler in Europe. So powerful, in fact, that he aroused anxi-

A portrait of Emperor Charles V, posing with his Ulmer boarhound, painted by the Austrian artist Jacob Seisenegger in 1532 (Bildarchiv Preussischer Kulturbesitz, Berlin / Art Resource, NY / Kunsthistorisches Museum, Vienna / Hermann Buresch)

ety among the German princes, who feared he might subordinate them and rule the empire as a centralized monarchy. Furthermore, he was not German but had been reared in the Low Countries. Finally, the empire was not his primary concern, since most of his revenue came from Spain and he was always distracted by endless campaigning against the French in the west and the Ottoman Turks in the east. Stern, haughty, and stubborn, this devout Catholic ruler would prove a dangerous adversary for the Protestants.

Luther traveled to the Diet under a safe conduct obtained by Elector Frederick the Wise from the young emperor, but as everyone knew, Jan Hus had been under such imperial protection when burnt at the stake at the Council of Constance a century earlier. When Luther appeared at the Diet, on April 16, he faced the emperor's representative, Johann Eck, a Catholic theologian who had been a longtime enemy of the Saxon reformer. Confronted with a pile of his writings Luther was ordered to recant the things he had written. He replied defiantly,

> Unless I am convinced by Scripture and by plain reason I do not believe in the authority of either popes or councils by themselves, for it is plain they have often erred and contradicted each other, I cannot and I will not recant anything, for to go against conscience is neither right nor safe. God help me, Amen. (Snyder 1958: 78)

The Habsburg emperor, Charles V, was a devout servant of the church. Determined to stamp out heresy and to enforce conformity within his troublesome realm, he condemned Luther.

At the conclusion of the Diet, on May 25, 1521, Emperor Charles issued the Edict of Worms, crafted with the help of the papal nuncio, Girolamo Aleandro (1480–1542). In the edict, the emperor proclaimed that:

> . . . we forbid anyone from this time forward to dare, either by words or by deeds, to receive, defend, sustain, or favor the said Martin Luther. On the contrary, we want him to be apprehended and punished as a notorious heretic, as he deserves, to be brought personally before us, or to be securely guarded until those who have captured him inform us, whereupon we will order the appropriate manner of proceeding against the said Luther. Those who will help in his capture will be rewarded generously for their good work. (Hunter 2010: 300)

Thus, the Edict of Worms made Luther an outlaw within the empire. Furthermore, the document made it illegal to publish or possess Lutheran

IN SILENTIO FORTITVDO   ET SPE ERIT VESTRA .

A 1532 portrait of the Protestant reformer Martin Luther by the Saxon court painter Lucas Cranach the Elder (Bildarchiv Preussischer Kulturbesitz, Berlin / Art Resource, NY / Regensburg Historisches Museum / Lutz Braun)

works. Still, it did not halt Luther's pen, much less the spread of the Reformation.

After the Diet, Luther left Worms, but given the strident language of the edict, it was feared that he could be arrested at any moment in spite of his safe conduct. To avoid this possibility, Frederick's men seized him on his way home and hid him in Wartburg castle, where he began his massive German translation of the Bible. Luther's German Bible was crucial to the Reformation, since it gave the "priesthood of all believers" access to the "pure Gospel." His New Testament, based upon Erasmus's Greek edition, was first printed in 1522, and the entire Bible was printed in 1530. By the time of the reformer's death, in 1546, more than 500,000 copies of the Luther Bible had been printed and sold. This publishing sensation not only furthered the Reformation but also helped to standardize the German language. Expressed in the clear German of the Saxon court, Luther's Bible gradually overcame the bewildering variety of dialects in the empire.

After Luther left the Wartburg and returned to Wittenberg, still under Frederick's protection, the emperor was not able to have him arrested. In fact, owing to the opposition of powerful German princes such as the Saxon elector and the rapid spread of Lutheranism among the German populace, the Edict of Worms was never stringently enforced in the empire. However, it was a different story in the Habsburg crown lands such as the Low Countries, where Charles's authority was more direct. There, several of Luther's supporters were tried for heresy. In December 1521, for example, Jacob Probst, an Augustinian prior, was prosecuted in Antwerp for violating the Edict of Worms and forced to publicly denounce Luther's teachings. Others did not get off so easily, and in July 1523, a pair of defiant monks, Johannes van Esschen and Hendrik Voes, refused to recant and were burnt as heretics in Brussels.

The Radical Reformation

Martin Luther returned to Wittenberg in 1522, accompanied by his closest follower, the humanist and theologian Philipp Melanchthon (1497–1560), to deal with the spread of radical religious enthusiasm in the town. In Luther's absence, three firebrand preachers, Thomas Dreschel, Nicolas Storch, and Mark Thomas Stübner, had come to the city and tried to push through a more radical brand of reform. According to these so-called Zwickau prophets, Luther's program to reform the church was not thorough enough. Most significantly, Luther retained infant baptism, while these Anabaptist prophets called for adult baptism, as a visible sign of membership in a community of saints. While Melanchthon remained loyal to Luther, some of the reformer's other associates, most notably Andreas Karlstadt (1486–1541), joined the Zwickau "enthusiasts," much to Luther's chagrin. When Luther returned to Wittenberg, in early March 1522, he interviewed the "prophets" and found them lacking. He banished the trio from Wittenberg and purged their followers from the territory. These radical reformers were thus scattered throughout the German countryside. Some of them, such as the radical preacher Thomas Müntzer (1490–1525), expressed increasingly extreme religious and political views that would soon set Germany aflame during the Peasants' War.

The first sign of the violent potential of the Reformation, however, was the Knights' Revolt of 1522. The free imperial knights were minor nobles who owed allegiance only to the emperor and who ruled their ancestral lands as sovereign lords. By the 16th century, with the advent of gunpowder weaponry and the development of professional armies, the military role of these imperial knights had become negligible, and their prestige had declined. Inspired by their Lutheran and humanist sympathies, and their declining political and social position within the empire, a faction of imperial knights led by Franz von Sickingen (1481–1523) took up arms against both the emperor and the church. Von Sickingen had fought under Emperor Maximilian in Venice and Emperor Charles in France, but once he became friends with Ulrich von Hütten, a fellow knight and prominent humanist, he joined the Lutheran cause. Soon his castle at Ebernburg became a refuge for reformers fleeing Catholic authorities, reformers including Johann Reuchlin, Martin Bucer (1491–1551), and Johannes Oecolampadius (1482–1531). In 1522, von Sickingen called a "Brotherly Convention" of knights and convinced them to use violence to support the Reformation and to regain their former stature in the empire. The knights' forces marched against the archbishop of Trier, a prince of the church and implacable enemy of Luther. The knights besieged Trier but failed to breach its defenses. Meanwhile, the imperial Diet placed von Sickingen, like Luther, under the imperial ban, and the powerful rulers of the Palatinate and Hesse marched against the knights. Von Sickingen retreated to his stronghold at Landstuhl, but the walls of this fortress fell before the cannons of Trier, the Palatinate, and Hesse. Grievously wounded during the siege, von Sickingen died the same day the city fell, and the power of the imperial knights was broken forever.

The failed Knights' Revolt proved to be but a prelude to a much more serious insurrection involving Germany's servile peasantry that erupted in Swabia in 1524, one that also sought to enact religious and social change through violence. The conflict, at its height in the summer of 1525, eventually raged across southern, western, and central Germany, and involved as many as 300,000 peasant insurgents. Chafing under the crumbling feudal system, and inspired by firebrand preachers such as Thomas Müntzer, the rebels called for the end of oppressive exactions from their feudal lords on the basis of the "brotherly love" advocated in the Gospels. In March 1525, the peasants, joined by dissatisfied townsfolk and renegade knights and clerics, met in Memmingen and published a list of their grievances, a mix of economic, political, and religious demands. Luther, already under the imperial ban, and blamed for stirring up the rebellion by Catholic authorities, was caught between the peasants and the princes.

While the reformer had initially sought to negotiate a peaceful settlement to the conflict, and had even expressed sympathy for the hard-pressed peasants' plight, the destructive potential of their rebellion to Germany and to his reform initiatives quickly became apparent. Luther issued a pamphlet, "Against the Robbing, Murdering Hordes of Peasants," which called upon the nobles to crush the rebels:

> Therefore let everyone who can, smite, slay, and stab, secretly or openly, remembering that nothing can be more poisonous, hurtful, or devilish than a rebel . . . For baptism does not make men free in body and property, but in soul; and the gospel does not make goods common, except in the case of those who, of their own free will, do what the apostles and disciples did in Acts 4. They did not demand, as do our insane peasants in their raging, that the goods of others—of Pilate and Herod—should be common, but only their own goods. Our peasants, however, want to make the goods of other men common, and keep their own for themselves. Fine Christians they are! I think there is

not a devil left in hell; they have all gone into the peasants.
Their raving has gone beyond all measure. (Luther in Perlikan
and Lehmenn 1955–1986: 52)

Fearing that the peasants' earthly excesses might swamp his theological movement, he ultimately sided with the princes, sanctioning their subsequent slaughter of the rebels by citing Romans 13, which reads in part:

Let every soul be subject to the governing authorities. For there
is no authority except from God and the authorities that exist
are appointed by God. Therefore, whoever resists the authority
resists the ordinance of God, and those who resist will bring
judgment on themselves. (Luther in Perlikan and Lehmenn
1955–1986: 52)

Abandoned by Luther, the peasant bands were decimated by combined armies of Catholic and Protestant princes, working together temporarily to stem the tide of revolution. The rebel armies were crushed in May 1525 at Frankenhausen, where the princes' trained armies reportedly butchered 100,000 peasants, and the ringleaders, including Luther's former follower, Thomas Müntzer, were tortured and executed.

Amid this swirling controversy, Luther cemented his repudiation of Catholic morality and papal authority by making a radical change in his personal life. On June 13, 1525, the 42-year-old Luther married a 26-year-old former nun, Katharina von Bora (1499–1552), whom he had helped to escape from her Cistercian convent the month before. While other reformers had already taken wives, Luther's marriage signaled his approval of clerical marriage and his denigration of the Catholic emphasis on chastity and virginity. Luther and his new bride soon started a family that eventually included four children who survived into adulthood. Luther's household would provide a potent symbol of the Protestant Reformation's emphasis on the family and the establishment of the so-called "Holy Household." At his wedding, Luther was feted by the new Saxon elector, Johann the Steadfast (1525–32), and the reformer soon began constructing a Lutheran church in Saxony.

The Princes' Reformation

With the destruction of the peasants' uprising in 1525, the initial popular phase of the German Reformation had come to a bloody end, and the so-called "Princes' Reformation" had begun. In 1526, with Luther's help, Elector Johann began to build a Lutheran state church in

Saxony, with a Lutheran service replacing the Catholic Mass, Lutheran clergy replacing the Catholic priesthood, and the confiscation of the enormous wealth of the Catholic Church, used to finance the development of a territorial ecclesiastical administration. Pastoral care and the instruction of parishioners was central to the Lutheran movement, and in 1529, Luther wrote the Large Catechism, a manual to instruct pastors on Lutheran theology and their pastoral duties, as well as the Small Catechism, a brief version that was to be memorized by the congregation, teaching them the rudiments of Protestant belief.

As Luther worked to establish the Saxon church, he came into conflict with another reformer, Huldrych Zwingli (1481–1531), who was busy building his own Protestant church in Zürich, Switzerland. Zwingli, who began his reform of Zürich in 1522, soon after Luther's confrontation at Worms, advocated a more radical break with Catholic tradition. His views on crucial theological issues such as the nature of the Eucharist, which Zwingli saw as a purely symbolic commemoration of the Last Supper, clashed with Luther's more conservative position, which asserted the real presence of Christ in the consecrated bread and wine. By the mid-1520s, several south German city-states had adopted the Reformation, but on a Zwinglian model, a development that threatened to split the Protestant camp. A prominent Lutheran prince, Philip of Hesse (1504–67), feared that the rift would leave the divided Protestants vulnerable to their Catholic enemies and arranged a meeting between Luther and Zwingli at Marburg in 1529, in an attempt to overcome their differences. The meeting, known as the Marburg Colloquy, was a dismal failure: The reformers reached an agreement on 14 of the 15 articles they discussed, but remained bitterly divided on the Eucharist question. As a result of their failure to reach a compromise, the German and Swiss branches of Protestantism would remain divided.

As the German and Swiss Reformations diverged, in the empire a growing number of princes began to build Protestant territorial churches modeled on the Saxon state church in open defiance of the Edict of Worms. The princes who established these new Lutheran churches often had mixed motivations: religious, political, and economic. Progress, however, was slow. In his earliest writings, Luther had called upon the ruling classes of Germany to implement a comprehensive plan of religious reform, and the princes, nobles, and city councils of the empire, who had been consolidating their authority since the late Middle Ages, grasped the usefulness of Lutheranism in increasing their power vis-à-vis both emperor and pope. Many princes outside of Saxony, however, initially proved reluctant to take up this "calling" for political reasons. After 1521, Luther was an excommunicate and outlaw, and at the Nuremberg Diets of 1522 and 1524, Charles V had confirmed his opposition to such "heresy." Most significantly, by 1525, peasant unrest had proven how dangerous spontaneous evangelical fervor could be in the hands of the "common man."

In the late 1520s, Emperor Charles V's policy toward the growing Protestant movement vacillated wildly, raising anxiety among the German princes. At the Diet of Speyer in 1526, he sought to defuse the growing tension by appeasing the Protestant minority in Germany. In an attempt to keep the empire from tearing itself apart along confessional lines, the emperor watered down the ban on Lutheran teachings imposed by the Edict of Worms, allowing each territorial prince to decide the issue for his own territory. To uphold the principle of imperial authority, he also added the caveat that they must each answer for this decision "to God and the emperor." In 1529, at the next Imperial Diet, again at Speyer, Charles V reversed himself again, withdrawing his concessions of three years before, and reinstated the Edict of Worms. A minority of staunch Lutherans among the delegates, five princes and 14 urban magistrates, issued a "protestation" against the emperor's decision, giving the fledgling reform movement its enduring name: the Protestant Reformation.

Despite this printed protest, few princes or reformers dared advocate open defiance against the emperor in the 1520s, since in the face of imperial legal and military power the Lutheran camp was quite vulnerable. At the Diet of Augsburg in 1530, Charles V stubbornly rejected any compromise with the Lutherans, despite Melanchthon's earnest attempt to find a middle ground between Lutheranism and a reformed Catholicism. Instead, the Diet decreed that by April 1531 all Protestant rulers must recant the Lutheran "heresy" and restore all properties that had been seized from the Catholic Church.

Facing this threatening prospect, and fearing that the emperor might seek to restore Catholicism in the empire by force, Protestant princes began to seek military alliances for mutual defense. In 1530, the German Protestants had signed the Augsburg Confession, based upon the Marburg Articles, which established Lutheran orthodoxy. With their religious unity codified, and fearing imperial aggression, in the following year the leading Protestant rulers sought a defensive league to protect their material security as well. Luther, against defying legitimate political authority on theological grounds, initially opposed the idea but in 1531 gave his blessing to an alliance of Protestant princes and towns, known as the Schmalkaldic League. Among these Protestant rulers, the most powerful of whom were Johann, elector of Saxony; Philip, land-grave of Hesse; and Georg, margrave of Brandenburg-Ansbach, resentment of the Flanders-born emperor, whom they viewed as a foreign lackey of the pope and as a tyrant trampling on the traditional liberties of the German princes, was growing.

As these religious tensions simmered, an outbreak of the sort of apocalyptic fanaticism that had been stamped out a decade before during the Peasants' War erupted in the Westphalian city of Münster. Terrifying Catholic and Protestant rulers and theologians alike, the Anabaptist theocracy established there in 1534 prompted these confessional rivals once again to destroy a mutually hated enemy: Anabaptism, hallmark of the so-called "radical Reformation." A group of radical Anabaptists in Münster had gained influence over the local Lutheran pastor and the town council, allowing a baker from Haarlem, Jan Matthys, and a tailor from Leiden, Jan Bockelson (both followers of the prominent spiritualist Melchior Hoffman), to seize power and declare an Anabaptist "New Jerusalem" in the city. Religious radicals from across Germany flowed into the city, and the theocrats preached eschatological sermons and introduced adult baptism, to the horror of Protestants and Catholics alike. Besieged by the combined forces of Münster's deposed Catholic bishop, Franz von Waldeck (1491–1553), and the Lutheran landgrave, Philip of Hesse, Matthys was killed in battle, and his former partner, the "tailor from Leiden," proclaimed himself a new David, the king of Münster, backing his edicts with frequent pronouncements of divine visions. Under Bockelson, the Anabaptist commune became even more radical when he introduced the community of goods and polygamy, reportedly taking 16 wives.

The city held out against its besiegers until June 1535, when its defenses crumbled and the Anabaptist ringleaders were captured by combined Catholic and Protestant forces. In January of the following year, Bockelson and his most important disciples were tortured and publicly executed. Afterward, their mutilated bodies were placed in iron cages exhibited on the facade of Münster's St. Lambert's Cathedral, cages that can still be seen there today. In the wake of the Münster Rebellion, the Anabaptist movement fragmented, forming a variety of isolated sects, which went underground in the empire, hunted as dangerous heretics by both Protestant and Catholic authorities. These scattered, elusive sects shunned established churches and, under the influence of the Dutch preacher Menno Simons (1496–1561), developed pacifist and spiritualist tenets that would eventually spawn the Mennonite, Amish, and Hutterite communities and influence later denominations as well.

Confessional Conflict and Compromise

While Protestant and Catholic rulers fought together to cleanse Münster of the Anabaptist heresy, the confessional divide in Germany was wider than ever in the second half of the 1530s. A final chance to heal this theological rift came at the Diet of Regensburg in 1541, where theologians from the two camps tried to hammer out a compromise that would bring Protestants back into the Catholic fold. They failed to reconcile, and Charles viewed this as the final straw: From this point on, he aimed at the destruction of the Schmalkaldic League. He began negotiating treaties with his hated enemies, the French, and even with the "infidel" Turks to prepare for war against the Protestants in Germany. The hammer fell in 1546, the year Martin Luther died, embittered and pessimistic about the survival of his movement, among the darkest hours for German Protestantism.

Determined to stamp out heresy in the empire once and for all, Charles V marched against the Schmalkaldic League in 1546 and won a spectacular victory over their forces at Mühlberg the following year. The two most powerful Protestant princes, Elector Johann Friedrich I of Saxony and Philip of Hesse, were captured by the triumphant emperor and imprisoned for five years each. In the wake of his crushing victory, Charles issued the Augsburg Interim, a 1548 imperial decree that sought to restore Catholicism throughout the empire but offered Protestants a few concessions, including marriage for the clergy and communion in both kinds for the laity. A compromise that truly pleased neither confession, and aroused the suspicions even of Catholic princes who feared the growing might of the emperor, the Interim faced unrelenting opposition. Worse yet, Charles V found himself betrayed by the new Saxon elector, Maurice (1521–53), whom he had placed in that dignity. Maurice allied himself with the Protestant princes and the Habsburgs' traditional enemies, the Valois dynasty of France, and defeated Charles's imperial forces in the so-called Princes' War of 1552. Thus, Charles was forced to capitulate and proved unable to stamp out religious heterodoxy through force of arms or to bring the fractious German princes to heel. In 1555, a year before abdicating and retiring to a monastery in Spain, the tired emperor accepted the Peace of Augsburg.

This enduring compromise, adopted at the Diet of Augsburg in 1555, acknowledged the religious and political changes that had taken effect in Germany in the four decades since the start of the Reformation. According to the Peace of Augsburg, each German prince or city council could choose between Catholicism and Lutheranism for their

Lutheran polemical woodcut contrasting the Protestant faith with Roman Catholic religiosity, 1545 (Bildarchiv Preussischer Kulturbesitz, Berlin / Art Resource, NY / Kupferstichkabinett, Staatliche Museen zu Berlin / Jörg P. Anders)

territory; their subjects had to abide by this decision or face persecution and exile. All other religious denominations, including Swiss Protestantism and Anabaptism, were forbidden. This settlement would hold the empire together for more than 60 years, before it unraveled in the face of an aggressive, resurgent Catholicism and a militant, zealous new brand of Protestantism from Geneva: Calvinism.

5

CONFESSIONAL GERMANY AND THE THIRTY YEARS' WAR

On May 20, 1631, as the violence and chaos of the Thirty Years' War embroiled Germany, Catholic troops sacked the Saxon city of Magdeburg. Founded by Charlemagne in 805, the city named for the Virgin Mary had served as the de facto capital of Emperor Otto the Great. Located on the Elbe, Magdeburg prospered, becoming one of Germany's wealthiest and most important medieval cities. In 1524, Luther preached in the city, and the populace quickly adopted the Reformation, expelling its Catholic archbishop. Magdeburg joined the Schmalkaldic League, taking a prominent place among the leading Lutheran cities and as a center of Protestant printing.

During the Thirty Years' War, the Protestant stronghold paid the ultimate price for its defiance against Catholic authorities. In 1629, Magdeburg had withstood a siege from the Catholic mercenary commander, Albrecht von Wallenstein (1583–1634). It was not so lucky in 1631, when Catholic League troops commanded by the Bavarian general Johann Tserclaes, count of Tilly (1559–1632), besieged the city. After a grueling six-month siege, Magdeburg finally fell, and Tilly's troops rampaged through the city, burning, looting, and slaughtering the unarmed townsfolk.

The horrors of the sack of Magdeburg were recorded by one of the survivors, Otto von Guericke (1602–86), the city's mayor and inventor of the vacuum pump:

> Then was there naught but beating and burning, plundering, torture, and murder. Most especially was every one of the enemy bent on securing much booty. When a marauding party entered a house, if its master had anything to give he

might thereby purchase respite and protection for himself and his family till the next man, who also wanted something, should come along. It was only when everything had been brought forth and there was nothing left to give that the real trouble commenced. Then, what with blows and threats of shooting, stabbing, and hanging, the poor people were so terrified that if they had had anything left they would have brought it forth if it had been buried in the earth or hidden away in a thousand castles. In this frenzied rage, the great and splendid city that had stood like a fair princess in the land was now, in its hour of direst need and unutterable distress and woe, given over to the flames, and thousands of innocent men, women, and children, in the midst of a horrible din of heartrending shrieks and cries, were tortured and put to death in so cruel and shameful a manner that no words would suffice to describe, nor no tears to bewail it. . . .
(Robinson 1906: 345)

The once proud city was burned to the ground, and more than 20,000 of its inhabitants were slaughtered. Just 15 percent of its population survived the fury of the siege. It is reported that it took 14 days to throw all of the burned bodies of the soldiers' victims into the Elbe. The traumatized survivors were driven into the devastated countryside to starve. By the end of the war, fewer than 500 Magdeburgers remained alive. Even in an age of religious violence, the gruesome atrocities that accompanied the sack of Magdeburg horrified all of Germany, galvanizing Protestant resistance to the imperial forces.

The Catholic Reformation

In the half century after the Augsburg settlement, the religious and political situation in Germany became increasingly unstable. At his abdication, Charles V, convinced that the sprawling Habsburg dominion was too much for any one man to rule, had split his patrimony. The eastern portion of the patrimony, including the Crown Lands in Austria and Bohemia, was ruled by the branch of the family known as the Austrian Habsburgs. Until the end of the empire in the early 1800s, the Austrian Habsburgs almost without exception enjoyed the imperial title. Accordingly, Charles's brother, Ferdinand (1503–64), who had been crowned king of the Romans in 1531 to safeguard his succession, officially became Holy Roman Emperor in 1558. Although able to focus more of his energies on administering the empire, Ferdinand I proved no more able to master the increasingly complex situation there than had his brother.

Bolstered by the official recognition gained through the 1555 Peace of Augsburg, Protestant rulers consolidated their position in the empire in the following decades. In response, Emperor Ferdinand supported the program of Catholic renewal and recovery, known as the Catholic or Counter-Reformation. A staunchly Catholic ruler, who despite the Augsburg settlement saw the growth and consolidation of Lutheranism as the persistence of heretical depravity, Ferdinand moved first in the Crown lands where his authority was more direct. In 1551, for example, he invited the militant Jesuit order into Vienna and five years later to Prague, a hotbed of defiant Protestantism.

Long known as the *Counter-Reformation* because it developed in part as a response to Protestant Reformation, scholars increasingly use the term *Catholic Reformation* to identify reformist aspects of the dramatic renewal that swept the Catholic Church during the 16th century. This is mainly because they recognize that it began before 1517, including the reform efforts of Christian humanists such as Erasmus and Reuchlin, and because at its height it always represented not only a counterattack against Protestantism but also a sincere attempt to rejuvenate religious practices and promote a distinctive revitalization of Catholic spirituality. In fact, even before Luther emerged as a reformer, kingdoms like Spain had already embarked upon an ambitious program of reforms, efforts that in large part inoculated them against the spread of Lutheranism in the 16th century. By 1492, Queen Isabella (1451–1504) and her able Franciscan spiritual adviser, Cardinal Francisco Jiménez de Cisneros (1436–1517), a devout Spanish cleric who wrote the mystical text *Exercises of the Spiritual Life,* had already begun rooting out clerical abuses such as absenteeism, concubinage, and simony and had begun to improve the intellectual caliber of the Spanish clergy.

Even in Italy, despite the prevalence of rampant clerical abuse—Erasmus had famously critiqued the Roman clergy for their worldliness and vanity in *The Praise of Folly*—and the deleterious effect of ambitious Renaissance-era prince-bishops and warrior-popes, tentative reform efforts took place before the Reformation began. Accordingly, Italian reform, unlike Spanish, did not come from the top but rather welled up from below. The revival of religious spirit began among the religious orders of monks (from the perspective of Christian humanists like Erasmus, perhaps the last place one might think), as they pursued a revitalized Catholic spirituality. Thus, between 1510 and 1512, the Benedictines revitalized their order by returning to the traditional, stringent practices of their founders, including discipline and rituals.

75

While these efforts helped pave the way for the comprehensive overhaul the church received in response to the Reformation, Catholic reform began in earnest under the pressure of the appearance of Protestantism in Germany. Paul III's pontificate (1534–49) witnessed the first real steps toward centralized reform and the high point of the Catholic Reformation. Paul III pursued a vigorous reform of the college of cardinals, supported efforts by Catholic rulers such as Charles V to suppress the spread of Protestantism, initiated a thorough (and much needed) cleanup of the clerical hierarchy in Rome, and even commissioned an embarrassingly frank report on clerical corruption in preparation for calling a general council of the church.

After a long series of negotiations, the General Council of the Roman Catholic Church convened at Trent in the Austrian Alps in March 1545 with several goals: to end the religious schism in Europe, to combat the spread of heresy, and to reform the church. The Council of Trent met on and off between 1545 and 1563, between outbreaks of the plague, and reached a number of far-ranging decisions that would profoundly affect religious life in Germany. First, it enacted serious reforms of clerical training and new standards of behavior. Second, it reaffirmed and reemphasized Catholic doctrines, confirming the centrality of the seven sacraments, as well as other orthodox elements such as indulgences, purgatory, and veneration of saints. Third, refuting Luther, it reaffirmed the supremacy of the pope within Christendom. Finally, it renounced Protestant theology and branded the reformers as notorious arch heretics.

The Council of Trent strengthened and reenergized the Roman Church by providing an authoritative definition of Catholic belief. This was expressed as positive reform or ecstatic forms of religiosity at times, but also as increased dogmatism and inflexibility. Thus, instead of healing the schism within Christendom, the council actually accentuated the division and inaugurated a violent counterattack against the spread of "heresy" in the empire and the rest of Europe. The Catholic Counter-Reformation, spearheaded by devout rulers such as Ferdinand and zealous orders such as the Jesuits, enjoyed considerable success during this period, rolling back the spread of Lutheranism in many areas of the empire. Catholicism was not the only energetic form of Christian devotion competing with Lutheranism in the empire after the Peace of Augsburg, however, as a vibrant new form of Protestantism spread from Geneva during this period.

The Second Reformation: Calvinism

Meanwhile, Protestantism was itself rejuvenated during the late 16th century by the spread of Calvinism within the empire, as several German princes adopted the denomination despite its exclusion from the Peace of Augsburg. In Geneva, a French reformer named Jean Calvin (1509–64), who had fled France to avoid persecution for heresy in 1534, had gradually established a reformed Protestant theocracy in the Swiss city by the 1540s. Calvin's theological vision was similar to Luther's, but the Genevan reformer accentuated predestination, providence, and discipline much more strongly. Word of Calvin's firebrand preaching and demanding theology spread throughout Europe, and people looked to Geneva, Calvin's "godly city," as a haven of right living in a troubled, sinful world. According to the Scottish Calvinist, John Knox (1513–72), the city was "the most perfect school of Christ that ever was on the earth since the days of the Apostles" (Smith 1920: 174). Geneva became a magnet drawing devout Protestants from France and beyond.

Besides religious zeal, these newcomers brought skills and capital, and the city prospered economically. It also eclipsed Wittenberg as a Protestant publishing center, becoming by the 1540s and 1550s what the Saxon city had been in the 1520s. At the high point of Calvin's career, his published output reached 250,000 words a year. By 1551, the French government had banned all Calvinist tracts, so Calvin began sending reformed missionaries, trained in Geneva, to infiltrate France and other areas, agents who nurtured and led underground Calvinist congregations. Thus, the fiery preacher and prolific writer spread his brand of Protestant theology throughout Europe using printed works such as his famous *Institutes of the Christian Religion* (1536) and trained missionaries from Geneva. These disciples risked life and limb promulgating the new faith in lands where it was prohibited, including both France and the empire.

Within the empire, these efforts soon paid off and threatened to upset the fragile settlement reached at Augsburg in 1555. In Germany, Calvinism was generally introduced by the ruling prince of a territory, who imposed it upon his subjects as Lutheran princes had done in establishing Protestant state churches during the first wave of the Reformation. Scholars have noted the appeal of Protestantism to nobles throughout Europe, including those in France and the Netherlands, who sought to reduce the power of central authorities. The situation was no different in the empire, where powerful princes adopted

Calvinism not only for its religious appeal but also in order to challenge imperial authority. The most important German prince to move towards adopting Calvinism in the years after the Peace of Augsburg was the elector of the Rhineland Palatinate, Frederick III the Pious (r. 1559–76). Frederick III gradually turned away from Lutheranism, eventually appointing Calvinists to posts in the Palatine Church and the University of Heidelberg. These theologians, some of whom studied in Geneva, created the Heidelberg Catechism, a statement of Calvinist religiosity that helped spread the new faith in Germany. The issuance of this catechism in 1563, and the adoption of a consistory in 1570, signaled the foundation of a Calvinist state church in the Palatinate. While Frederick III's successor, Louis VI (1539–83), undid many of his father's reforms and tried to return the territory to the Lutheran fold, under Johann Casimir (r. 1583–92), Calvinism was restored, and Heidelberg became the capital of German Calvinism. During the 17th century, the international connections fostered by the electors of the Rhineland Palatinate, and particularly Frederick V (1596–1623), would help engulf Germany in bloodshed.

The clash between reenergized Catholicism and this fervent new brand of Protestantism, Calvinism, destabilized the empire and helped set the stage for its devastation during the Thirty Years' War, where the religious tensions within the empire were resolved through violent destruction. At the same time, the conflict was the product of Europe's dynastic rivalries, as the Habsburgs of Spain and Austria clashed with their Danish, Swedish, and French rivals on German soil. Thus, the Thirty Years' War, like the Reformation in general, was fueled by a mixture of religious and political motivations.

Dangerous confessional tensions had been simmering in the empire since the first decade of the 1600s. In December 1607, Bavarian forces, led by the powerful duke of Bavaria, Maximilian I, occupied the city of Donauwörth. Acting with imperial support to protect the rights of the city's Catholic minority, Maximilian began to forcibly restore Catholicism in the city. In response, in May 1608, Germany's Protestant rulers formed a military alliance known as the Protestant Union. The alliance was to be led by Frederick IV, the elector Palatine (1574–1610), a powerful Protestant prince. Alarmed, the Catholic powers of the Holy Roman Empire formed a rival alliance, the Catholic League, at the Diet of Munich in July 1609. The Catholic League was to be led by Maximilian. Ironically, Frederick and Maximilian were cousins, scions of the rival Protestant and Catholic branches of the Wittelsbach dynasty. Formed to pursue collective diplomacy and to ensure joint

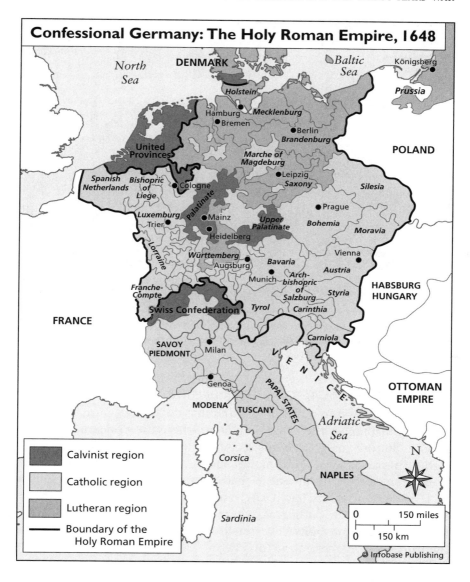

Confessional Germany: The Holy Roman Empire, 1648

security, these confessional alliances devolved to a pair of armed camps within Germany, itching for war.

Bohemia and the Start of the Thirty Years' War

The great conflict finally came in 1618, with a revolt in Bohemia. The insurrection began when an aggressive Habsburg emperor,

An engraving of the Michaelskirche and Jesuit College in Munich, a center of the Counter-Reformation in Catholic Bavaria, 1701 (Bildarchiv Preussischer Kulturbesitz, Berlin / Art Resource, NY)

Ferdinand II (1578–1637), sought to force his subjects to accept the forced re-Catholicization of the territory. Habsburg rule was resented in Prague, the city of Jan Hus, where the Bohemian aristocracy, including many Calvinists, sought to protect their traditional rights in the face of Ferdinand's harsh Counter-Reformation centralization efforts. Ferdinand II had been crowned king of Bohemia in 1617 and, with his Jesuit advisers, sought to restore the Catholic Mass in Bethlehem Cathedral, where Hus had once preached, enraging the local Protestants. The revolt began in earnest in 1618, with the famous "Defenestration of Prague," when rebellious Protestant Bohemians cast a trio of royal officials representing the Catholic Habsburg Crown out of the window of the royal Hradčany palace, the seat of the Habsburg government in Prague. The regents reportedly only survived because they fell on a dung heap in the moat.

The conflict escalated in 1619, the same year Ferdinand II was elected Holy Roman Emperor, when an assembly of Protestant nobles in Prague issued a startling proclamation. Declaring that the Bohemian monarchy was elective, the nobles deposed Ferdinand. They chose as their new king the Calvinist Frederick V, the elector of the Rhineland

Palatinate and head of the Protestant League, a military alliance of Protestant territories within the empire.

Frederick rashly accepted the Bohemian throne and was crowned in Prague in November 1619, infuriating Ferdinand. The Habsburg had been elected Holy Roman Emperor three months before and viewed Frederick's coronation as an affront to his dynastic claims, as well as a challenge to his imperial authority. Ferdinand raised an army in nearby Bavaria, a staunchly Catholic territory ruled by his ally, the Wittelsbach duke Maximilian I, and invaded Bohemia. Frederick's Protestant allies refused to come to his aid, and the imperial forces overwhelmed Bohemia, crushing his army at the Battle of White Mountain outside Prague in November 1620. Thus ended Frederick's reign. Having ruled only a year and four days, he fled back to the Palatinate, and he was derisively called the Winter King. After imperial forces invaded the Palatinate, he was forced into exile in Holland. By imperial edict, Ferdinand II seized the Palatinate and in gratitude granted Frederick's territories—and his position as an imperial elector—to Maximilian.

After his crushing victory at the Battle of White Mountain, and his successful invasion of the Rhineland Palatinate, Ferdinand II reasserted his control over Bohemia. He ruthlessly punished the Bohemians, restoring Catholicism by force and extracting a steady stream of revenue from the occupied kingdom. As Ferdinand re-Catholicized Prague, with the help of the Jesuits, thousands of Bohemian Protestants fled their homeland. The victorious emperor appointed a minor Czech nobleman and military commander, Albrecht von Wallenstein, governor of Bohemia, who then began raising a massive mercenary army to serve the imperial cause. This new army was put to the test in the spring of 1525, when the forces of the Lutheran king of Denmark invaded Germany.

Imperial Triumph and the Edict of Restitution

The Danish king Christian IV (1577–1648) decided to invade North Germany for a variety of reasons, political as well as religious. While he certainly hoped to help his Lutheran coreligionists, threatened by Ferdinand's growing might, he also sought to conquer territory in northern Germany and protect his Baltic interests. Unfortunately for Christian, his invasion force proved no match for the imperial armies he faced: a Bavarian army fighting for the Catholic League, commanded by Johann Tserclaes, count of Tilly, and the imperial army led by Wallenstein. The two imperial commanders defeated Christian's forces in a series of crushing victories, driving the Danes from Germany and back into Denmark. On the heels of this military success, and at the height of his power, Ferdinand II issued the Edict of Restitution in March 1629.

The Edict of Restitution demanded the return of all Catholic lands that had been seized by Protestant rulers since the Peace of Augsburg in 1555. According to the "Ecclesiastical Reservation" clause of the Augsburg settlement, no further Catholic lands were to be appropriated by Protestants, but this part of the edict had not been enforced for the last 80 years. So, in a sense, Ferdinand was seeking to use his military might, bolstered by Wallenstein's massive imperial army, to retroactively enforce this controversial provision. Had he succeeded, it would have entailed a staggering transfer of property and a stunning reversal of Protestant fortunes, with the re-Catholicization of a pair of former archbishoprics, a dozen former bishoprics, and more than 100 monastic territories. Furthermore, the edict supported attempts to compel Protestants in these territories back to Catholicism, with the support of imperial troops, angering Protestants throughout the empire and beyond.

The great princes of Germany, Protestant and Catholic alike, feared the growing might of the emperor and pressured Ferdinand to release the hated Wallenstein. Needing the support of the electors for the election of his son, Ferdinand III, as king of the Romans, and fearing the growing power of his ruthless commander, the emperor complied, informing Wallenstein of his dismissal in September 1630. With the arrival of a new Protestant champion on German soil, the Swedish king Gustavus Adolphus Vasa, or Gustav II (1594–1632), this proved to be a very costly decision.

The Lion of the North

Gustavus Adolphus, a brilliant commander known as the Lion of the North, landed in northern Germany in July 1630 with just 4,000 Swedish troops. A pious Lutheran, one of his aims in invading Germany was undoubtedly to serve as a champion for his fellow Protestants, suffering under the Edict of Restitution. However, Gustavus was also an ambitious ruler, who had carved out a Baltic empire in wars with Poland, and who no doubt also wished to counter the growing strength of the emperor and his Catholic allies in northern Germany. As the Swedish king slowly gained the support of Protestant rulers in the north, Catholic forces, including the armies of Bavaria and the Catholic League combined under Tilly's command, were busy putting Saxony

Wer kan   wider Gott

A broadsheet from the period of the Thirty Years' War depicting the Imperial commander, Johann Tserclaes von Tilly, with the siege of Magdeburg in the background (Bildarchiv Preussischer Kulturbesitz, Berlin / Art Resource, NY)

to the torch. Finally, in September 1631, Swedish and Catholic forces clashed at the Battle of Breitenfeld.

At Breitenfeld, Gustavus Adolphus unleashed innovative new tactics that overwhelmed his Catholic adversaries. Deploying more nimble, linear formations than the traditional Spanish arrangements used by Tilly, the Swedish warrior-king used mobility and firepower to crush the imperial armies. Having swept Tilly from the field, Gustavus Adolphus invaded Bavaria in March 1632, a stunning reversal of fortune for the once triumphant Catholic rulers, Ferdinand II and Maximilian I. Seemingly invincible, Gustavus crushed the forces of the Catholic League again at the Battle of Rain on the banks of the River Lech in April 1632. Again, the Swedish king's skillful use of cannon, infantry, and cavalry in coordination overwhelmed the plodding Catholic armies, and when Tilly fell on the battlefield, his troops fled in disarray. The battle was a disaster for the Catholic League, leaving Bavaria open to Swedish occupation and allowing Gustavus to launch attacks into Austria, the Habsburg heartland.

The dramatic Swedish victories rejuvenated the Protestant Union. In May 1632, as Gustavus entered Munich, Maximilian's capital, the elector of Saxony, Johann Georg I (1585–1656), took Prague. Alarmed, Ferdinand II was forced to recall Albrecht von Wallenstein, the brilliant general and military entrepreneur he had fired two years before. The able Wallenstein quickly raised a new imperial army and took the field, driving Saxon forces from Bohemia and marching against the Swedes. After a series of inconclusive clashes, Wallenstein and Gustavus met in battle at Lützen, near Leipzig, in November 1632. While Wallenstein's forces got the worst of the exchange, and had to retreat, Gustavus Adolphus was shot and killed in the aftermath of the battle, leading a cavalry charge. The death of Gustavus did not cause the Swedish forces to leave Germany, but without their charismatic leader, the Protestants lost their momentum, and the war bogged down into a miserable stalemate.

Wallenstein's success, and the formidable mercenary force he commanded, caused Ferdinand once again to fear his general's growing power. In 1634, the emperor conspired with his lieutenants to assassinate his able but ambitious general, and a group of imperial officers tracked Wallenstein down and murdered him in his bed in Eger. On the heels of Wallenstein's assassination, Ferdinand enjoyed his greatest battlefield victory since the Battle of White Mountain in 1620. At the Battle of Nördlingen, in September 1634, imperial forces, bolstered by veteran Spanish infantry, crushed a combined Saxon-Swedish force. The battle was among the most crushing defeats suffered by the Protestants in the entire war and ended Swedish dominance in Germany. The imperial victory drove the weary German Protestants to seek a separate peace with Ferdinand, and in the Peace of Prague, signed in 1635, the emperor agreed to grant a major concession to the Protestants in an attempt to secure peace in the empire. While Ferdinand had decreed in the Edict of Restitution in 1629 that Catholic properties seized by Protestants since 1555 must be returned to the church, he now demanded only the return of properties taken since 1627. Had the conflict been strictly a German affair, the Peace of Prague may have ended hostilities, but unfortunately for the German princes and their subjects, foreign rulers had no intention of allowing the war to end.

French Intervention and the Peace of Westphalia

The Peace of Prague did not concern the Spanish Habsburgs, who had resumed their war against the rebellious Dutch in 1621 and were also engaged within Germany in support of their Austrian cousins. It also excluded the Swedes, whose troops were still fighting against imperial forces, largely financed through subsidies paid by the French. The French, longtime rivals to the Habsburgs, had no interest in fostering peace within the empire or allowing Ferdinand to consolidate his position. Despite his Catholic allegiance, the French statesman, Cardinal Richelieu (1585–1642), formed an open alliance with the Protestant Dutch and Swedes to keep the war going in the empire. He also declared war on the Spanish and Austrian Habsburgs, leading to the final, devastating phase of the long-running conflict in Germany.

Between the abortive Peace of Prague in 1635 and the Peace of Westphalia that finally ended the Thirty Years' War in 1648, the agony of Germany's long-suffering civilian population became catastrophic. The last dozen years of the conflict proved indecisive, marked primarily by the destruction of the countryside and the misery of its inhabitants. Pitched battles were few and far between, as rapacious mercenary armies burned and looted their way across the empire, savagely requisitioning supplies and burning towns and villages to deny support to their enemies. Supported by French money, the Swedes devastated wide swaths of Germany, some of which were completely depopulated as thousands of terrified and starving villagers took to the roads to escape the destruction. Disease followed the roving armies and also claimed the lives of tens of thousands of malnourished peasants throughout the empire who were in their path. While it is impossible to arrive at accurate figures, given the poor state of record-keeping during these chaotic times, Germany's total population loss may have been reduced by as much as one-third during the Thirty Years' War, destruction on par with the onslaught of the Black Death three centuries before.

The period of the Thirty Years' War, a time of religious fervor and rising fear, also witnessed the great European witch hunts, and nowhere was the panic more deadly than in Germany. Unchecked by central authorities, territorial princes and magistrates, ranging from powerful prince-bishops in mighty city-states to minor potentates in backwater counties, tried and executed thousands of suspected witches between 1550 and 1650. Scholars suggest that some 90,000 people suffered execution for witchcraft in early modern Europe and that half of these witch burnings took place in Germany, the true "heartland of the witchcraze." In the prince-bishopric of Würzburg, for example, 160 suspected witches died at the stake between 1627 and 1629 after delivering forced confessions under torture. The social dislocation and terror caused by the witch trials, prosecutions that reached a fever pitch in the empire during the Thirty Years' War, only added to the misery of the age.

In the last, frenzied years of the war, the conflict also spilled beyond the borders of the empire, embroiling much of the Continent, from the Netherlands to Bohemia and from Denmark to Italy. French troops fared poorly in Germany, and Spanish and imperial forces quickly pursued them back into France, ravaging the countryside and even threatening Paris in 1636. After the death of Richelieu, his successor, Cardinal Mazarin, sought to end the conflict, which had proven quite costly for France. By 1643, all of the major combatants were eager to end hostilities, and peace negotiations began in the Westphalian cities of Osnabrück and Münster in that year, although warfare continued during the negotiations unabated. After a series of defeats in 1645, Ferdinand III (r. 1637–57), successor to Ferdinand II as Holy Roman Emperor, began to seek peace in earnest. After years of complicated negotiations, conducted while warfare still raged throughout Germany, the Peace of Westphalia was finally signed in 1648. The treaty was signed by more than 150 delegates, representing the emperor, the rulers of Spain, France, and Sweden, the United Provinces of the Netherlands, and the major German princes, ending 30 years of warfare in the empire and 80 years of hostilities in the Netherlands. The settlement established a new political order in the empire that would dominate German affairs until its dissolution in 1806.

The Peace of Westphalia enacted a series of sweeping changes in territorial borders and political arrangements in Europe and the empire. Sweden, which gained important territory along the Baltic, and France, which got most of Alsace and Lorraine from the emperor, profited the most. Other winners included the Calvinist Wittelsbach line of Frederick

GERMANY: THE "HEARTLAND OF THE WITCHCRAZE"

Germany was the "heartland of the witchcraze," the site of the most deadly witch hunts of early modern Europe. The Catholic prince-bishoprics of southern Germany experienced the most virulent outbreaks of witch hunting. A chilling letter written to the prince-bishop of Würzburg, Germany, by one of his court officials in 1629 gives a sense of the fear and anxiety that fueled the witch hunts:

As to the affair of the witches, which Your Grace thinks brought to an end before this, it has started up afresh, and no words can do justice to it. Ah, the woe and the misery of it—there are still four hundred in the city, high and low, of every rank and sex, nay, even clerics, so strongly accused that they may be arrested at any hour. It is true that, of the people of my Gracious Prince here, some out of all offices and faculties must be executed: clerics, electoral councilors and doctors, city officials, court assessors, several of whom Your Grace knows. . . . The notary of our Church consistory, a very learned man, was yesterday arrested and put to the torture. In a word, a third part of the city is surely involved. . . . A week ago a maiden of nineteen was executed, of whom it is everywhere said that she was the fairest in the whole city, and was held by everybody a girl of singular modesty and purity. She will be followed by seven or eight others of the best and most attractive persons. . . . And thus many are put to death for renouncing God and being at the witch-dances, [defendants] against whom nobody has ever before spoken a [disparaging] word.

To conclude this wretched matter, there are children of three and four years, to the number of three hundred, who are said to have had intercourse with the Devil. I have seen put to death children of seven, promising students of ten, twelve, fourteen, and fifteen, but I cannot and must not write more of this misery. There are persons of yet higher rank, whom you know, and would marvel to hear of, nay, would scarcely believe it; yet justice must be done. . . .

P.S. [A]t a place called the Fraw-Rengberg, the Devil in person, with eight thousand of his followers, held an assembly and celebrated mass before them all, administering to his audience (that is, the witches) turnip-rinds and parings in place of the Holy Eucharist. There took place not only foul, but most horrible and hideous, blasphemies, whereof I shudder to write. . . .

Source: Kors, Alan Charles and Edward Peters, eds. *Witchcraft in Europe, 400–1700: A Documentary History* (Philadelphia, Pa.: University of Pennsylvania Press, 2001), pp. 353–354.

V, who regained the Rhine Palatinate, and the Dutch, who finally won recognition of their independence from Spain. Within Germany, the Peace of Westphalia restored the provisions that the Peace of Augsburg had established in 1555, with a few important modifications. Rulers of individual territories could still choose the religion in their domain, but their subjects were now granted the freedom to worship a different brand of Christianity or to emigrate lawfully. Furthermore, the Westphalian settlement also reflected the new confessional realities within the empire by allowing rulers to adopt Calvinism, which had been prohibited by the Peace of Augsburg in 1555. As Holy Roman Emperor, Ferdinand III alone gained the right to impose Catholicism within his own lands. This proved to be one of the few concessions that the emperor was to gain from three decades of war.

The Peace of Westphalia also fundamentally changed the nature of imperial politics. It diminished the authority of the emperor by making the 300 princes of the empire formally sovereign within their own territories and allowing them to conduct their own independent foreign policies. During the final convulsive period of war, in 1644, Ferdinand III had granted the German princes the right to pursue their own international diplomacy in an attempt to garner their support. This wartime concession, codified in the Peace of Westphalia, eroded imperial authority and prestige, effectively ending forever the Habsburgs' dream of transforming the Holy Roman Empire into a centralized territorial monarchy like France or Sweden. Distracted by the incursions of the Turks on their eastern frontier, the Austrian Habsburgs retreated from imperial politics for much of the 17th century. These developments would also spark a competition among the most important German principalities, Saxony, Bavaria, and upstart Prussia, which struggled to challenge the Austrian Habsburgs for dominance within the empire.

6

ABSOLUTISM AND ENLIGHTENMENT

Maria Theresa was born on May 13, 1717, the eldest daughter of the Austrian Habsburg emperor Charles VI (1685–1740). By 1713, Charles had not produced a male heir and issued an imperial edict known as the Pragmatic Sanction that decreed that if an Austrian ruler did not have living sons, the throne should pass to his eldest daughter upon his death. After his sole male heir died in infancy in 1716, Charles spent the rest of his reign ensuring that the crowned heads of Europe would accept Maria Theresa as his successor, despite widespread opposition to female succession. After lengthy negotiations, and even a series of territorial concessions, most neighboring monarchs agreed to the Pragmatic Sanction. One of the few to refuse to agree to it was the king of Prussia, Friedrich Wilhelm I (1713–40), an ambitious monarch who hoped to profit from the Habsburg dynastic instability.

Upon the death of her father in October 1740, the 23-year-old Maria Theresa assumed the Austrian throne. When Maria Theresa claimed her crown, however, Prussia contested her claims and in December invaded the strategic Austrian territory of Silesia, sparking the War of Austrian Succession. Maria Theresa was also forced to fight the rulers of France, Spain, Bavaria, and Saxony, although most of them had previously agreed to the Pragmatic Sanction. Facing these powerful enemies, and with the Austrian army in disarray, Maria Theresa, as newly crowned queen of Hungary, had to appeal to the Hungarian diet to support the war effort or risk disaster. She had just given birth to her first child, as Bavarian troops advanced on Vienna and French soldiers invaded Bohemia, but she traveled with the infant to the September 1741 diet to make a dramatic personal appeal to the Hungarian nobles. Holding her son in her arms, the young queen pleaded for the nobles' support, reportedly saying:

Portrait of Empress Maria Theresa (Bildarchiv Preussischer Kulturbesitz, Berlin / Art Resource, NY)

The clouds of danger gather above us from all directions. I do not want to hide this fact from my beloved Hungarians, as you also are affected by it. The Holy Crown is in danger, I am in danger with my child and—abandoned by all others—I solicit the help of Hungarian arms whose fame shines throughout history. I appeal to the well-known gallantry of the Magyars and to their loyalty, it is in this fidelity that I herewith lay my future and my child's future. (Sisa 1995: 124)

Her famous appeal did not fall upon deaf ears, and with drawn swords Hungary's nobles pledged their loyalty to Maria Theresa and soon rode to the defense of Austria. While the Austrians lost Silesia to the Prussians, Maria Theresa successfully defended her claim to the Austrian throne after eight grueling years of warfare. She would ultimately emerge as one of the greatest Habsburg rulers. While Salic law prevented her election to the imperial dignity, in 1745 she secured the election of her husband, Francis I, and as empress consort Maria Theresa was de facto ruler of the Holy Roman Empire for decades.

The Rise of Prussia

The Thirty Years' War left much of Germany in ruins, many of its princes in debt, and the authority of the Habsburg emperors in doubt. One German principality used its wartime experience as a crucible, however, forging a powerful barracks-state that would emerge to become the dominant power within the empire. This state was Prussia, ruled by the ambitious Hohenzollern dynasty. Initially, the scattered dynastic lands of the Hohenzollerns were quite weak and fared poorly in the war. Brandenburg-Prussia, commonly known as Prussia, was not a contiguous state, and its territories, including Prussia, Brandenburg, and Pomerania, were scattered across northern Germany. His far-flung territories ravaged repeatedly by the mercenary armies of the imperial forces and the Swedes, the Hohenzollern margrave Georg Wilhelm (1619–40) was even forced to flee his own capital, Berlin, for Königsberg (a city known today as Kaliningrad, Russia) in 1637. His successor, Friedrich Wilhelm (1640–88), sought to safeguard Prussia by rebuilding its feeble military. He gradually transformed the Prussian army from a laughingstock into a juggernaut.

Friedrich Wilhelm also consolidated the Hohenzollern's political situation. Upon his ascension, the duchy of Prussia was still held in fief from the king of Poland. After aiding the Polish Crown in its struggle with Sweden during the Northern Wars, Friedrich Wilhelm obtained full sovereignty over Prussia and was released from his feudal obligations in the Treaty of Wehlau in 1657. Given free rein in his domain, Friedrich Wilhelm, known as the Great Elector, was an absolutist ruler who dominated political affairs. Above all, he militarized the state, seeing a powerful army as the key to defending his scattered possessions and to realizing his lofty ambitions.

The Great Elector's successor, Elector Friedrich III (1657–1713), built upon his father's successes and in January 1701 crowned himself King Friedrich I, transforming his realm from a duchy into a kingdom. Frederick convinced Emperor Leopold I (1640–1705) to sanction his use of the new title, one that technically referred to the eastern territories the Hohenzollerns ruled that lay outside the borders of the empire, in exchange for Prussian support for the Habsburgs against the French in the War of the Spanish Succession. Since most of the Hohenzollern state was still part of the Holy Roman Empire, and subject to imperial authority, the Habsburg emperor Leopold I only allowed Friedrich to adopt the title "King in Prussia," rather than the more grandiloquent "King of Prussia." Despite the semantics, Friedrich's new royal title, made official with the Treaty of Utrecht in 1713, signaled the growing might of Prussia and the declining power of the emperor to bring such ambitious princes to heel. Befitting his new station, King Friedrich I was a lavish patron of the arts and sought to create a glittering court that reflected his new royal dignity. Unfortunately, his efforts to emulate the splendor of Versailles in northern Germany had dire consequences for the Prussian treasury.

His successor, Friedrich Wilhelm I, had completely different aspirations, and this spartan "Soldier King" eschewed the arts and literature for the parade ground. Through mandatory conscription and rigorous drill, Friedrich Wilhelm I turned the Prussian military into one of the most formidable armies in Europe. While this military machine only saw brief action during the Great Northern War, the Soldier King managed to expand his realm considerably. He wrested territories from Sweden in 1720, pushing the borders of Pomerania to the Peene River. Friedrich Wilhelm also extended the boundaries of eastern Prussia to the Memel River, settling this frontier with thousands of Protestant refugees fleeing Catholic Salzburg.

Friedrich II (1712–86) succeeded his father in 1740. A rebellious crown prince who had devoted his youth to philosophy and the arts, Friedrich II, who would come to be known as "Friedrich the Great," proved to be a worthy successor to the Soldier King. In the very first year of his reign, his troops marched on Silesia, an Austrian Habsburg possession. Friedrich II used an old and dubious treaty, the 1537 Treaty of Schwiebus, to justify the campaign, a flimsy pretext at best. Prussia triumphed in the three Silesian Wars waged between 1740 and 1763, even managing to hold on to Silesia against a combined force fielded by Austria, France, and Russia.

The last of these conflicts, known as the Seven Years' War, which raged from 1756 to 1763, escalated into an early modern world war involving all the major European powers and fought in Europe, Asia, and North America. Still fuming over the loss of Silesia in 1748, Austria began mobilizing its armies and gaining allies for a campaign to retake its valuable former possession. Having gained support from Russia, France, Spain, Saxony, and later Sweden, the Habsburgs prepared to march against the Prussians, who were supported by a single ally, Britain. Friedrich preempted the Austrians, however, invading Saxony in 1756. The Prussian forces proved invincible in the early years of the war, handing crushing defeats to the French at Rossbach and the Austrians at Leuthen in 1757, and beating the Russians at Zorndorf the following year. This impressive string of victories alarmed Prussia's neighbors, and at this point, Sweden joined the conflict. Soon Prussia's fortunes changed, and by 1759, eastern Prussia fell to the Russians. With Berlin itself in enemy hands, Prussia seemed on the verge of collapse, until England turned the tide of war again by handing a series of defeats to the French in their overseas colonies. Meanwhile, in 1762, Empress Elizabeth of Russia (1709–62), a formidable foe of the Hohenzollerns, died and was succeeded by her son, the incompetent Peter III (1728–62), who was an ardent admirer of the Hohenzollerns. Soon after Peter ascended the Russian throne, Russia pulled out of the conflict, followed by Sweden. With his eastern front secure, Friedrich defeated the Austrians at the Battle of Burkersdorf and managed to negotiate a settlement that restored the prewar situation. Friedrich had emerged victorious from the Seven Years' War, a global conflict that cost between 900,000 and 1,400,000 lives and changed the balance of power in Europe. Having held on to its Silesian possession, and humbled the mighty Austrians and their allies, Prussia claimed its place among Europe's greatest powers.

The conquest of Silesia, a prosperous region, not only increased the territorial expanse of Prussia but also augmented her population and her economic might. Furthermore, Prussia's triumph in battle against a mighty coalition of imperial states demonstrated that it belonged among the great powers of Europe. On the heels of this great victory, Friedrich II consolidated these gains by further increasing the territory and wealth of the Prussian state. He did this by developing the economically backward and sparsely populated possessions of his kingdom, as well as by conquering new territories. Thus, he welcomed immigrants from across Europe fleeing religious persecution, such as the Huguenots, French Protestants who had been leaving France ever since the revocation of the Edict of Nantes by Louis XIV (1638–1715) had denied them royal protection. Migrants like these brought valuable skills and a pioneering spirit that helped develop backward areas like the marshy region along the Oder known as the Oderbruch. Meanwhile, in 1772, Friedrich II also participated in the first of several partitions of Poland, sharing the spoils of the dismembered kingdom with Austria and Russia as these rivals sought to establish a stable balance of power in the east.

Between 1772 and 1795, Prussia participated in three such partitions of Poland, occupying vast areas of the Polish-Lithuanian Commonwealth. The Hohenzollerns feared the growing power of Russia, and its increasing influence over a moribund Poland. In response, in 1772, Prussia participated with Russia and Austria in the First Partition, annexing the province of Royal Prussia, which the Hohenzollerns had long held as a fief of the Polish monarchy, renaming it West Prussia. This pivotal acquisition linked East Prussia, the area of Prussia that was part of the Holy Roman Empire, with Pomerania, making the Hohenzollern state contiguous for the first time. Subsequent partitions of Poland, under Friedrich's successor, led to even greater Prussian expansion. In 1793, Friedrich Wilhelm II (1744–97) gained extensive territory in western Poland in a second annexation. In the Third Partition of Poland, a treaty completed on October 24, 1795, at St. Petersburg, Russia, the rest of Poland was swallowed up by the signatories, with Prussia gaining a large swath of territory to the south of East Prussia, an area it arranged into the provinces of New Silesia, South Prussia, and New East Prussia. In 1786, at the end of his long reign, having forged Prussia into a major European power, Friedrich II died childless, passing the crown to his nephew, Friedrich Wilhelm II.

Prussia was not alone in its efforts to fashion itself into a European power during this period. As the empire lost its primacy in German affairs, individual German principalities began to ignore imperial politics and to operate instead on the larger European stage. The most powerful German polities increasingly sought to increase their power and protect their interests by forming alliances and waging wars outside the traditional boundaries of the Holy Roman Empire. Meanwhile, with imperial cooperation at low ebb in the wake of the Thirty Years' War, foreign powers took advantage of German disunity and once again sought to claim territory in central Europe. Thus, the absolutist ruler Louis XIV, the preeminent monarch of Europe in his day, campaigned in Alsace between 1678 and 1681 and ravaged the Palatine between 1688 and 1697. While the Sun King eventually had to abandon the Palatinate, he established French control over Alsace, including the great city of Strasbourg. His intrusion into Germany also demonstrated to the German princes the feeble protection that the empire afforded them. The inability of the Habsburg emperors to assert their authority within the moribund empire was exacerbated by the depredations of the Ottoman Turks in the 1680s. In 1683, the Turks had even besieged Vienna itself, the Habsburgs' imperial capital, almost taking the city before being routed by a relief army led by King Jan Sobieski of Poland (1629–96). To counter this Turkish threat, the Habsburgs turned their attention to their eastern frontier and fought a series of wars aimed at retaking Hungary. Increasingly, the imperial dignity became secondary to safeguarding and extending their own dynastic lands.

As the Holy Roman Empire fell into irrelevance, individual German states, especially the rival powerhouses of Austria and Prussia, competed for recognition among the major powers of Europe. Without the protective framework of a vigorous empire to defend their interests, the hundreds of minor states of the empire drifted into obscurity. Meanwhile, the most prominent German princes competed for influence and prestige within Germany. The rulers of Saxony and Bavaria constructed lavish palaces and courts at Dresden and Munich, their respective capitals, and also constructed efficient state bureaucracies and potent military establishments. Ultimately, however, during the 18th century, German history was increasingly marked by dualism, with its two strongest states—Prussia and Austria—vying with one another for control of Germany. Prussia's dramatic rise set the stage for a titanic struggle between Prussia and Austria, the Hohenzollerns and the Habsburgs, for dominance within the empire, one that would rage for the next century.

Aufklärung: German Enlightenment

Amid Prussia's efforts to become a great power, cultural and intellectual life within Germany was undergoing a change. Beginning in the late 17th century, the Enlightenment, an intellectual movement marked by its efforts to reform society by applying the power of reason, had spread to Germany from France and Britain. The German Enlightenment, known as the Aufklärung, started with the work of a pair of contemporaneous intellectuals.

The first, Christian Thomasius (1655–1728), became a professor of law at the university of Leipzig in 1681 and, with the support of the Prussian elector Friedrich III, helped found the university of Halle in 1694. Throughout his career as a jurist and academic, Thomasius always emphasized the capability of human reason. Eager to apply his principles to social reform, Thomasius was instrumental in ending witchcraft prosecution in Germany, using rational arguments to expose the dubious foundations of such fantastic beliefs.

Working at roughly the same time as Thomasius, the German philosopher and mathematician Gottfried Wilhelm von Leibniz (1646–1716) was also instrumental in spreading the spirit of the Aufklärung throughout Germany. An innovative thinker, Leibniz left his mark in mathematics and is credited alongside Newton with inventing infinitesimal calculus. In philosophy, he developed the approach known as optimism, the idea that the universe, created by an omniscient God, is the best possible one. Although this philosophical position was savagely ridiculed by the French philosopher Voltaire (1694–1778) in *Candide,* in his day, Leibniz was considered to be among the giants of rationalism, along with French philosopher and scholar René Descartes (1596–1650) and Dutch philosopher Baruch Spinoza (1632–77).

The next generation of German Enlightenment thinkers was dominated by three intellectual giants, Gotthold Ephraim Lessing (1729–81), Moses Mendelssohn (1729–86), and Immanuel Kant (1724–1804). The first of these, the writer, dramatist, philosopher, and critic, Gotthold Ephraim Lessing, was born in Saxony in 1729, the son of a pastor. Instrumental in the development of a distinctively German theater, Lessing's most influential critical writings explored aesthetics, and his most important philosophical works advocated the freedom of thought. A true Enlightenment thinker, in matters of religion, Lessing relied upon the power of reason and boldly called for the toleration of other religious faiths within Christian society, a stance that drew strident protests from prominent clergymen and prompted the censorship of his works.

Prevented from publishing further philosophical works advocating tolerance, Lessing used the stage to express his views, penning his most famous work, the play *Nathan the Wise.* The play, published in 1779 and set in medieval Jerusalem, illustrates the themes of religious toleration, cross-cultural understanding, and moral relativism through the story of a Muslim sultan, a Christian knight, and a Jewish merchant who come to mutual understanding during a dispute over a priceless ring. *Nathan the Wise* was suppressed by German religious censors during Lessing's lifetime and by the Nazis long after his death. The title character, the pious and prudent Jew Nathan the Wise, was based upon the playwright's friend, the brilliant philosopher Moses Mendelssohn.

Moses Mendelssohn, born in 1729 in Saxony like his friend Lessing, became a leading figure in the German Aufklärung in his own right.

Raised in poverty, the young Mendelssohn was educated by a local rabbi and by learned Jews within his community, eventually moving to Berlin and acquiring knowledge of Latin, French, and English. Mendelssohn was exposed to the Enlightenment writings of British political philosopher John Locke (1632–1704) and in 1754 met Gotthold Ephraim Lessing, forging a lifelong friendship with the philosopher and playwright. Lessing, whose works arguing that Jews could have the same moral character as Christians met with derision and scorn in 1750s Berlin, admired Mendelssohn and encouraged him to publish several early writings anonymously. Gradually, Mendelssohn emerged as one of the great intellects of the German Enlightenment, even edging out the famous philosopher Immanuel Kant for the coveted Berlin Prize in a 1763 literary competition. In the same year, the Prussian monarch, Friedrich the Great, no friend of Prussia's Jews, rewarded Mendelssohn by granting him unrestricted permission to reside in Berlin unmolested as a "protected Jew"; the fact that the celebrated thinker needed such royal protection is an indication of the precarious position of Jews in Prussia at the time. In 1767, Mendelssohn published an important philosophical treatise on the immortality of souls, and its success cemented his place in the German Aufklärung.

Having made his name as a philosopher, the celebrated thinker soon became embroiled in a controversy that caused him to confront the status of Germany's Jewish community. In October 1769, a zealous young Swiss theologian named Johann Kaspar Lavater (1741–1801) sent Mendelssohn, whose brilliance and moral stature he admired, a book by the Christian metaphysician Charles Bonnet (1720–93), demanding that he either refute the book's premises in public or convert to the Christian faith. The renowned Jewish intellectual responded with an open letter to Lavater, arguing that it was possible to admire the morality of worthy men without converting to their religion (or, by extension, demanding that they convert to one's own). While Mendelssohn won the support of many of Germany's leading thinkers, the stress of the public confrontation taxed his health. Despite his flagging health, in the wake of the Lavater controversy, Mendelssohn began to use his considerable influence to improve the condition of Prussia's Jews, who suffered under the crushing weight of official restrictions and special taxes. In 1783, the great intellectual contributed a new German translation of the Pentateuch, the Jewish Scriptures, hoping to encourage Jews to use High German. For Mendelssohn, mastery of the German language, rather than the German-Jewish dialect known as Yiddish, was essential to the assimilation of the Jews into German culture and their eventual emancipation. Meanwhile, Mendelssohn promoted and published works advocating religious tolerance within Germany and calling for the emancipation of Germany's Jews by lifting the array of discriminatory laws that barred them from full participation in society. These Prussian government edicts, enforced throughout the reign of Friedrich II and similar to anti-Semitic measures issued by other European monarchs at the time, prohibited Jews from settling in certain cities, barred them from practicing certain restricted trades, and required them to pay exorbitant fees and exactions to the state. Regardless of his efforts, Mendelssohn's religiosity remained controversial within his homeland, and when he died in 1786, he was engaged in a bitter dispute with detractors who had accused him of atheism.

Without question, one of the greatest and most influential minds of the Aufklärung was the eminent German philosopher Immanuel Kant, who was a rough contemporary of Lessing and Mendelssohn born in the Prussian city of Königsberg in 1724. Pushing the Enlightenment to its very limits, Kant's monumental work, the *Critique of Pure Reason*, challenged traditional epistemology, the branch of philosophy concerned with the nature and grounds of knowledge, especially regarding its limits and validity, by investigating the limits and meaning of reason itself. In his philosophical works, Kant sought a compromise between empiricists, who believed all knowledge to be derived from experience, and rationalists, who thought it was always the product of human reason. He posited that both experience and reason are essential to arrive at knowledge that is both valid and objective. Kantian thought was tremendously influential in German intellectual circles in his own day and has continued to influence philosophic thought in the centuries since his death.

The spread of the Aufklärung in Germany was a reflection of the growing power of the bourgeoisie in the empire, the educated class of civil servants, jurists, and businessmen who formed a ready audience for the progressive ideas of philosophers like Thomasius and Kant. The growing wealth and influence of the middle classes, becoming more apparent in the 18th century, helped foster the spread of the cult of reason in Germany, along with strident calls for reform of the empire's increasingly anachronistic institutions. In German coffeehouses and on the pages of enlightened gazettes, the reading public eagerly consumed progressive notions of social reform. Influenced by Enlightenment ideals, the educated bureaucrats and technocrats who staffed the administrations of the German states constantly pressured their aristocratic rulers to enact enlightened reforms.

Enlightened Absolutism in Germany

Responding to this emerging bourgeois public, and influenced by Enlightenment thinkers in their own right, some German rulers began to enact progressive reforms within their realms. Known as enlightened absolutism or enlightened despotism, the efforts of rulers to modernize their governments and to ameliorate the effects of monarchical rule by enacting "enlightened" reforms changed the nature of political life in the empire during the 18th century. Rulers influenced by these principles often afforded their subjects religious toleration, freedom of the press, and the right to speak their minds without fearing punishment. Enlightened despots also fostered advancements in philosophy and the arts through generous patronage, sometimes even inviting leading Enlightenment thinkers to live at court.

While these enlightened despots proved willing to extend these sorts of rights to their subjects, they were despots nonetheless. Accordingly, most believed as fervently in their own divine right to rule as absolutist monarchs, and consistently refused to acquiesce to their liberal subjects' demands for written constitutions. For most 18th-century German princes, any such document would place an unacceptable brake on their free exercise of power. Thus, enlightened absolutists generally accepted a variety of progressive reforms, viewing themselves as instruments for improving the lives of their subjects. At the same time that they worked to reform aspects of the legal system or economic policies, often with the intent of augmenting their own authority, these enlightened rulers invariably rejected one of the most important principles of the Enlightenment: the social contract. Ironically, the progressive reforms realized by Prussian and Austrian rulers in the 18th century, intended to improve society, met with dogged resistance from the nobility and commoners alike, due to the populace's resentment of the reforms' autocratic nature and their reckless disregard for custom and traditional liberties.

The king of Prussia, Friedrich the Great (1740–86), is often cited as an enlightened absolutist, since he absorbed the principles of the Enlightenment and practiced the arts in his youth. He even tried to flee his domineering father before being dragged back to court. Once he took the throne, many of his policies can indeed be viewed as enlightened, including his benevolent legal reforms, which included the abolishment of judicial torture and his establishment of a state-sponsored system of secondary education. He modernized the Prussian civil service and even extended religious tolerance to his subjects. Furthermore, Friedrich corresponded with the great French philosopher Voltaire and provided generous support to progressive writers and artists. Despite these enlightened policies, it must be remembered that his reign was marked above all by autocratic rule and stifling militarism.

A pair of Austrian Habsburg monarchs, Maria Theresa (1717–80) and Joseph II (1741–90), came closer to the ideal of the enlightened ruler. Maria Theresa was archduchess of Austria, queen of Hungary and Bohemia, grand duchess of Tuscany, and, by virtue of her marriage to Francis of Lorraine (1708–65), empress consort of the Holy Roman Empire. Maria Theresa had to fight bitterly to secure the Austrian Crown. Since she was the only surviving heir of Holy Roman Emperor Charles VI, her succession was ratified after her father negotiated with the major European powers, issuing the Pragmatic Sanction in 1713 that declared her his heir to the Austrian throne. Once Maria Theresa assumed the throne, however, after the death of her father in 1740, Friedrich the Great of Prussia refused to recognize the claim of a woman to the Austrian Crown. This sparked the War of the Austrian Succession that raged from 1740 to 1748, a conflict that eventually involved all of the major powers of Europe, with Prussia, France, and the Electorate of Bavaria ranged against Austria and its English, Dutch, and Saxon allies. The war finally ended with the treaty of Aix-la-Chapelle, which ratified Maria Theresa's succession and Prussia's seizure of the valuable territory of Silesia.

Despite her success in defending her claim to the Austrian Crown, there was no question of a woman ascending to the imperial dignity. As a result, Maria Theresa had her husband, the duke of Lorraine, elected emperor in 1745. While Maria Theresa was technically empress consort, there is little doubt that she was the real power behind the throne. Ruling as de facto empress, Maria Theresa enacted a variety of enlightened reforms in her realms, including educational, economic, and agricultural initiatives. She also reinforced the Austrian military, which was still locked in the ongoing struggle with Prussia throughout her reign. During her reign, Maria Theresa helped restore Austrian power and ensured the future of the ruling dynasty, bearing 16 children. After the death of her husband in 1765, Maria Theresa became dowager empress, helping her son, crowned Holy Roman Emperor Joseph II, to administer the empire.

Joseph II, who reigned as emperor from 1765 to 1790 and as archduke of Austria from 1780 to 1790, was perhaps the German ruler most dedicated to enlightened absolutism. He was untiring in his attempts to modernize the administration of the Habsburgs' Austrian Crown lands and to bring rational reform to society. Influenced by his admiration for Voltaire and the French Enlightenment, he sought to extend religious toleration, to reduce the exactions of the church and the vestiges of feudalism, and to enhance both free trade and free thinking in his domain. Throughout his reign, Joseph II believed that it was his destiny, and the destiny of Austria, to change the world; guided by reason and unfettered by law, he sought to build a better state and society. Until the death of his domineering mother in 1780, however, he could not pursue these progressive programs without raising her opposition. Once she had died, Joseph pursued his reform program with reckless abandon, issuing thousands of new edicts. Exerting autocratic control over the state, he reformed the entire legal system, revamped the state's financial institutions, abolished serfdom, secularized numerous church properties, and established compulsory elementary education. In 1781, Joseph issued the Patent of Toleration, which guaranteed limited freedom of worship. He even abolished capital punishment in 1787, although like most of his enlightened reforms, this did not last long after his reign.

In his foreign policy, Joseph II was not so enlightened and eagerly pursued Austrian territorial expansion through bloody warfare and cunning diplomacy. Thus, he embroiled Austria in the costly struggle known as the Seven Years' War, a struggle that involved all the great powers of Europe and brought bloodshed to Europe, Asia, and North America from 1756 to 1763. Joseph also took part in the cynical dismemberment of Poland in the First Partition in 1772 and plunged Austria into the War of Bavarian Succession between 1778 and 1779, where Prussia and Saxony thwarted his attempts to add Lower Bavaria to his patrimony. In concert with his Russian ally, Joseph spent the next decade embroiled in expensive and ultimately fruitless campaigning against the Ottoman Turks on the Habsburgs' eastern frontier. Another reckless attempt to acquire Bavarian territory led to the formation of the so-called Fürstenbund, a league of German princes formed by Friedrich the Great of Prussia, united by their shared opposition to Austrian territorial expansion. This German alliance, the first led by Prussia, included the rulers of Saxony, Hanover, and later Saxe-Weimar, Saxe-Gotha, Palatinate-Zweibrücken, Brunswick, Baden, Hesse-Kassel, Anhalt, Ansbach, Mecklenburg, and the electorate of Mainz. Meant to check Joseph II's ambition, the short-lived Fürstenbund demonstrated the growing might of Prussia, the state that would eventually unify Germany, and the emperor's waning prestige. By 1790, rebellions against Joseph's centralizing initiatives and sweeping reforms had begun to break out on the fringes of the Habsburg realm, to the west in Belgium and to the east in Hungary. Fearing the fragmentation of his domain, Emperor Joseph was forced to repeal many of his reforms and died disillusioned at 48 in February 1790. His successor, Emperor Leopold II (1747–92), proved himself to be a more cautious and careful reformer.

As Joseph II pursued his failed reform initiatives, the Enlightenment project itself was coming into question in Germany, as writers and artists of the Sturm und Drang (storm and stress) movement—named after *Der Wirrwarr, oder Sturm und Drang,* a play by Friedrich Maximilian von Klinger (1752–1831) in which the action took place during the American Revolution—turned from rationality to emotionality, from reason to passion. This cultural movement, sustained by the philosopher Johann Georg Hamann (1730–88) and the polymath Johann Wolfgang von Goethe (1749–1832), flourished from the 1760s to the 1780s, foreshadowing the revolutionary passions and anxieties of the next quarter century. The literature, drama, and music of these artists

Johann Heinrich Wilhelm Tischbein's romantic 1787 portrait of the famous German writer and thinker Johann Wolfgang von Goethe, entitled Goethe in der Campagna *(Bildarchiv Preussischer Kulturbesitz, Berlin / Art Resource, NY / Städelsches Kunstinstitut, Frankfurt am Main)*

BEETHOVEN AND THE GERMAN AUFKLÄRUNG

Germany's place in the history of music is arguably unparalleled, as the country has produced many of the world's greatest composers. German-speaking Europe has produced the brilliant composers Johann Sebastian Bach (1685–1750), Georg Friedrich Handel (1685–1759), and Wolfgang Amadeus Mozart (1756–91). Another famous German composer, Ludwig van Beethoven (1770–1827), was deeply influenced by the German Aufklärung and the emerging romantic movement. Born in Bonn in 1770, Beethoven moved to Vienna in his youth, the musical capital of the day. Recognized as a virtuoso as a child, by the early 19th century, Beethoven had established himself as one of the greatest composers in history, despite the fact that he began losing his hearing in the 1790s.

The great composer wrote many of his most famous works as the Napoleonic Wars raged, including his iconic "Ode to Joy," a piece that links Germany's artistic heritage with today's unified Europe. This famous 1824 composition, the fourth movement of his Ninth Symphony, set Friedrich Schiller's poem "Ode to Joy" to music. Schiller's moving verse, written in 1785 as a rousing call for brotherhood among men, was an expression of the optimistic spirit of the Enlightenment. Beethoven's brilliant choral composition is considered one of the greatest masterpieces in the history of music and in 1985 was chosen as the official anthem of the European Union.

explored extremes of human emotion, seeking to elicit terror or unease in audiences through evocations of primal passion and violence. In this vein, Goethe's celebrated 1774 novel, *The Sorrows of Young Werther,* provides a painful depiction of unrequited love and suicide. In the novel, inspired by a painful episode from Goethe's youth, a sensitive young artist recounts his passion for the beautiful Charlotte, who is engaged to another man. Distraught, Werther leaves the village of Wahlheim, where Charlotte lives, and settles in Weimar. When he returns and finds Charlotte married, the pain is overwhelming. Werther continues to visit Charlotte, tortured by the knowledge that she will never be his, until she asks him to stop seeing her. Overcome by feelings, Werther decides to commit suicide and, after writing an emotional farewell letter, shoots himself with a borrowed pistol. The novel ends on a somber note, with Werther's lonely funeral, as his beloved Charlotte refrains from visiting his grave.

Goethe disavowed the novel in later life, but it became an instant sensation, making him an international celebrity. In the decades after its publication, young men across Europe sought to emulate Werther's romantic style and youthful angst. Despite the popularity of their works, both Goethe and his closest associate, the poet, philosopher, and playwright Johann Christoph Friedrich von Schiller (1759–1805), eventually abandoned the Sturm und Drang movement in favor of a rejuvenated classicism. The radical rejection of Enlightenment rationality they initiated with their early works, however, helped foster later romantic aspirations for German nationalism and liberalism.

At the close of the 18th century, Germany lay disunited amid the simmering rivalry between Prussia and Austria. Having emerged from the trauma of the Thirty Years' War, the empire was once again the "cockpit of Europe," where the great powers of the era waged their dynastic wars. As the Holy Roman Empire gradually pulled itself apart in the course of these struggles, its medieval institutions increasingly appeared irrelevant in an era of dynastic warfare and cynical diplomacy. However, the rivalry between the Hohenzollerns and the Habsburgs, and the failed reforms of Germany's enlightened despots, would soon give way to a wave of radical change from the west: the French Revolution.

7

NAPOLEONIC GERMANY
AND THE REVOLUTION
OF 1848

The March Revolution of 1848 pitted the forces of absolutism against radical liberals and nationalists, bringing mass demonstrations and violent clashes to the streets of Germany's cities. The previous six decades had brought bewildering change to Europe, beginning with the turmoil and terror of the French Revolution, an upheaval inspired by the ideals of the Enlightenment that toppled France's monarchy in 1792. The wave of revolutionary fervor that transformed France swept across Europe during the Napoleonic Wars, shaking the Continent's political and social order to its core and stirring nationalist passions in Germany after the dissolution of the Holy Roman Empire in 1806. After the defeat of Napoléon (1769–1821) in 1815, however, the hopes of Europe's revolutionaries were dashed when the great powers met in Vienna and established the "Concert of Europe," an alliance of monarchs that established a balance of power and suppressed liberal political agitation. In the spring of 1848, however, this conservative order was threatened by the outbreak of spontaneous revolts across Europe, as angry mobs took to the streets, demanding everything from moderate liberal reforms to radical political change.

In Dresden, capital city of the Kingdom of Saxony, the revolution began quietly enough. Once the German Confederation approved a general election for delegates to a National Assembly that would meet in Frankfurt to draft a constitution, however, the mood quickly changed. In April 1848, a new nationalist political organization known as the Patriotic Association emerged, and its candidates won election to all but one of the seats in the Frankfurt Parliament. The Association's leaders were bourgeois intellectuals, content with constitutional monarchy, but its base was made up of more radical laborers, who agitated for republican government. Radical newspapers, including the *Volksblätter* published by the conductor at the Dresden Opera House, August Röckel (1814–76), stirred the passions of the populace and helped the Patriotic Association gain new members.

By the winter of 1849, Dresden had become a hotbed of radical politics, and a cadre of revolutionaries began plotting to overthrow the Saxon monarchy. These conspirators included the republican jurist Samuel Erdmann Tzschirner (1812–70), the radical publishers August Röckel and Ludwig Wittig (1815–74), as well as the Russian anarchist Mikhail Bakunin (1814–76). Alarmed by the growing radicalism in the city, on April 28, 1849, King Friedrich Augustus II (1797–1854) refused to accept the liberal constitution issued by the Frankfurt Parliament and suspended the lower house of the Saxon assembly. This move sparked widespread outrage, and amid the gathering storm the Prussians offered military assistance to the Saxon monarch to quell the disturbance. In response, angry demonstrators filled the streets of Dresden, marching on the municipal armory, where on May 3 they demanded weapons to defend themselves from the expected arrival of Prussian soldiers in the city. When frightened Saxon troops opened fire on the protesters, the crowd went wild and began barricading Dresden's streets. The May Uprising of 1849 had begun.

As Friedrich August hesitated, the revolutionaries elected a democratic provisional government, headed by Tzschirner. The revolutionaries hoped that the king would be forced to recognize the revolutionary government and accept the Frankfurt constitution, but instead he holed up in a royal fortress at Königstein. While the provisional government tried to arrange a diplomatic solution, the military governor of Dresden mobilized Saxon military units and awaited the arrival of crack Prussian infantry so he could end the insurrection by force. Unable to convince the rest of Saxony to come to their aid, or to convince the army to join the revolution, the revolutionaries manning the barricades waited grimly for the soldiers to begin their assault. Fighting began around midday on May 5, and the 5,000 professional troops supporting the monarchy quickly crushed the rabble of around 3,000 disorganized and poorly equipped revolutionaries. At least 250 of the revolutionaries died, and hundreds were wounded in the street fighting. By May 9, the rest had fled into exile in Switzerland, like the famous composer Richard Wagner (1813–83), or in the United States, or were captured and sentenced to long prison terms.

The May Uprising in Dresden was the bloodiest episode in the wave of revolutionary fervor that spilled over Germany in 1848–49.

These uprisings erupted in all the major capitals of the empire, Berlin, Vienna, Dresden, Frankfurt, Stuttgart, and forever changed the course of German history.

The French Revolution and Germany

The French Revolution of 1789–99 swept away monarchy in France and transformed life there forever. Fostered by discontent with social inequality and inspired by Enlightenment principles, this dynamic outburst of revolutionary zeal not only changed life for the French but also for all of Europe. The Age of Revolution transformed Europe, sweeping away the vestiges of the feudal system and bringing radical political, social, and economic change. Founded on progressive principles, the revolution descended into violence and oppression, sparking a generation of bloodshed on the Continent. Perhaps nowhere was more affected by these events than Germany, where the flames of revolution brought an end to a political system that had stood for 1,000 years: the Holy Roman Empire.

In the early years of the French Revolution, France's neighbors, including German powers Austria and Prussia, proved reluctant to intervene. Despite his aristocratic distaste for insurrection, Emperor Leopold II took a cautious approach, hoping to turn the domestic disorder within France to his advantage in the old struggle between the Habsburgs and the French Crown. Meanwhile, eyeing the prospect of another partition of a hapless Poland, Prussia was distracted as well. By 1791, however, Leopold was growing increasingly concerned about the situation in France, not least because he was the brother of the French queen, Marie Antoinette (1755–93). In August of that year, Leopold approached Austria's rival, Prussia, and the two German powers jointly issued the Declaration of Pillnitz. In this decree, Leopold and Friedrich Wilhelm II warned the revolutionaries in France of serious repercussions if they harmed the royal family. The Pillnitz decree, along with the agitation of French nobles within Germany who had fled their homeland, raised tensions between France's revolutionary government and Austria to the boiling point.

The revolutionaries struck first, and in April 1792, the Revolutionary Assembly voted to declare war on Austria and began preparing for an invasion of the Austrian Netherlands. The French revolutionaries expected the Dutch to rise against their Habsburg overlords and embrace the spirit of liberty, equality, and fraternity. The armies of the revolution did not prove up to the task, however, since the radicals in France had purged its aristocratic officer corps, and discipline had broken down among the rank and file. Soon after taking the field, most of the French soldiers deserted. As the revolutionary government scrambled to rebuild its forces, an allied army commanded by the duke of Brunswick, and made up mostly of crack Prussian infantry, invaded France in June 1792. Quickly taking a series of French fortresses, including Verdun, the duke delivered the so-called Brunswick Manifesto to the revolutionary government. Instead of breaking the will of the revolutionaries, this ill-considered document, declaring that the allied forces intended to restore the French king and execute any rebels who resisted, actually endangered the royal family and rallied the French populace around the fragile new government.

On January 21, 1793, the revolutionaries executed Louis XVI and Marie Antoinette, and a rejuvenated revolutionary army took the field. The desperate French government relied upon mass conscription to raise a massive army, hoping to overwhelm the relatively small professional armies of their German adversaries. The execution of the French monarch prompted Spain and Portugal to join the alliance against France, and in February 1793, France declared war on Britain and the Dutch Republic. The stage was now set for a cataclysmic struggle that would transform Europe, known as the French Revolutionary Wars.

The ragtag French revolutionary armies found themselves outclassed again by their professional adversaries in the early campaigns of 1793, taking heavy losses and sparking revolts against the revolutionary government in the French countryside. However, by the end of the year, learning from these initial defeats, their massive conscript armies began to turn the tide, beating the allied armies, expelling them from French territory and bringing savage repression to the restive French provinces. In 1794, the French went on the offensive, and their troops invaded Italy and Spain and overran Belgium and the Rhineland. The following year, French armies conquered the Netherlands, installing a revolutionary regime called the Batavian Republic. The establishment of this puppet government prefigured their intrusion into German politics a decade later, under Napoléon. On the heels of this dramatic French victory, Portugal and Prussia withdrew from the alliance: The revolutionary government had averted collapse and safeguarded the borders of their new nation-state.

In 1796, the revolutionary armies launched a daring triple assault on Austria, weakened by the departure of Portugal and Prussia. Two French armies crossed the Rhine, and a third, under a young officer named Napoléon Bonaparte, moved through Italy. All three of these great armies had a single goal: to meet on Austrian soil and take Vienna, capital of the Habsburg emperors. After a string of victories in Germany, French forces advanced through Bavaria and into the Tyrol before being defeated by an Austrian army commanded by the able Archduke Charles (1771–1847). While these French armies had to withdraw over the Rhine, Napoléon's forces fared much better in Italy, defeating Austrian armies there and besieging the city of Mantua. After the fall of Mantua, and the surrender of 18,000 Austrian troops, the Tyrol was open to Napoléon's troops, and the Austrians sued for peace, signing a humiliating settlement. In the Treaty of Campo Formio, signed in October 1797, the Austrians handed over Belgium to the revolutionary government and recognized the French occupation of the Rhineland and northern Italy. Furthermore, France and Austria partitioned the territories of the Republic of Venice. While this treaty signaled the collapse of the First Coalition against France, it did not end hostilities for long, and the Austrians began gearing up for war again.

In 1798, Napoléon launched his quixotic Egyptian campaign, to the relief of the revolutionary government, which was happy to have the ambitious general far from the seat of power. In his absence, the French intervened in Switzerland, riven by political strife, and established another puppet government, known as the Helvetic Republic. The French annexed Geneva and turned on Rome, daring to depose Pope Pius VI (1717–99) before erecting a pro-French republic in the Eternal City. Anxiously watching these developments and fearing similar French intrusion into Germany, the Austrians joined a powerful Second Coalition against the revolutionary government in June 1798. The alliance included former allies Austria and Britain, joined by a new partner, imperial Russia. These allies attacked the French on several fronts in 1799.

In Italy, the Russians won several important victories, pushing the French forces back to the Alps. While the revolutionary armies fared better against the British in the Netherlands and the Russians in Switzerland, Archduke Charles's Austrian forces in Germany quickly drove the French back across the Rhine. Things looked bleak for the revolutionary government of France, until internal squabbling among the allies caused the Russians to pull out of the Second Coalition. Meanwhile, at the end of 1799, Napoléon returned from his Egyptian debacle and launched a military coup, seizing power in France. Declaring himself First Consul, head of the French government, Napoléon immediately went on the offensive.

In 1800, French troops commanded by Napoléon himself reversed Austrian fortunes in Italy, defeating Habsburg forces at the Battle of

Marengo and driving them back to the Austrian Alps. After another major French victory over the Austrians in Germany, at Hohenlinden, near Munich, Napoléon marched on Vienna. This reversal shattered the Second Coalition and forced the Habsburgs to capitulate once again. In the Treaty of Lunéville, signed in February 1801, the Austrians recognized French control of German territory to the Rhine and accepted the French client republics in the Netherlands and Italy. After the capitulation of the Austrians, the British were also forced to the peace table.

Napoléon and the Dissolution of the Holy Roman Empire

Flush with victory, Napoléon subverted the revolutionary government and was proclaimed emperor of the French by the Senate in May 1804. In December of that year, he crowned himself, becoming a new Caesar. Rather than pacify Europe, however, the new emperor's ambition brought an intensification of violence that devastated the Continent in the following decade. These conflicts, known collectively as the Napoleonic Wars, would change life in Germany forever.

In the preceding year, 1803, the map of Germany had been redrawn as the Holy Roman Empire passed one of its last comprehensive pieces of legislation, the Final Recess of the Imperial Deputation. This legislation represented an attempt to deal with harsh realities dictated by the Treaty of Lunéville in 1801, which had ceded German territories west of the Rhine to the French. Emperor Francis II (1768–1835), the last Holy Roman Emperor, who had taken the imperial throne after the death of Joseph II in 1790, commissioned the Imperial Deputation to arrange compensation for the Rhineland princes deposed when the French were granted their hereditary lands. In February 1803, the commission compensated secular princes with new territories at the expense of the imperial cities and ecclesiastical rulers. While most secular rulers were thus restored, only six of the empire's 48 imperial cities remained and all but three ecclesiastical rulers were dispossessed. In effect, the Imperial Deputation effected a massive transfer of territory, political allegiance, and economic resources within the borders of the empire. Upsetting the status quo and stirring up anxieties, it even helped spread revolutionary fervor within the teetering empire. In the following year, 1804, several German states, including Bavaria, Württemberg, and Baden, even made separate alliances with the French. The Holy Roman Empire was quickly unraveling.

Alarmed by these developments, Austria, Portugal, and Russia joined Britain in a third alliance against the French in 1805. This coalition proved no more successful than its predecessors, suffering a series of crushing defeats at the hands of Napoléon and his generals. While Britain averted a possible French invasion with its glorious naval victory at Trafalgar, in Germany the French proved their dominance on the battlefield. In a series of rapid actions near the south German city of Ulm, Napoléon's forces outmaneuvered and captured an entire Austrian army before crushing the main Russo-Austrian force at Austerlitz in early December. The defeat at Austerlitz knocked the Austrians out of the war, and the Habsburgs were forced to sign the costly Treaty of Pressburg on December 26, 1805. This capitulation reaffirmed the earlier Lunéville settlement, forcing Austria to cede territory to Napoléon's German allies and to pay ruinous reparations to France. Austerlitz also sounded the death knell of the Holy Roman Empire, an institution that had governed Germany for 1,000 years.

The first blow came on July 12, 1806, when Napoléon signed a treaty with 16 of his German allies, including the major states of Baden, Bavaria, Hesse-Darmstadt, Saxony, and Württemberg. By signing this agreement, the 16 German principalities formally withdrew from the Holy Roman Empire and formed a coalition known as the Confederation of the Rhine (Rheinbund), a buffer intended to secure France's eastern frontier. Primarily intended as a military alliance, the confederation formally allied itself with the French emperor. In return, the member states were permitted to expand by gobbling up the many small territories that the empire had long protected, and the great princes, including the rulers of Bavaria, Saxony, and Württemberg, were proclaimed kings. In the wake of these traumatic developments and faced with an ultimatum from Napoléon, on August 6, 1806, Francis II formally abdicated as emperor and proclaimed the dissolution of the Holy Roman Empire. With the breakdown of the empire and the dubious protection it had afforded to its constituents, a score of other German states flocked to join the Confederation of the Rhine. In the end, only Austria, now ruled by Francis II as the Austrian Empire, Prussia, Danish Holstein, and Swedish Pomerania remained outside its orbit to defy Napoléon.

Napoléon defeated the fourth coalition formed to thwart his domination of Europe between 1806 and 1807. This time, Prussia joined Britain, Russia, Saxony, and Sweden. The Hohenzollerns feared the growing might of France and resented the formation of the Confederation of the Rhine, which threatened their power within Germany. In the end, even the formidable Prussian military made little difference, as Napoléon won a series of crushing victories over the coalition. His forces defeated the Prussians at Jena-Auerstedt in October 1806, took Berlin, and occupied East Prussia. Launching an attack on Russia from Prussian territory, Napoléon forced the Russians to capitulate in June 1807. The subsequent settlement, the Treaty of Tilsit, had major ramifications for Germany. According to the terms of the treaty, the French received half of Prussia, which Napoléon reorganized as the Kingdom of Westphalia. This new principality, a French puppet state, was given to Napoléon's brother, Jérôme Bonaparte (1784–1860). Named king, he immediately joined the Confederation of the Rhine and enacted a series of social, economic, and legal reforms modeled on Napoleonic France.

In 1809, in the War of the Fifth Coalition, the Austrian Empire, its armies newly reorganized and its tactics and equipment modernized by Archduke Charles, joined Britain against Napoléon and his imperial dominions. Napoléon received the most significant support from the Kingdom of Bavaria, a demonstration of the growing divisions within Germany during the Napoleonic period. After a series of bloody campaigns against the Austrians in central Europe and the British in Iberia, the French gained the upper hand with their victory at the Battle of Wagram outside Vienna, where some 300,000 troops clashed. With the French again on their doorstep, the Austrians were forced to sign yet another humiliating capitulation, the Treaty of Schönbrunn. In return for the preservation of the Habsburg Empire, the Austrians ceded a host of valuable territories to France and its allies, including Carinthia, Carniola, its Adriatic ports, and Galicia. Bavaria received much of the Tyrol. Humbled, Austria lost more than 3 million subjects with the transfer of these territories. Furthermore, Austrian emperor Francis II was forced to pay a crushing indemnity to the French, to recognize Jérôme Bonaparte as king of Spain, and to adhere to Napoléon's embargo on British goods.

While German troops from Prussia, Austria, and Bavaria had fought on opposite sides of the Napoleonic Wars, the era's revolutionary upheavals and military struggles, as well as the dissolution of the Holy Roman Empire, also helped foster a growing sense of German nationalism. As French troops triumphed on the battlefields of Germany, they also had to waste resources suppressing revolts in the puppet state, the Kingdom of Westphalia, and in the former Austrian territory of the Tyrol, as their German subjects chafed under French domination. By the time that the allies formed their victorious Sixth Coalition in 1812, the German populace was increasingly united in its opposition to French intrusion across the Rhine.

A German "Stahlhelm" paramilitary unit assembles at the Battle of the Nations monument outside Leipzig in September 1932. A ponderous monument to the 1813 Battle of Leipzig during the Napoleonic Wars, the site was completed a century later and long inspired aggressive nationalist sentiment. (Bundesarchiv, Bild 102-13867)

On the heels of Napoléon's disastrous debacle in Russia, the bulk of his armies destroyed, he faced this Sixth Coalition, made up of Austria and Prussia, as well as Britain, Russia, and Sweden. The ensuing Battle of Leipzig, in October 1813, proved to be the largest battle on European soil before World War I, involving more than half a million troops. Also known as the Battle of the Nations, the confrontation provided a mythical rally point for German nationalists of the late 19th century, who romanticized it as a struggle of the "German people" to expel the French invaders and commemorated it with the massive 300-foot-high Völkerschlachtdenkmal, a monument begun in 1898. In fact, Napoléon's French armies were supported by troops supplied by his German allies from the Confederation of the Rhine. While Napoléon won a few minor victories in the lead-up to the major action, he suffered a catastrophic defeat at the hands of the allied armies at the Battle of Leipzig. The allied victory pushed the French back over the Rhine and prompted the leading German states of the Confederation of the Rhine, including Bavaria, Saxony, and Württemberg, to switch sides and to join the coalition. Having broken the French military, the coalition invaded France and deposed Napoléon, restoring the Bourbon monarchy in France and exiling him to the isolated island of Elba in 1814. Meanwhile, Russian forces overran and dissolved the French puppet state in northern Germany, the Kingdom of Westphalia, restoring the political map of 1806. Finally, without French support, the Confederation of the Rhine collapsed, most of its remaining members having joined the victorious allies after the Battle of the Nations.

In the aftermath of the Napoleonic Wars, the Congress of Vienna would redraw the map of Europe. For the Germans, this meant restoring the prewar borders of most belligerents and the creation, in 1815, of the German Confederation, which replaced the defunct Confederation of the Rhine and set the stage for the eventual unification of Germany.

Congress of Vienna and the German Confederation

The Congress of Vienna, intended to restore order to a Europe destabilized by the meteoric rise and fall of Napoléon, was convened in July 1814. Attended by representatives of all of the Continent's great powers, including Austria, Prussia, Britain, Russia, and France, it had been arranged by the Treaty of Paris, the settlement between the victors of the Sixth Coalition and France. Alongside these major participants, virtually every state and aristocratic dynasty in Europe had a delegation in

Vienna, with more than 200 separate groups and a horde of representatives from individual cities, religious orders, and associations.

Austria's foreign minister, Klemens Wenzel von Metternich (1773–1859), the preeminent statesman of the age, chaired the Congress. It had three main objectives: to redraw Europe's territorial borders jumbled by Napoléon's conquests; to settle lingering political disputes raised by a quarter century of conflict; and to deal with the destabilization of central Europe caused by the dissolution of the Holy Roman Empire. Despite Napoléon's escape from Elba and his last desperate gamble at Waterloo in June 1815, the Congress continued uninterrupted, a sign of its significance. Its Final Act, negotiated in a series of face-to-face meetings between the most prominent delegates and signed in June 1815, set the stage for European affairs for the next century and had important consequences for German history.

The delegates from the most important allied states, Austria, Britain, Prussia, and Russia, tried initially to exclude France and other, lesser states, such as Portugal, Spain, and Sweden. However, the cunning backroom diplomacy of France's shrewd representative, Charles Maurice de Talleyrand-Périgord (1754–1838), thwarted their efforts. Talleyrand had managed to survive amid the turbulent political intrigue of France, serving Louis XVI, the revolutionary government, Emperor Napoléon, and the restored Bourbon monarch, Louis XVIII (1755–1824). Vienna, however, was his masterstroke, and he contrived to insert France among the allies, as a major player in the proceedings. With Talleyrand and Metternich playing the major roles in the deliberations, the Congress of Vienna issued its Final Act on June 9, 1815, just days before Napoléon's defeat at Waterloo.

The Final Act of the Congress of Vienna instituted a sweeping range of provisions, remaking the European political and diplomatic landscape. Britain gained valuable colonial possessions in Africa and Asia. Russia obtained most of Napoléon's Polish puppet state, the Duchy of Warsaw, as well as Finland. The House of Orange-Nassau was to rule the reconstituted Netherlands, made up of the old United Provinces and the former Austrian possessions in the southern Netherlands. Switzerland's neutrality was guaranteed. In Italy, Victor Emmanuel I (1759–1824), king of Sardinia, was given control of Piedmont, Nice, Savoy, and Genoa. Ferdinand IV, king of Sicily (1751–1825), was given the Kingdom of Naples, and the pope was restored as ruler of the Papal States. The most far-reaching changes, however, were in Germany.

Austria had suffered grievously during the Napoleonic Wars and saw most of these reverses erased. Metternich regained the Tyrol,

Salzburg, Lombardy-Venetia in Italy, and key territory in Dalmatia for the Habsburgs. Prussia, having played a key role in the final defeat of Napoléon, gained significant territory: the Hohenzollerns gained much of Saxony, a share of the former Duchy of Warsaw and former Duchy of Westphalia, Swedish Pomerania, and the strategic port of Danzig. The leading German states of the Confederation of the Rhine, having abandoned Napoléon after his defeat at the Battle of Leipzig, also obtained territorial concessions. The Congress recognized the wartime acquisitions of Baden, Bavaria, Hesse-Darmstadt, and Württemberg, gains confirmed by the Imperial Deputation of 1803. Most important, the Final Act established a new German Confederation to take the place of the old empire. This confederation, made up of more than 30 German states, was to be governed by the emperor of Austria, who served as its president. Ironically, its dominant states, Austria and Prussia, old rivals, both drew their strength from the extensive territories they held outside of Germany.

The German Confederation formed from the wreckage of the Holy Roman Empire by the Congress of Vienna was a conservative institution intended to prevent the sort of radical fervor unleashed by the French Revolution and Napoleonic Wars. The 38 sovereign states and four free cities that comprised the confederation were only loosely aligned, meeting at an assembly in Frankfurt with the Austrian representative presiding as president. Metternich, the Austrian statesman and architect of the Congress of Vienna, dominated the German Confederation for its first 30 years. Working to snuff out the spread of the liberal ideals that had ravaged Europe in the Age of Revolution, Metternich issued a torrent of repressive legislation. His Carlsbad Decrees of 1819, for example, shored up the conservative, aristocratic order in Germany by enacting rigid censorship of the press. In the 1820s, he forged the so-called Holy Alliance, binding the rulers of Austria, Prussia, and Russia to the cause of maintaining autocratic, monarchical control within central Europe.

As Metternich labored to uphold the status quo within Germany, however, powerful political, intellectual, and economic trends were fostering the spread of liberal ideologies and pushing Germany toward unification. Within the German states, an increasingly wealthy and vocal bourgeois class was pushing for liberal reforms, as they had during the era of Enlightened Absolutism. These reforms, often based upon Napoleonic policies in the Rhineland, included the establishment of laissez-faire economic policies, the protection of free speech rights, and even the formation of constitutional governments within the individual states that made up the confederation. The most successful of these demands, pushed by Germany's rising business class, called for the removal of impediments to trade within the confederation. Germany's businessmen sought the end of restrictive guild monopolies within German cities, the adoption of a common currency and system of weights and measures throughout the confederation, and the abolition of the rapacious river and road tolls and customs duties that crippled commerce. Facing stiff economic competition from the British, German merchants faced hundreds of complicated and expensive customs and tolls that hampered domestic trade. By the 1830s, the commercial class had made significant strides in meeting this last goal, the reduction of customs barriers within Germany, with the aid of Prussia, efforts that helped lead to the eventual unification of the German nation.

Since the Congress of Vienna had not addressed economic activity within the newly created German Confederation, in 1818 the Prussians had established a customs union to facilitate trade among their own scattered territories. This Prussian-dominated Zollverein, or Customs Union, gradually expanded as more and more German states joined between the 1820s and 1860s. By 1835, it had come to encompass most of the states of the German Confederation, including leading constituents like Baden, Bavaria, Saxony, Thuringia, and Württemberg. The Zollverein stimulated the German economy and fostered rapid industrialization. Between 1840 and 1860, steel and coal production climbed sharply in Germany, and German factory output increased exponentially. The flood of manufactured goods produced by German factories caused the expansion of the middle class, breeding ground for nationalist and liberal ideals. As the Zollverein expanded, the Prussians were careful to exclude their Austrian rivals, however, sowing the seeds of German unification under the Prussian aegis. The German Customs Union was intended to promote trade within the confederation by reducing trade barriers, but economic integration gradually began to foster a sense of shared German identity within the member states.

The development of nationalist sentiment among Germany's liberal intellectuals and educated professionals also cultivated dreams of unification. This liberal intelligentsia was deeply influenced by the writings of authors such as the Prussian philosopher Johann Gottfried Herder (1744–1803). Herder's passionate nationalism was based upon the German people's shared language and historical experience, steeped in romantic visions of medieval Germany. His influential cultural nationalism served to foster a desire for unification in the decades after his death. Meanwhile, the painful experience of the Napoleonic

Wars taught the Germans that their disunited principalities were no match for a unified France, bolstered by ardent nationalist fervor. These nationalistic impulses were amplified by a diplomatic crisis in the Rhineland in 1840. The first murmurs of modern German nationalism had surfaced during the Napoleonic Wars, in opposition to French occupation. Consequently, when the foreign minister of King Louis-Philippe's (1773–1850) France issued statements regarding his country's Rhine border, it aroused fears of a French invasion of the Rhineland. The result was an outburst of German nationalistic fervor in print and song, as presses churned out patriotic newspapers, including the *Deutsche Zeitung,* and crowds sang stirring "Rheinlied" songs such as "Die Wacht am Rhine." Another of these nationalistic hymns, the "Deutschlandlied," which opens with the line "Deutschland über alles" (Germany above all), would one day become the national anthem of a united Germany. These patriotic expressions served to spread nationalistic sentiments throughout the German populace in the decade before the March Revolution of 1848.

As these liberals and nationalists agitated for political reform and advocated German nationalism, conservative forces sought to maintain the status quo. Perhaps no one was more opposed to these radical ideas than Metternich, since in the multicultural Austrian Empire, Croats, Czechs, Hungarians, Slovaks, and Serbs outnumbered Germans. Thus, the Austrian Empire would not fit easily into a united Germany, where inclusion was based upon shared German culture and language. Accordingly, Metternich sought to maintain the German Confederation, loosely integrated and dominated by Austria. Ironically, the haughty Austrian aristocrat's aversion to German unification was shared by many of the farmers, craftsmen, and workers who made up Germany's lower classes. Without a voice in politics, and impoverished by the spread of industrialization in the region after 1815, these laborers had little interest in German unification and clung to the parochial institutions that had sustained their forefathers: village, family, and guild.

Despite these objections, powerful political and economic forces were sweeping Germany, emboldening the businessman and bureaucrats, jurists and academics, who advocated liberal reforms and parliamentary government. These educated men of the bourgeoisie viewed a unified German "Fatherland" as a better vehicle for realizing these aims than the hidebound, aristocratic regimes of the confederation. Among these liberals, who sought more representative government, there was a range of political views. While many moderate liberals advocated constitutional monarchy, the more radical ones called for the establishment of a German republic governed by a parliamentary democracy. This growing agitation among the German bourgeoisie eventually boiled over, causing the revolution of 1848.

The Revolution of 1848

The forces of conservatism in Germany, bolstered by the Congress of Vienna and embodied in Metternich's direction of the German Confederation, had worked relentlessly since the end of the Napoleonic Wars to repress the revolutionary impulses the wars unleashed. By 1830, however, the stability that Metternich had imposed in Europe was beginning to break down. A pair of successful revolutions, fueled by a combustible mix of liberal ideology and nationalist fervor, broke out that year in France and Belgium. Seeing monarchs unseated in these revolutions, Europe's remaining rulers contemplated a military intervention, while another rebellion began in Poland. In response, the autocratic monarchs of central and eastern Europe met secretly in Berlin in 1833 to reaffirm the "Holy Alliance" of the emperor of Austria, the king of Prussia, and the czar of Russia. This alliance, engineered by an aging Metternich, was intended to preserve monarchical government in the face of rising revolutionary sentiments.

These reactionary efforts bought only a temporary reprieve, and the revolutions of the 1830s were just a prelude to a mighty wave of revolution that gripped Europe in the next decade. Once again, revolutionary currents emanating from France buffeted Germany. In March 1848, riots broke out in a number of German cities, as radicals pressed for political and social reforms. The revolution of 1848 pitted the conservative, aristocratic order against a hodgepodge of revolutionaries, including both radical firebrands inspired by the French Revolution and learned liberals who sought political and economic reform. In the period before the outbreak of the 1848 revolution, known as the Vormärz era, romantic poets such as August Heinrich Hoffmann von Fallersleben (1798–1874), who wrote the pan-German anthem, "Das Lied der Deutschen," fired the nationalist imagination. Somewhat ironically, the nationalist lyric poetry of Heinrich Heine (1797–1856) also stirred these passions, despite the fact that the poet had converted from Judaism to Lutheranism at 25 and had fled the censorship and oppression of Germany for France at 33. Thus, despite his role in promoting German nationalism, later the Nazis would include Heine's writings in their massive public book-burnings in Berlin in 1933. Nationalist youth organizations also proliferated within Germany before 1848, ranging from the gymnastic clubs run by the Prussian liberal Friedrich Ludwig Jahn (1778–1852) to the college fraternities known as Burschenschaften, which promoted nationalistic and democratic ideals. Ominously, these fraternities denied admission to Jews, deriding them as non-German despite their shared language and historical experience, on the basis of their distinctive religious and cultural practices.

As early as 1819, Metternich had sought to stamp out these nationalist embers by issuing a repressive edict known as the Carlsbad Decrees. This legislation placed restrictions on universities, considered hotbeds of subversive nationalist and liberal thinking, throughout the German Confederation. The decrees made membership in Burschenschaften illegal and authorized university inspectors to monitor students' activities and professors' lectures on each German campus. More broadly, the Carlsbad Decrees introduced tight censorship of the press throughout the confederation and led to the discharge of reformers from university and government posts in its constituent states.

The Carlsbad Decrees could not stifle the radical passions that animated the Vormärz period, and a mass protest erupted at Hambach Castle in the Rhineland in May 1832, an uprising that foreshadowed the March Revolution of 1848. Known as the Hambacher Fest, the meeting attracted nationalists and liberals drawn from throughout German society. Some 30,000 people took part in the festival, including politicians, students, and workers, who called for a unified German state with a representative government and personal freedom for its citizens. While the spontaneous uprising did not achieve concrete results, it signaled the growing influence of liberal and nationalistic ideals among the German populace. In the spring of 1848, as a wave of revolution swept across Europe, the spirit of the Hambacher Fest gripped all of Germany.

The March Revolution of 1848 unleashed powerful forces of discontent against the conservative order in the German Confederation. The wave of revolution spread from France, tapping into widespread agitation within Germany. Industrialization had transformed the German economy and created a new sort of working class that was growing slowly during this period. Poorly organized and at the mercy of their industrialist bosses, these factory laborers were subject to the writings of socialists among the radical left. Karl Heinrich Marx (1818–83), for example, published his masterwork, *The Communist Manifesto,* amid the unrest of 1848, in an attempt to appeal to this burgeoning industrial proletariat. Poor craftsmen, displaced by increasing industrial production, and rural farmworkers alike had suffered from economic depression and crop failures since 1846 and flocked to urban slums in search of work. Together, the impoverished masses of Germany's small but cramped cities made for a volatile audience for the revolutionary appeals of the middle classes, a restless mob ready for change. Joining the liberal intelligentsia, whose radical ideals animated the revolution, the masses took to the streets of Germany's cities during the March Revolution. In the south and west of the German Confederation, in mass demonstrations, protesters called for a bevy of sweeping changes, including national unity, freedom of the press, and the formation of a parliamentary government.

The wave of revolution that would engulf Europe began in France in February 1848, sparked by a coup that toppled King Louis-Philippe. As word spread of the triumph of the Parisian revolutionaries, revolts erupted across Europe, spreading quickly throughout the German Confederation. At the end of February, in the city of Mannheim, an assembly of

KARL MARX AND *THE COMMUNIST MANIFESTO*

Karl Heinrich Marx, born in Trier in 1818, stands as one of the most influential—and controversial—thinkers in modern history. Trained as a philosopher, Marx is better known as a revolutionary who laid the foundations for modern communism. Karl Marx's most famous work, *The Communist Manifesto,* was written on the eve of the revolution of 1848 as an impassioned call to arms to the workers of the world. Marx was troubled by the plight of the factory workers laboring in Europe's industrial slums and begins his fateful tract with the basic premise of Marxist thought: "The history of all hitherto existing society is the history of class struggles." Thus, Marx interpreted all of human history as an ongoing economic conflict and prophesied that just as capitalism supplanted feudalism it would in turn succumb to socialism. In other works, Marx presented a vision of a communist future, in which the workers would control the means of production and establish a temporary "dictatorship of the proletariat," that would in turn develop into a stateless and classless society, a society defined by Marx as pure communism. While Karl Marx remained obscure during his own lifetime, after his death his revolutionary theories exerted a tremendous influence on the history of Germany, as well as the rest of the world.

demonstrators from the state of Baden issued a resolution demanding a constitution. Setting the stage for Germany's March Revolution, this protest quickly spawned similar protests in the grand duchy of Hesse, the duchy of Nassau, and the kingdom of Württemberg, calling for liberal reforms. Caught off-guard by the spontaneity and scale of these demonstrations, rulers throughout the German Confederation made concessions, seeking to appease the protesters as the revolution spread. In Baden, however, a violent confrontation between ducal troops and a republican army presaged the violence that would soon engulf Germany. On April 20, 1848, soldiers from Baden and Hesse met a revolutionary militia raised by the radical firebrand Friedrich Hecker (1811–81) at Kandern, near the Black Forest. While the aristocratic army's commander fell in the fighting, the revolutionaries were thoroughly routed. Defeated, Hecker eventually emigrated to America, like so many of his fellow disappointed German nationalists and liberal "Forty-Eighters," and even commanded a Union regiment in the American Civil War.

Even in Berlin, capital of the autocratic Kingdom of Prussia, demonstrators took to the streets demanding liberal concessions from their ruler, King Friedrich Wilhelm IV (1795–1861). The Prussian ruler gave in to their demands, addressing the crowd and pledging to grant them a constitution, a representative parliament, and freedom of speech. Responding to their nationalistic fervor, he even promised to help form a unified German nation-state. By March 18, however, the situation in Berlin boiled over when anxious Prussian troops fired into a crowd. The demonstrators erected barricades, and the Prussian capital became a war zone, with soldiers killing hundreds of protesters. Fearing a dangerous escalation, Friedrich Wilhelm went to the streets of Berlin three days later, reaffirming his promises of concessions, and even visited the graves of the demonstrators who had died at the barricades.

In the Austrian Empire, Metternich and Emperor Ferdinand I had been watching events in Germany with alarm. Leader of the German Confederation and lynchpin of the conservative order, Austria was the site of increasing revolutionary foment that raged from March 1848 to July 1849. Sparked by nationalist agitation among the Habsburgs' diverse subjects, including Croats, Czechs, Germans, Hungarians, Italians, Poles, Romanians, Slovaks, and Serbs, who sought autonomy, the unrest threatened to unravel the Austrian Empire. Meanwhile, the rising tide of nationalist sentiment within the confederation also threatened to undermine the Habsburgs. In the end, the popular uprising of 1848 put an end to Metternich's long diplomatic career. When the Viennese demonstrators demanded his ouster, Emperor Ferdinand acquiesced, and on March 13, 1848, Metternich was relieved of his duties and went into exile in England. Ferdinand appointed more liberal ministers to replace the fallen statesman, but this did not quell the disturbance. Shortly afterward, the ineffective emperor agreed to abdicate and named as his successor his nephew, Franz Joseph (1830–1916), who would reign for the next 68 years, among the most turbulent in the dynasty's history.

As tensions simmered in Berlin and Vienna, Frankfurt emerged as a hotbed of revolutionary fervor. In early March 1848, German liberals met in Heidelberg to arrange elections for a national assembly that would meet in Frankfurt. They demanded free elections for delegates to the National Assembly to be conducted throughout Germany, and in an attempt to quell the growing demonstrations, the German Confederation's states surprisingly permitted them to proceed. The diet of the German Confederation quietly disbanded, its duties transferred to the planned National Assembly.

On May 18, 1848, the new National Assembly, known as the Frankfurt Parliament, convened there, in St. Paul's Church. The general elections had produced a distinguished body of 586 delegates, drawn from the liberal intelligentsia. The Frankfurt representatives elected the prominent Hessian statesman Heinrich von Gagern (1799–1880) as their chair and immediately set to work on a German constitution, intended as the foundation for building a unified nation-state with a single parliament. The debate on the constitution bogged down, however, amid disagreements about the inclusion of Austria in the united Germany. For many delegates, admitting the multicultural Austrian Empire, with its large Slavic population, into the new nation was incompatible with their sense of cultural nationalism based upon shared language, customs, and history. The discussions dragged on for months, until the delegates narrowly approved a plan for a provisional government that would exclude the Austrian Empire but bind it through a treaty of union with the unified Germany. After a year of contentious deliberation, the Frankfurt Parliament, which powerful foreign states like France and Russia had failed to recognize, was also rapidly losing prestige among the German masses, as Austria and Prussia ignored it and began to ruthlessly suppress demonstrations in Vienna and Berlin. Amid these repressive measures, the parliament finally ratified the new constitution on March 28, 1849, one that created a constitutional monarchy, offering a hereditary crown to King Friedrich Wilhelm IV of Prussia. Ominously, the constitution had barely passed the vote in the parliament, and while it was recognized by most of the confederation's minor states, the major powers, including Austria, Prussia, Bavaria, and Saxony, refused to do so.

While Friedrich Wilhelm IV had positioned himself as a friend of the revolution when demonstrations first broke out in Berlin and had even promised to issue a Prussian constitution, the Hohenzollern monarch was no radical. Consequently, when formally offered the crown on April 3, 1849, the autocratic Friedrich Wilhelm refused to accept it, disparaging it as "a crown made of mud and clay." The Prussian monarch's refusal signaled that the tide had turned against the revolutionaries, and a crushing conservative backlash soon followed. The Frankfurt Parliament collapsed in disarray, and the revolution splintered into a score of separate movements scattered across the German states. In April 1849, all Austrian delegates withdrew from the parliament, and in May, the Prussians joined them. Later that month, even the committed liberal Gagern and his associates resigned from the ill-fated parliament. The most radical leftists formed a rump parliament in Stuttgart that met for several weeks in June, before being driven out of Württemberg by royal dragoons.

The fragmentation of the revolution allowed the German princes to stifle the demonstrations, often with ruthless violence. In Baden, for example, where radicals from the defunct National Assembly had formed a revolutionary council in Stuttgart, and forced the grand duke to flee the territory, Prussian troops acting on behalf of the German Confederation finally intervened to restore order in 1849. In Saxony, a more serious revolt erupted in the same year, known as the May Uprising, when the Saxon king Friedrich Augustus II (1797–1854) tried to use troops to disperse crowds calling for him to accept the constitution drafted by the Frankfurt Parliament. The municipal troops sent to quell the demonstration joined the revolutionaries. In response, the Saxon monarch called in Prussian troops for support, escalating the tension. As the crowds grew more violent, Friedrich Augustus withdrew to the fortified municipal armory, guarded by royal soldiers. When the demonstrators marched on the armory, the royal troops fired on the crowd, and Dresden erupted into anarchy, with revolutionaries manning barricades throughout the city, bracing for the arrival of the Prussians. Once the king fled the city, the revolutionary leaders formed a provisional government to arrange the defense of the city and to force the monarch to accept liberal reforms. Once Saxon and Prussian troops arrived, the city was torn apart by vicious street fighting. By May 9, the ragtag revolutionary forces had disintegrated: Many of the radicals had been slaughtered at the barricades, the rest had surrendered or fled the country. One such exile was the ardent nationalist and composer Richard Wagner, who fled to Switzerland to avoid arrest for his part in the May Uprising.

By June 1849, the abortive revolution was over, and the forces of conservatism tightened their grip on the populace. The revolution's major ringleaders dead, imprisoned, or in foreign exile, and its achievements proved fleeting as the German states reversed the concessions they had reluctantly accepted under duress in March 1848. In 1850, the diet of the German Assembly reconvened and set to work rebuilding the conservative order envisioned by Metternich 50 years before. By 1851, most German states had even repealed the timid bill of rights adopted by the Frankfurt Parliament, its only real accomplishment. Disappointed German nationalists and liberals, known as Forty-Eighters, emigrated to

An 1870s portrait of the German revolutionary and American statesman Carl Schurz. Schurz fled to the United States after the failed revolution of 1848 and took up the abolitionist cause. After serving as a Union general in the American Civil War, Schurz was elected to the U.S. Senate in 1869. (Library of Congress)

the United States, with thousands settling in the Hill Country of Texas. Leading revolutionaries, including Carl Schurz (1829–1906) and Friedrich Hecker, fled Germany, taking with them their radical aspirations and remarkable talents.

As generations of German historians have pointed out, the dismal failure of the March Revolution changed the course of German history. As a result of the defeat of the revolution, the coalition between German liberals and nationalists broke down. Increasingly, the aim of unifying Germany was uncoupled from the dream of establishing a liberal constitutional government. The failure of the Frankfurt Parliament to arrive at a consensus or to convince Germany's princes to accept their political vision exacerbated the heated rivalry between Austria and Prussia for dominance and doomed any peaceful attempt to build a united Germany informed by liberal ideals. Instead, the German nation-state would be born in bloodshed and autocracy.

8

UNIFICATION AND EMPIRE

On September 30, 1862, the great German statesman Otto von Bismarck (1815–98) gave a fateful speech before the Prussian Parliament that foreshadowed the violence that would accompany Germany's unification. Bismarck had recently returned to Berlin from a diplomatic post abroad to take up his appointment as Prussian minister president. Serving under Wilhelm I (1797–1888), a crown prince who had just become king of Prussia the year before, Bismarck immediately set about the monumental task of unifying Germany under the Prussian monarchy. Prussia had been thwarted by its Austrian rival a decade before in an attempt to unify Germany, when it was forced to sign a humiliating capitulation at Olmütz, in Moravia. Bismarck understood that he had to redress this failure, since the only way that Prussia could compete with the great powers of Europe was as the head of a unified German nation-state. This shrewd and cynical statesman also recognized that a new German empire would have to be forged in the crucible of war.

Standing in Bismarck's way, however, were the delegates of the budget commission of the Prussian Parliament, who resisted a costly reform of the Prussian military proposed by Wilhelm I and demanded liberal reforms from the new monarch. In response, Bismarck confronted the delegates and delivered one of the most famous speeches in German history. While he had only been in office for a few days, Bismarck argued for the unification of Germany under the Prussian aegis, a new German empire that would exclude the Austrians. Bismarck stressed Prussia's need for military strength, informing the delegates that "it is not by speeches and majority resolutions that the great questions of the time are decided—that was the big mistake of 1848 and 1849—but by iron and blood" (Snyder 1958, 202). In the coming decades, Bismarck would demonstrate time and again his willingness to resort to war to achieve Prussia's ends. While the delegates refused to vote in favor of the military expenditures, Bismarck's speech inflamed patriotism within Prussia and desire for unification within the fragmented German states. Showing a single-minded determination and an authoritarian mindset, the Prussian minister president ultimately raised the funds without the consent of the Parliament, ignoring their vote and subverting their authority. The bloody course of German unification was set.

The Humiliation of Olmütz

In the wake of the revolutions of 1848, Germany lay disorganized and disunited. Austria's German Confederation and the Frankfurt Parliament both dissolved in 1849. In the absence of these collective institutions, the individual German states struggled to deal with the profound political and social change that had recently swept through Germany. In this crisis of leadership, the Hohenzollern king of Prussia had turned down the crown offered by the liberal Frankfurt delegates because of the constitutional restrictions it would impose on the exercise of royal authority. Instead, he sought to form his own German federation, one firmly under Prussian control. The architect of this federation, which would come to be known as the Erfurt Union, was a Prussian military officer and diplomat named Joseph Maria von Radowitz (1797–1853).

Von Radowitz was a member of the Prussian delegation to the German Confederation who, with the outbreak of the March Revolution, had served as the Prussian representative to the Frankfurt Assembly. Once the Prussian monarch, Friedrich Wilhelm IV (1795–1861), refused to accept the leadership of the German Empire envisioned by the Frankfurt Assembly, von Radowitz engineered an attempt to unify Germany under Prussian control that was not hobbled by a liberal constitution. By early 1849, the Prussian diplomat had convinced Friedrich Wilhelm that Germany could be united under Hohenzollern imperial authority. Like the Frankfurt scheme, this new German Union would exclude Austria, making Prussia dominant within Germany itself, but would also link the Austrian Empire to Germany through a series of treaties. To appease German liberals, the German Union would have a constitution and a parliament, but both would be subordinate to a conservative council of the six leading German princes.

In a series of negotiations in the summer of 1849, as Austria struggled to suppress a revolt in Hungary, von Radowitz convinced 28 of Germany's 39 states, still haunted by the specter of revolution, to join this federation. Just as it seemed that this Prussian-led union might come to fruition, however, the fluid political situation within central Europe thwarted von Radowitz's efforts. Alarmed by the prospect of Prussian domination in Germany, Russia assisted Austria in putting down the Hungarian revolt, allowing the Habsburgs to focus their attention on hampering their Hohenzollern rivals. The Austrians stirred fears of Prussian domination among the German princes and offered an alternative to the proposed union: a revived German Confederation headed by the Austrian ruler. When the delegates elected to von Radowitz's federation, which would come to be known as the Erfurt Union, finally convened in March 1850, several important German states had already broken with Prussia and gone over to the Austrians. These deserters joined with the German states that had refused to join the union at its inception and revived the defunct German Confederation, headed by Austria. By November 1850, Germany was split into two antagonistic camps, and their leading states—Prussia and Austria—were on the brink of war.

Fearing that Russia would enter the conflict in support of Austria, Friedrich Wilhelm IV was forced to the negotiating table and obliged by the conservative Prussian nobility to discharge von Radowitz. Meanwhile, the abortive Erfurt Union, on the eve of its inception, collapsed as its remaining members pulled out, most notably the powerful kingdoms of Saxony and Hanover, who abandoned the Prussians in the face of Austrian and Russian pressure. Prussian and Austrian diplomats met at the Moravian city of Olmütz, where on November 29, 1850, the Prussians were forced to accept a humiliating settlement that forced them to rejoin the German Confederation under Habsburg control. Smarting under this reversal, Prussian resentment of the "humiliation of Olmütz" would serve later as an impetus for Prussia's aggressive drive toward the subjugation of Austria and toward German unification under the Hohenzollern dynasty.

Germany's Wars of Unification

In 1850, keeping the promise that he made to Berlin's demonstrators during the March Revolution, Friedrich Wilhelm IV issued Prussia's first constitution. This conservative constitution made certain concessions to the liberals, but ultimately preserved royal authority. It established a parliament composed of two houses: a lower house, known as the Landtag, and an upper house, called the Herrenhaus. The delegates who served in the Landtag were to be elected, but a stringent property qualification ensured conservative control by giving the most votes to those who paid the highest taxes. Meanwhile, members of the

Herrenhaus were to be appointed by the king. Furthermore, the king's authority was augmented by his complete control over the cabinet of ministers, all of whom he appointed, as well as the Prussian civil service and the army.

Along with these political developments, the 1850s were also a time of rapid economic and technological change as well. At the Congress of Vienna in 1815, Prussia had gained territories in the Rhineland and Westphalia, including the Ruhr, a region rich in coal deposits that would become the cradle of German industrialization. Disunited and fragmented, the German states had lagged far behind Britain in industrial development, but by the 1840s, Germany began to experience rapid industrialization. By the 1850s, some 300 coal mines in the Ruhr Valley fueled massive blast furnaces, turning iron ore into steel for the manufacture of machinery, steam engines, and armaments. The rapid growth of Germany's railway system drove increasing industrialization and fostered urbanization, as German cities swelled with masses of factory workers and their families. Germany's industrial production increased dramatically, and the Saar region, in Upper Silesia, joined the Ruhr as one of the most important centers of heavy industry in all of Europe. By the end of the 1850s, Germany was gaining on Britain in industrial production. Within two decades, Germany would match British production, eventually becoming Europe's leading industrial power, its cities and countryside transformed by the spread of railways and the proliferation of factories, mines, and foundries.

Having weathered the turbulent period since the March Revolution, Friedrich Wilhelm IV was incapacitated by a stroke in 1857, and his younger brother, Wilhelm (1797–1888), ruled Prussia as prince regent. When Friedrich Wilhelm IV died in 1861, the crown prince, who had fought with distinction against the armies of Napoléon, took the Prussian throne as King Wilhelm I. Amid a dispute with parliament about Prussia's soaring military expenditures, the new monarch was persuaded to appoint Otto von Bismarck, a brilliant statesman serving as ambassador to France, to the post of minister president. Bismarck took the reins of the Prussian government in September 1862, beginning a meteoric career that would transform German history.

Bismarck resolved the budget impasse caused by Friedrich Wilhelm IV's controversial army reform and immediately began to work toward the unification of Germany under Prussian control, a goal that had languished since Olmütz. The conservative Junkers, who dominated the Prussian officer corps and civil service as completely as they did their own landed estates, opposed unification. The Junkers feared that within a unified Germany, their beloved Prussia's stature would be diminished. They were also concerned that the Hohenzollern monarch, their feudal lord and patron, would be forced to accept liberal reforms imposed by a German assembly. An aristocrat and archconservative, Bismarck's primary concern was the destiny of Prussia. He understood, however, that Prussian power would be enhanced if the Hohenzollerns could make themselves rulers of a unified Germany. A practitioner of *Realpolitik,* a realistic and pragmatic brand of power politics, he was more than willing to appease Prussia's liberals to advance this agenda, despite his distaste for their political views. The 1850s had been disastrous for Prussia, which was marginalized by the other Great Powers, Britain, France, and Austria, during the Crimean War against Russia in 1854–55 and again during the Italian War of 1859. According to Bismarck, the only way that Prussia could regain its former power in Europe was as the head of a unified German nation-state that could vie with these imperial powers on an even footing. In September 1862, the Prussian statesman, arguing the need for military spending, gave his famous "iron and blood" speech before the Landtag, foreshadowing the violence that would accompany Germany's unification. In the coming decades, Bismarck would demonstrate time and again his willingness to resort to war to achieve Prussia's ends.

The Wars of Schleswig

In 1864, the Second War of Schleswig, also known as the Danish-Prussian War, pitted the German Confederation against Denmark. Bismarck instigated the war and shrewdly gained unlikely support from Austria, in a bid to redress Prussian frustration in the First Schleswig War of 1848–51. This earlier conflict arose from the issue of who should possess the largely German provinces of Schleswig and Holstein that were under Danish control. Prussia intervened in a nationalist uprising in the region but was forced to withdraw after three years of fruitless military operations under mounting pressure from Russia, Austria, and Britain. Forced to sign the London Protocol of 1852, a settlement that reestablished the prewar status quo by confirming the Danish heir to the throne as the future monarch of the two duchies while precluding Denmark from absorbing the German provinces, the defeated Prussians were eager for revenge.

The crisis that gave Bismarck the opportunity to make up for Prussia's embarrassing losses in the First Schleswig War began with the death of Danish king Frederik VII (1808–63), who had not left a male heir. The Prussians used this as a pretext to contest the Danish succession and the claim of the new Danish ruler, Christian IX (1818–1906), on the territories of Schleswig and Holstein. In response, the Danish king signed a new constitution that tightened Denmark's control over Schleswig, violating the terms of the London Protocol of 1852. Furthermore, Holstein, populated almost entirely by ethnic Germans, had been held before 1806 as a German fief and was part of the German Confederation, complicating the situation. Thus, Bismarck was able to convince the confederation to join in the conflict, using German nationalist sentiment to stoke the flames of war, and even convinced the Austrians to support the war effort to "liberate" ethnic Germans in the two Danish duchies. Meanwhile, support from Europe's great powers, so important in thwarting Prussia in the First Schleswig War, was faltering. The Russians were still reeling from their defeat in the Crimean War, and the French were not inclined to intervene on Denmark's behalf. Only Britain, somewhat reluctantly, supported the Danes, fearing the potential Baltic naval threat from a resurgent Prussia. On December 24, 1863, at Bismarck's urging, Saxon and Hanoverian forces occupied Holstein, supporting the claim of a local aristocrat as duke of the territory. Several days later, Prussia and Austria offered a motion in the assembly of the German Confederation authorizing them to occupy Schleswig to ensure that the Danes complied with the settlement of 1852. When the motion failed, the two powers declared their intention to operate independently in the matter.

On February 1, 1864, the Prussians invaded Schleswig after the Danish government refused an ultimatum issued by Bismarck to revoke the new constitution. Austrian forces also moved into the territory alongside the Prussians, fighting the Danes in harsh winter conditions. By mid February the war had spilled over into Denmark, and Bismarck convinced the Austrians that the conflict presented an opportunity settle the issue once and for all. Thus, the allies declared that the protocol of 1852 was no longer valid and that the status of Schleswig and Holstein was to be determined by force of arms. Abandoned by the major powers of Europe, and assaulted by the combined forces of Prussia and Austria, the Danish defenses crumbled. Despite the success of the Danish navy, which won a narrow victory at the Battle of Heligoland over the Austrians in May, the Danish army was outnumbered almost 2 to 1 by the combined forces of the Prussians and Austrians. In addition, the Prussians were armed with the latest military equipment and held a decisive advantage in heavy artillery, pounding Danish positions with unrelenting fire. While the outmanned Danes fought valiantly, the invaders soon overwhelmed their defenses, and by July, the Prussians occupied all of Denmark. By the summer of 1864, the war was effectively over, and on October 30, the belligerents signed the Treaty of Vienna, which ceded Schleswig to Prussia and Holstein to Austria.

The Second Schleswig War had several important consequences for German history. Most important, it demonstrated the formidable power of the recently reorganized Prussian army, a force armed with state-of-the-art breech-loading rifles that gave them unprecedented firepower. The war also brought valuable territory into the German orbit, as these productive regions, including several strategic Baltic ports, were absorbed into the Hohenzollern and Habsburg realms. The war was also the last time that the Prussians and Austrians cooperated. A conflict between the two German powers would erupt over a dispute regarding the administration of these newly conquered regions.

The Austro-Prussian War

Just 18 months after the end of the Second Schleswig War, the Austro-Prussian War began. Pitting the Austrian Empire and a roster of German allies against the Kingdom of Prussia and its German and Italian allies, the Austro-Prussian War was waged in 1866, when the Austrians brought a dispute over the administration of the former Danish territories of Schleswig and Holstein before the German Confederation for mediation. The Prussians charged that they had thereby violated the postwar settlement and used this action as a pretext for invading Holstein. In response, the German Confederation authorized its members to mobilize against Prussia, hoping to force the Hohenzollerns to back down. Bismarck refused to be intimidated, however, and declared the German Confederation dissolved as Prussia geared for war. Seizing the chance to force Austria into a military confrontation, he convinced the Prussian monarch, Wilhelm I, to enter the fray, as most of the leading German states joined Austria's side, including Baden, Bavaria, Hanover, Hesse-Darmstadt, Hesse-Kassel, Nassau, and Württemberg. As the Prussians mobilized for war, they were supported militarily by only a handful of north German states and the Kingdom of Italy, which hoped to wrest the Veneto from Austrian control to further Italian unification. Europe's great powers stayed on the sidelines as these two German powerhouses struggled for dominance.

Bolstered by new industrial technologies, including railroad transport and telegraph communication, the Prussians mobilized quickly, following campaign plans drawn up by General Helmuth von Moltke the Elder (1800–91), the Prussian army's innovative chief of staff. As the Austrian troops massed for an invasion of Silesia, located mostly in modern-day Poland with minor sections in the Czech Republic and Germany, the Prussians invaded Saxony and Bohemia. The armies met at Königgrätz, on July 3, where well-trained Prussian troops armed with modern breech-loading rifles overwhelmed a larger force of Austrians equipped with outdated muzzle-loaders, which took four times as long to reload as the Prussian rifles. Suffering a costly defeat, their army in tatters, the Austrians were forced to sue for peace as Prussia turned against Austria's allies. Prussian forces had defeated the Hanoverian army by the end of June and had pushed the Bavarians back to the River Main.

Emperor Wilhelm I in military uniform, 1884 (Bundesarchiv, Bild 146-1970-077-18 / W. Kuntzemüller)

Hostilities between the Prussians and Austrians ceased with the Peace of Prague on August 23, ending the short-lived Seven Weeks' War that excluded Austria from any future role in a united Germany. The Italians gained important concessions from the Austrian Habsburgs with the subsequent Treaty of Vienna on October 12 and, despite battlefield reverses against the Austrians during the conflict, gained Venetia. The Prussians, now the unquestioned leading state within Germany, enjoyed even more valuable spoils of war. The settlement led to the dissolution of the German Confederation, freeing the Prussians to form a new German confederation in its place. This alliance, known as the North German Confederation, formed the year after the Peace of Prague, included all 21 of the German states north of the River Main, uniting them under Hohenzollern control. The North German Confederation soon became the best hope of German nationalists, who increasingly looked to Prussia to unify Germany as a *kleindeutsch* state, excluding Austria's multinational empire. Prussia also absorbed the territory of Schleswig-Holstein; annexed Austria's former allies, Hanover, Nassau, and Hesse-Kassel; and forced several other German states, including Saxony, to join the new North German Confederation. These territorial gains allowed Prussia to form a contiguous kingdom that encompassed all of northern Germany, and its dominance within the North German Confederation gave it an unrivaled political mastery in central Europe. As Prussian minister president, Bismarck, in turn, used his influence to dominate the North German Confederation.

The Franco-Prussian War and German Unification

Prussia's startling victory over the Austrians, and the growing unity of Germany under Hohenzollern control in the aftermath of the Austro-Prussian War, alarmed the French. As the emperor of the French Napoléon III (1808–73) grew increasingly wary of Prussia's growing power, Bismarck worked to alienate France, seeing a conflict with Germany's traditional enemy as a means to bring the south German states into the Prussian fold. Employing shrewd diplomacy to isolate France, the Prussian minister president ensured that Europe's other major powers, namely Great Britain and Russia, would not interfere in the coming contest. As Prussia and France geared for war, the pretext for hostilities presented itself in distant Spain.

The Spanish throne, vacant since a revolution in 1868, was offered to Prince Leopold (1835–1905) of the House of Hohenzollern-Sigmaringen, a relative of the Prussian monarch. Faced with the prospect of a Prussian-Spanish axis encircling them, the French threatened to take up arms against Prussia unless Leopold refused the crown. The French government sent its ambassador, Vincente Benedetti (1817–1900), to confront Wilhelm I at Ems, a north German spa. Benedetti demanded that the Prussian monarch order his relative to withdraw his claim on the Spanish throne. Infuriated, but reticent to go to war with the French, Wilhelm allowed the French ambassador to contact Leopold directly, and he sent a telegraph expressing France's demands. Leopold's candidacy had already been formally withdrawn, but the French wanted an assurance that no Hohenzollern would ever mount the Spanish throne.

With this aim, Napoléon III had his foreign minister, Antoine Agénor Alfred, demand that the Prussian monarch issue a written apology that would guarantee that a Hohenzollern would never pursue the Spanish claim. Insulted, Wilhelm rejected France's demands. The impasse gave Bismarck the opportunity he needed, and he stirred anti-French sentiment within Germany by publishing the notorious Ems Dispatch. Supposedly divulging the correspondence between the French and Prussian governments regarding the Spanish succession, Bismarck edited them to insult France.

THE EMS DISPATCH

The notorious Ems Dispatch provides a lucid example of Otto von Bismarck's ruthless brand of power politics, as well as the role that the defense of national pride and the manipulation of mass media played in German unification. Here, we can compare the original description of the meeting at the German spa town of Ems, where the French ambassador asked Wilhelm I for assurances that the Hohenzollerns would not claim the vacant Spanish throne, with the edited text that Bismarck released to the press and foreign diplomats. We can see how Bismarck's editing of the exchange between King Wilhelm I and the French ambassador, Count Benedetti, at Ems on the morning of July 13, 1870, stoked passions on both sides, pushing France into declaring war:

The report of the meeting sent to Bismarck by the king's secretary, Heinrich Abeken, on July 13, 1870:

His Majesty the King writes to me:

M. Benedetti intercepted me on the Promenade in order to demand of me most insistently that I should authorize him to telegraph immediately to Paris that I shall obligate myself for all future time never again to give my approval to the candidacy of the Hohenzollerns should it be renewed. I refused to agree to this, the last time somewhat severely, informing him that one dare not and cannot assume such obligations á tout jamais. Naturally, I informed him that I had received no news as yet, and since he had been informed earlier than I by way of Paris and Madrid, he could easily understand why my government was once again out of the matter.

Since then His Majesty . . . decided not to receive the French envoy again but to inform him through an adjutant that His Majesty . . . had nothing further to say to the ambassador. His Majesty leaves it to the judgment of Your Excellency whether or not to communicate at once the new demand by Benedetti and its rejection to our ambassadors and to the press.

The abridged version of the events crafted by Bismarck and released to the press and the diplomatic corps:

After the reports of the renunciation by the hereditary Prince of Hohenzollern had been officially transmitted by the Royal Government of Spain to the Imperial Government of France, the French Ambassador presented to His Majesty the King at

(continues)

THE EMS DISPATCH (continued)

Ems the demand to authorize him to telegraph to Paris that His Majesty the King would obligate himself for all future time never again to give his approval to the candidacy of the Hohenzollerns should it be renewed.

His Majesty the King thereupon refused to receive the French envoy again and informed him through an adjutant that His Majesty had nothing further to say to the Ambassador.

Decades later, in his memoirs, Bismarck explained his thinking as he goaded the French into war, writing that:

. . . we must fight if we do not want to act the part of the defeated without a battle. However, success depends essentially upon the impression that the beginning of the war makes upon us and others. It is most important that we be the ones attacked.

Source: Snyder, Louis L., ed. Documents of German History (New Brunswick, N.J.: Rutgers University Press, 1958), pp. 215–216.

The Prussian statesman got the reaction he wanted. On July 19, 1870, the French declared war on Prussia. In the face of this French declaration—portrayed as French "aggression" by Bismarck—nationalist sentiment flourished in Germany. In a stirring speech addressed to the German people on the eve of war, Wilhelm I stoked the fires of nationalist fervor to drum up support for Prussian arms:

From all tribes of the German Fatherland, from all circles of the German people, even from across the seas, from societies and guilds, from organizations and private individuals, I have received so many messages of devotion and willingness to make sacrifices on the occasion of the coming struggle for the honor and independence of Germany. . . . The love for our common Fatherland and the unanimous uprising of the German people and their princes have reconciled all differences and opposition; and, unified, as seldom before in her history, Germany will find that the war will bring her lasting peace, and that, out of the bloody seed, will come a God-blessed harvest of German freedom and unity. (Snyder 1958, 218–219)

As Wilhelm I delivered his speech, rallying the German people to the Prussian cause, the Prussian military prepared for war.

Prussia's forces, augmented by the troops of their allies in the North German Confederation and the southern German states who had signed treaties with the Hohenzollerns, took the field quickly. Following the meticulous prewar plans prepared by von Moltke, the German armies mobilized rapidly, while the French struggled to marshal their forces. Three massive German armies invaded France, under the supreme command of King Wilhelm I. After an initial setback in a border skirmish on August 2, the German forces began to gain the upper hand, overwhelming the badly outnumbered French. The French supreme commander,

Otto von Bismarck, chancellor of Germany, 1890 (Bundesarchiv, Bild 146-2005-0057 / Jacques Pilartz)

General Edme Mac-Mahon (1808–98), suffered a series of crushing defeats the following week at Weissenburg, Wörth, and Spichern and was forced to withdraw to Châlons. On the heels of these setbacks, the French forces in the east, under the command of Marshal François-Achille Bazaine (1811–88), who had been given supreme command over the French armies after Mac-Mahon's retreat, also suffered a series of crushing defeats by the Germans. After these clashes, at Vionville (August 15) and Gravelotte (August 18), the French forces retreated to the fortified city of Metz, a strategic stronghold on the frontier with Germany. A pair of Prussian armies, numbering 150,000 troops, besieged Metz. As disease spread among the French troops packed in squalid conditions within the city, a newly formed French army, the Army of Châlons, under the personal command of Emperor Napoléon III, marched on the city in an effort to lift the siege. Maintaining pressure on Metz, the Prussians split their forces and ambushed advance elements of the French relief force at Beaumont on August 30. After this stinging defeat, the French retreated to Sedan to regroup, setting the stage for the war's decisive clash.

On the morning of September 1, 1870, the German and French forces clashed outside the French town of Sedan, in a battle that would alter the history of France and Germany. Surrounded by the rapidly advancing Prussians and exhausted after unrelenting marching, the desperate French forces sought to break out of Sedan. French troops under Mac-Mahon advanced on the city of La Moncelle, hoping to break the Prussian encirclement. The French forces set up defensive positions in the town, and in the early hours of September 1, Saxon and Prussian troops crossed the Meuse on pontoon bridges and attacked La Moncelle. Bitter street fighting ensued, as the French and Germans both committed large numbers of troops to the engagement. Mac-Mahon was wounded in this early fighting and handed command of the French defense to General Auguste-Alexandre Ducrot (1817–82). Ducrot ordered a retreat, but the French general Emmanuel de Wimpffen (1811–84) disregarded this order, mounting a successful attack against the Saxon forces pressing La Moncelle. This French rally proved short-lived, however, as fresh Prussian troops poured onto the battlefield and German artillery decimated the Army of Châlons. Surrounded, and pressed under relentless attacks by the Prussians and their Bavarian allies, the French launched a series of fruitless and costly counterattacks. By midday, the situation appeared hopeless for the beleaguered French.

As evening fell, Napoléon III arrived in Sedan and, seeing the senseless slaughter of the French troops, called off the counterattack. The French had suffered more than 17,000 casualties—more than twice as many as the Germans—in the engagement. Another 21,000 French troops had been captured. On September 2, Napoléon III surrendered and, along with some 83,000 French soldiers, was taken into custody by the Prussians. Without its leader, France's Second Empire collapsed, but the provisional government in Paris continued the war effort for five months, although the military situation was hopeless after Sedan. By the end of September, the French stronghold at Strasbourg had fallen, and by the end of October, Marshal Bazaine surrendered Metz as well. German troops besieged Paris, shelling the city. After enduring bombardment and starvation, the city finally surrendered on January 19, 1871. Back in Germany, jubilant crowds thronged the streets celebrating King Wilhelm's victory over the hated French.

With nationalist fervor sweeping Germany, one of the seminal events in German history occurred on French soil. On January 18, in the Hall of Mirrors at the palace of Versailles, the Hohenzollern monarch,

Anton von Werner's famous painting of the proclamation of the German Empire in the Hall of Mirrors at Versailles on January 18, 1871 (Bildarchiv Preussischer Kulturbesitz, Berlin / Art Resource, NY / Bismarck-Museum, Friedrichsruh / Hermann Buresch)

Wilhelm I, was crowned emperor of a united Germany. In the Imperial Proclamation of January 18, 1871, the new kaiser declared:

> *We, Wilhelm, by the grace of God, King of Prussia, do hereby proclaim that we have considered it to be a duty to our common Fatherland to respond to the summons of the unified German Princes and cities and to accept the German imperial title. As a result, we and those who succeed us on the throne of Prussia, henceforth shall bear the imperial title in all our relations and in all the activities of the German Empire, and we trust in God that the German nation will be granted the ability to construct a propitious future for the Fatherland under the symbol of its ancient glory. (Snyder 1958, 222)*

The second *Reich* that Wilhelm proclaimed at Versailles was born in iron and blood, as Bismarck had predicted. It was through his machinations that Germany was finally unified under Prussian leadership.

The German Empire

Flush with victory over France, Bavaria, Württemberg, and Baden joined with the states of the North German Federation to form the German Empire, with Wilhelm I serving as German emperor. This new *Kaiserreich,* or monarchial empire, thus included all the states of the old German Confederation, except for Prussia's long-standing rival, Austria, and the tiny states of Luxembourg and Liechtenstein. Exploiting German nationalist fervor, Bismarck harnessed it to Prussian interests, forming a unified German state that was decidedly autocratic. The imperial constitution that Bismarck engineered in 1871 was based upon that of the North German Confederation and ensured Prussian domination within the newly formed empire. Bismarck granted some democratic concessions, including the formation of a bicameral imperial parliament with a lower house, known as the Reichstag, whose delegates would be elected through universal male suffrage. He also allowed the formation of political parties. He was careful, however, to preserve the old North German Confederation's conservative aspects and to ensure Prussian control with other provisions included in the new constitution. For example, all legislation had to be ratified by the Bundesrat, a federal council composed of deputies appointed by the German princes, who could effectively block liberal reform. Meanwhile, the Prussian emperor enjoyed wide-ranging executive powers, as did his chosen chancellor, Bismarck. According to the imperial constitution, the German chancellor oversaw virtually all of the activities of the government and had sole authority to enact legislation. The most powerful and populous German polity by far, Prussia dominated the empire through its veto power within the Bundesrat. According to the imperial constitution, just 14 votes were required to block any constitutional changes, and Prussia had 17 delegates in the Bundesrat. Thus, while the other German states technically remained sovereign entities, most of their functions, including passing legislation, conducting diplomacy, and issuing currency, passed through the Prussian-dominated imperial government. Thus, Bismarck created an imperial structure with the trappings of constitutional government, but ensured that it retained an essentially authoritarian nature.

On May 10, 1871, the Treaty of Frankfurt, a settlement signed by the government of France's new Third Republic, ended hostilities between Germany and France. According to the provisions of this treaty, France was forced to cede the provinces of Alsace and Lorraine to Germany and to pay an indemnity of 5 billion francs. German troops occupied France until these reparations were paid, returning to Germany only

A view of the Borsigwerke locomotive machinery factory in Berlin in 1837, one of the most important early industrial sites in Germany (Bundesarchiv, Bild 102-12816)

in September 1873. As Germany reveled in its triumph over France, their victory sowed the seeds of future conflict within Europe and signaled the emergence of a united Germany as a global power. The dramatic events of 1871 upset the balance of power on the European continent so carefully maintained since the Congress of Vienna, alarming Europe's great powers. The humiliation suffered by France, and especially its territorial losses in Alsace and Lorraine, stoked the fires of enmity between France and Germany. Finally, Germany's battlefield success in the Franco-Prussian War reinforced the militaristic tendencies of the Prussian regime.

Having taken its place in the first rank of European powers, and established itself as the dominant power on the Continent, imperial Germany quickly emerged as an industrial and economic powerhouse as well. The regions that it had wrested from France in Alsace and Lorraine, aside from their Germanic heritage and strategic importance, were major centers of industrial production with valuable iron ore deposits. Economic activity flourished within the newly united Germany, and amid the rising prosperity, the nation's population base expanded, and its urban centers experienced rapid growth. Making up for lost time, Germany gradually transformed itself into an industrial power that could rival Britain, which had dominated global production since the

Industrial Revolution of the 18th century. In the age of steam, a nation's economic might was measured in terms of steel and coal production. Germany had become a force to be reckoned with on both counts and also made great strides in its production of industrial machinery, chemicals, and manufactured goods. Likewise, German exports tripled in the decades after unification, as German manufacturers began to compete with British imports at home and abroad. By the turn of the century, Germany had passed Britain to become the dominant economic power in Europe and was second only to the United States among the world's exporting nations.

The Iron Chancellor

As Germany's burgeoning economy expanded in the decades after 1871, Bismarck pursued a series of political and cultural initiatives intended to unify the German people and centralize the German state. To achieve these goals, Bismarck championed conservative Prussian values, moving to suppress the spread of religious activism among Germany's Catholic minority and socialist agitation among the nation's working classes. Both Catholics and workers were disaffected groups within a rapidly changing Germany, with nationalist ideology challenging traditional religiosity, and industrialization and urbanization revolutionizing labor.

Bismarck turned first against the influence of Catholicism, in an effort known as the Kulturkampf. In 1864, Pope Pius IX (1792–1878) wrote the *Syllabus of Modern Errors,* decrying the increasingly secular nature of European society and calling upon Catholics to adhere to traditional values. The pope's opposition to state-sponsored education and civil marriage, expressed in this declaration, as well as the Vatican's proclamation of the doctrine of papal infallibility in religious matters in 1871, angered Bismarck. In the following year, 1872, he responded by expelling Prussia's Jesuits. In 1873, Bismarck issued the May Laws, which gave the state control over the training and appointment of clergy within Germany, closing Catholic seminaries and jailing Catholics who sought to contravene the law. Seeking to break Catholic resistance to state intrusion, he confiscated church property, increased state control over education and marriage, and regulated the activities of the Catholic clergy. Pope Pius declared the May Laws invalid and responded by calling upon German Catholics to resist official repression. As a result, Catholics joined the Catholic Center Party, a political vehicle for southern Germany's numerous Catholics, to Bismarck's chagrin. For Bismarck, conservative

Catholicism was an impediment to German unification, fostering dissatisfaction with Germany's changing political and economic landscape and offering a competing locus of loyalty that rivaled the German nation-state. By the late 1870s, Bismarck's efforts to suppress Catholicism had foundered, since the repression actually strengthened the resolve of beleaguered Catholics. Therefore, when faced with the growing radicalism of organized labor, in the form of the burgeoning popularity of the socialist movement in Germany, Bismarck changed course. Abandoning the unsuccessful Kulturkampf, he united with his former enemies in the Catholic Center Party against the socialists.

Bismarck's unlikely alliance with Germany's most prominent Catholic party brought an end to the ill-fated Kulturkampf and also signaled his growing concern with the spread of radical socialism among Germany's workers. In 1863, a socialist leader named Ferdinand Lassalle (1825–64), who had been jailed for his role in the 1848 revolution, founded Germany's first workers' party, the General German Workers' Association, or ADAV. The prominent Marxists Wilhelm Liebknecht (1826–1900) and August Bebel (1840–1913) opposed the Lassaleans, forming their own socialist party, the Social Democratic Workers' Party of Germany, or SDAP, in 1869. Despite bitter disagreement over socialist ideology and how it should be implemented within Germany, the two rival parties joined together at the May 1875 meeting of the Socialist Congress at Gotha to discuss the future of Germany's working classes and the creation of a new socialist program. The meeting produced revolutionary demands for republican government and socialist legislation, an attempt to realize socialist aims by working within the established political system. Banding together to pursue this new agenda, the delegates formed a new party, the Socialist Workers' Party of Germany, or SAPD. By the 1890s, this reinvigorated socialist party had changed its name to the Social Democratic Party of Germany (SPD) and was growing rapidly as members of the burgeoning working class were recruited in Germany's industrial cities.

Bismarck was alarmed by the socialists' growing strength and looked for an excuse to crack down on leftist political activity. In 1878, Emperor Wilhelm survived a pair of assassination attempts by anarchist radicals. While the socialists were not responsible for these failed attacks, they gave Bismarck the opportunity he needed to suppress socialism. Blaming the socialists for the attempts on the kaiser's life, Bismarck issued the Exceptional Laws aimed at eradicating German socialism. The first article of these laws declared that "Organizations which, through Social Democratic, Socialist, or Communist activities, aim to overthrow the established state or social order are hereby forbidden" and granted the state wide-ranging powers to suppress working-class political activities (Snyder 1958, 235). Using this legislation, Bismarck disrupted socialist political organizations, closed radical newspapers, and broke up workers' assemblies.

As with his earlier efforts to suppress Catholic agitation, Bismarck's attempt to stamp out socialism in Germany also proved fruitless, as leftist leaders went into hiding and membership socialist parties continued to grow unabated in defiance of official repression. Thus, he was forced to change tactics. In order to undercut the appeal of socialist political parties among Germany's budding working class, Bismarck made another surprising move. He enacted a series of progressive social welfare programs, preempting the demands of the socialist parties. The first of these came in 1881, when Bismarck proposed a bill in the Reichstag authorizing the establishment of a program that would ensure factory workers and miners against workplace accidents. In 1883, Bismarck introduced a national health care system and in the following year unveiled a state disability insurance program. By 1887, he had added a retirement pension plan, giving the conservative Kaiserreich the most comprehensive social security system in the world. Ironically, the social welfare programs put in place by the stodgy Bismarck were far more progressive than those introduced in liberal nations like Britain or France.

Bismarck's efforts to contain conservative Catholicism and radical socialism were part of a larger aim: to foster national unity within Germany. Through policies known collectively as Germanization, Bismarck sought to forge the various German states, with a history of political autonomy and cultural exclusivity, into a single, unified nation-state. Bismarck sought to achieve this through promoting new national institutions and by repressing heterogeneous elements within Germany. Accordingly, Bismarck established a commission in 1881 to create a single legal code for the empire, one that would supersede the bewildering array of local legal instruments that survived from before unification. The product of these efforts, a comprehensive civil code known as the Bürgerliches Gesetzbuch, was enacted in 1900, furthering German unification.

Bismarck also promoted cultural nationalism, requiring the use of German in all aspects of public life, and especially in government and education. The Germanization program also had a darker side, as he pressured Germany's ethnic minorities, including Danes in the north, French in the west, and the large Polish community inhabiting Prussia's eastern provinces, to assimilate. These efforts eventually culminated in the forced resettlement of Poles. In 1885, a government commission was established to relocate Poles living in lands that had been acquired from Poland during the partitions and to colonize these areas with ethnic Germans. In a controversial move, the imperial government even authorized the forced expulsion of more than 20,000 Poles to Russia's Polish possessions. While these measures led to widespread misery among Germany's Polish population, in the end they proved just as futile as Bismarck's efforts to suppress the Catholic and socialist movements. In fact, official repression seems to have fostered resistance by ethnic Poles, who formed pro-Polish political organizations in the Reichstag and clung to their traditions more tightly in the face of government intrusion.

Foreign Policy

While Bismarck's domestic initiatives, aimed at the suppression of Catholics, socialists, and ethnic minorities, ended in failure, he proved more successful in foreign policy. After unification, the chancellor of the new German nation-state forged a complex series of alliances intended to safeguard Germany from foreign aggression. Aware that France was still smarting from its humiliation in the Franco-Prussian War and the costly loss of Alsace-Lorraine, Bismarck was always careful during his tenure to isolate the French diplomatically. Meanwhile, he carefully maintained a series of military alliances with a succession of European powers to protect Germany's security. Thus, in the early 1870s, Bismarck avoided challenging Britain's naval supremacy or its colonial possessions. In 1872, Bismarck forged an alliance known as the Three Emperors League that united the emperors of Germany, Russia, and Austria, Prussia's one-time enemy, in a military alliance. In 1878, after the Russo-Turkish War, Bismarck negotiated the Treaty of Berlin, a postwar settlement that frustrated Russia's main war aim: gaining a warm-water port in the Dardanelles in northwestern Turkey. With relations between Germany and Russia increasingly tense, the Three Emperors League unraveled. In response, in 1879, the German chancellor negotiated the Dual Alliance between the German Empire and the Austro-Hungarian Empire, with each promising to support the other in case of Russian aggression. With the addition of Italy in 1882, the alliance became known as the Triple Alliance and was strengthened by the so-called Mediterranean Agreement that linked Austria and Italy with Britain. Seemingly prescient, Bismarck always feared that Germany would face a two-front war against France and Russia, and despite lingering animosities with Russia, he negotiated the Reinsurance Treaty late in his career. In this important secret treaty, signed in 1887, the emperors of Germany and Russia pledged to remain neutral if either went to war with a third power, unless Germany attacked France or Russia attacked Austria-Hungary.

While Bismarck was initially disdainful of colonies, arguing that their acquisition would cost Germany more than they were worth, by the 1880s, he had changed course. Persuaded by powerful business interests within Germany, Bismarck hurried to catch up with Britain and France in claiming overseas colonies. A signal of Germany's increasing influence, the great powers met on German soil to lay the ground rules for the so-called Scramble for Africa at the Berlin Conference in 1884. Germany established several colonies as the era's great powers carved up the African continent, claiming areas that make up the modern nations of Cameroon, Burundi, Ghana, Namibia, Rwanda, Tanzania, and Togo. Germany also claimed a handful of Pacific territories, including German New Guinea, the Bismarck Archipelago, and the Marshall Islands, having joined the other great powers of Europe in the rapacious "New Imperialism" of the 19th century.

Friedrich III

Kaiser Wilhelm I died in March 1888, at the age of 90, and the imperial crown passed to his son, Friedrich III (1831–88). As crown prince, Friedrich had served with distinction as a military commander during Prussia's Wars of Unification. While Friedrich embraced his military duty, he often proclaimed a personal distaste for war and proved far more liberal in his politics than his father. He often clashed with Bismarck in policy discussions and even denounced his repressive measures in public, and his father virtually excluded him from politics as long as he lived. Friedrich was a great admirer of Britain and its constitutional monarchy, and even married the eldest daughter of Queen Victoria in 1858. Thus, for Germany's liberals gradually gaining strength in the Reichstag, Friedrich was their great hope. By the time he ascended to the imperial throne, however, Friedrich was 57 years old and dying of throat cancer.

During his short reign, one that lasted only 99 days, Friedrich attempted to push through a series of ill-fated liberal reforms, but few of his efforts outlived him. Soon after he took the throne, for example, he dismissed Prussia's interior minister, Robert von Puttkamer (1828–1900), a conservative ally of Bismarck. Liberals within Germany and abroad were delighted by this move, which they hoped was a prelude to a more sweeping series of constitutional reforms. The most important of these would be to reduce the immense influence of the chancellor, written into the German constitution by Bismarck, by establishing a British-style cabinet answerable to the Reichstag. Unfortunately, weakened by his illness and left incapable of speech by a botched surgery, Friedrich was unable to make lasting reforms or to curb the authoritarian and militaristic tendencies inherent in the Kaiserreich. Friedrich's tragic career has long fascinated scholars who speculate about how he might have changed Germany's path had he enjoyed a longer reign. Upon Friedrich's death in 1888—known in Germany as the Year of the Three Emperors—his son was crowned Emperor Wilhelm II (1859–1941). Fascinated by military life but without battlefield experience, the young Wilhelm repudiated his father's liberal sentiments. Deeply influenced by Otto von Bismarck, the new kaiser openly proclaimed his intention to return Prussia to the conservative and bellicose policies of his grandfather and namesake, Wilhelm I.

9

THE GREAT WAR AND WEIMAR GERMANY

On the first of July 1916, the Battle of the Somme began with a weeklong British artillery bombardment. The terrifying barrage, comprising more than 1.7 million high-explosive shells, was intended to clear German trenches and destroy barbed-wire entanglements in preparation for a massive assault that the British generals hoped would break the deadlock on the Western Front. Since the start of World War I, the belligerents had been unable to break through the lines of trenches that marked the front lines, despite the slaughter of hundreds of thousands of young soldiers. The First World War had degenerated into hellish trench warfare, as the Germans, British, and French devoted the full destructive might of the modern industrial nation-state to the extermination of their enemies.

After the allied guns fell silent, thousands of British and French soldiers clambered from their trenches and advanced across the shrapnel-torn wasteland of No Man's Land toward the German trenches. Unfortunately for the British and French troops, the German defenders had survived the artillery bombardment, sheltering in deep underground bunkers. Once the British barrage ended, the German defenders knew an assault was commencing and rushed to man their trenches and set up machine-gun emplacements. A deadly hail of machine-gun bullets decimated the first wave of allied soldiers, advancing in ragged lines across a 25-mile front as the Germans fired into their ranks. More than 60,000 British troops died on the first day of the battle alone. One British survivor described the gruesome aftermath of the initial assault: "The Germans always had a commanding view of No Man's Land. The attack had been brutally repulsed. Hundreds of dead were strung out like wreckage washed up to a high-water mark. Quite as many died on the enemy wire as on the ground, like fish caught in a net. They hung there in grotesque postures. Some looked as if they were praying; they had died on their knees and the wire had prevented their fall. Machine-gun fire had done its terrible work" (Coppard 1980, 82).

The Battle of the Somme dragged on for months, but subsequent assaults proved just as costly—and just as futile—as the first. By the time the battle finally ended, in November 1916, the British had lost more than 400,000 men, their French allies had lost almost 200,000, and the Germans had lost half a million dead. For the cost of more than a million young soldiers, the British and French had advanced barely seven miles. The Battle of the Somme demonstrates the horrors unleashed during World War I, a conflict that would destroy the German Empire.

The Reign of Wilhelm II

Once the new kaiser, Wilhelm II, took the throne in 1888, he was determined to prove himself master of his German Empire. Son of Friedrich III and grandson of Britain's Queen Victoria, Wilhelm spent his reign in an attempt to prove himself the worthy successor to the great Hohenzollern rulers of the past. Born with a deformed left arm, the self-conscious Wilhelm was obsessed with the Prussian military, appearing throughout his reign in ostentatious military regalia, his malformed limb resting on the scabbard of a ceremonial sword to conceal his disability. An arrogant and tempestuous man, the young kaiser identified with his grandfather, Wilhelm I, believing that he ruled Germany by the grace of God. Wilhelm's fascination with the military and his overweening confidence in his own divine purpose exacerbated the authoritarian and bellicose political culture of Wilhelmine Germany, ultimately leading to disaster.

As crown prince, Wilhelm had increasingly fallen under the influence of Otto von Bismarck, who convinced him to eschew the progressive policies advocated by his parents. By the time Wilhelm took the throne, at 29, he was determined to return Germany to the course of his grandfather, Wilhelm I, whom he idolized. The haughty young monarch soon clashed with Bismarck, impatient with the aging chancellor's cautious foreign policy and chafing at his interference in imperial politics. Wilhelm scorned Bismarck's painstaking attempts to maintain peace among Europe's great powers and demanded aggressive action. The final straw, however, proved to be a domestic controversy.

In early 1890, Bismarck tried to pass a bill through the Reichstag that would make his antisocialist laws permanent. Given Bismarck's influence among the conservative parties in the Reichstag, the bill was certain to pass, but during the deliberations, a split emerged among the delegates regarding the police powers authorized by the legislation. As the debate became more heated, Wilhelm intervened, arguing against Bismarck's measures against the socialists in an effort to curry favor among Germany's working classes. Bismarck eventually acquiesced, but the disagreement strained his relationship with his monarch. It also signaled Wilhelm's intention to take a more active role in government than the old chancellor would have liked.

Reeling from the conflict with Wilhelm, Bismarck sought to shore up his support within the Reichstag by forming a new coalition that included his former enemies in the Catholic Center Party. He held a secret meeting with their leading delegate, one that enraged Wilhelm when he learned of it. Wilhelm felt that as monarch he should have been informed of the meeting and confronted Bismarck. After a heated exchange, the 79-year-old Iron Chancellor resigned in 1890, complaining bitterly of Wilhelm's interference in both diplomacy and domestic policy.

With Bismarck out of the way, Kaiser Wilhelm endeavored to rule Germany himself, appointing a more docile chancellor, Leo von Caprivi (1831–99), to oversee the implementation of his increasingly reckless policies. Once Caprivi took over, he learned of the secret Reinsurance Treaty Bismarck had brokered in 1887 between Russia and Germany. On Caprivi's advice, Wilhelm allowed this crucial agreement, one that guaranteed that Russia would remain neutral if France attacked Germany and safeguarded Germany from the specter of a two-front war, to lapse. Abandoned by Germany and diplomatically isolated, the Russians reached out to France, a nation that had recovered its strength and still sought to avenge its defeat in the Franco-Prussian War. In August 1892, the two nations signed the Franco-Russian Alliance, promising each other military support in case of war, just the sort of agreement Bismarck had worked for decades to preclude.

In 1894, the incompetent Caprivi was replaced with Chlodwig zu Hohenlohe-Schillingsfürst (1819–1901), before Wilhelm settled on a more able chancellor in 1900, Bernhard von Bülow (1849–1929). In the decade that followed, as the impatient and impulsive Wilhelm meddled in diplomacy, German foreign policy veered from crisis to crisis. The first of Wilhelm's diplomatic blunders came in 1896, with the publication of the Kruger telegram. Wilhelm resented the British monarchy his father had so revered and rashly sent a telegraph to the president of the Transvaal Republic in South Africa, congratulating him on defeating a coup by a band of English adventurers. Once made public, the telegram embarrassed the British government and enraged the English public, needlessly undoing Bismarck's policy of avoiding conflict with Britain.

On the heels of this debacle, Wilhelm II began a costly endeavor to make Germany into a naval power of the first order. Jealous of the powerful fleet controlled by his uncle, King Edward VII (1841–1910) of England, Wilhelm dreamed of possessing a naval force that could rival Britain's mighty Royal Navy. Meanwhile, the Germans viewed a powerful navy as essential in acquiring overseas colonies and protecting maritime commerce. In 1897, the kaiser appointed Grand Admiral Alfred von Tirpitz (1849–1930), an energetic naval commander, to run the Imperial Naval Office, entrusting him with this daunting task. Under von Tirpitz, Germany passed a succession of naval laws between 1898 and 1912, spending bills that financed the rapid construction of a world-class imperial navy. Admiral von Tirpitz focused his efforts on building massive battleships that could ply the Baltic and North Atlantic, and challenge the capital ships of the Royal Navy. Since British strategy during this period required them to maintain a navy that was as powerful as the combined naval forces of any two other nations, the result was a tense arms race between Germany and the United Kingdom.

The competition heated up in 1900, amid the tension surrounding the Boer War, when von Tirpitz pushed a second naval law through the Reichstag that called for doubling the size of Germany's navy. The planned naval construction would give Germany the world's second-largest navy, a fleet capable of challenging Britain's dominance on the high seas. As an island nation dependent upon its foreign colonies, the British were deeply alarmed and accelerated their own naval construction to keep pace. Using the frequent diplomatic crises of the early 1900s, von Tirpitz kept up the pace of German naval armament, issuing ambitious new naval laws in 1906, 1908, and 1912.

Alarmed by Germany's increasing aggressive stance and growing naval might, the British and French governments established the Entente Cordiale, a series of agreements that brought an end to their historic animosity. Addressing the colonial ambitions of the two partners, the agreements divided contested areas into British and French spheres of influence, in order to forestall conflict. Having already signed an alliance with Russia, the French used their new relationship with Britain, reeling from the disastrous Boer War, to counter the growing power of Germany. In fact, British and French diplomats had been discussing the possibility of forming an alliance against Germany since the early 1880s, but amid colonial rivalries, these efforts had faltered. At the insistence of Britain's King Edward VII, who acceded to the throne in 1901, his country ended its "splendid isolation," and the agreement, the Entente Cordiale, meant to restore the balance of power on the Continent, was finally signed in April 1904. For the French, the backing of Russia and Britain gave them the confidence to adopt a more aggressive stance against Germany.

In 1905, France's growing confidence and Wilhelm's active involvement in diplomacy caused another spectacular blunder, the so-called First Moroccan Crisis. On a state visit to Tangiers, Wilhelm made remarks that seemed to suggest his support for Moroccan independence, angering the French, who considered the region to be within their sphere of influence and were in the process of establishing a protectorate over the area. The German chancellor Bernhard von Bülow sought to use the ensuing crisis to test the Entente Cordiale between Britain and France. He wagered that the two nations would find themselves unable to set aside their traditional animosity or their colonial rivalry. As tensions between France and Germany heightened, von Bülow proposed an international conference that would resolve the issue, but France refused to submit to such an arrangement. By mid-June, the crisis threatened to boil over, as France and Germany geared for war, but the British convinced the French to attend the conference, which would meet at Algeciras in southern Spain in January 1906. The Algeciras Conference proved to be a disaster for Germany and demonstrated its growing isolation from the other major powers. Only Austria-Hungary stood by Germany, while France enjoyed the support of Britain, Italy, Russia, Spain, and the United States. In the final agreement of May 31, 1906, France was granted effective control over Morocco, and Germany suffered yet another embarrassing diplomatic setback.

In the following year, 1907, another ominous event helped pave the way for the First World War. Just as Britain had put an end to its long-running adversarial relationship with France with the Entente Cordiale, the Anglo-Russian Convention, signed in St. Petersburg in August 1907, now ended Britain's rivalry with the Romanovs. The Anglo-Russian Convention accord defined the two powers' spheres of influence in Central Asia and also guaranteed mutual military support against Germany. With this 1907 Anglo-Russian agreement, along with the earlier Franco-Russian Alliance of 1892 and the Entente Cordiale of 1904, Germany increasingly found itself at odds with the combined clout of three great imperial powers: Britain, France, and Russia, a situation that would come to a head with the Second Moroccan Crisis of 1911.

The growing rift between Germany and Britain came to the fore once again a year later when Kaiser Wilhelm gave a damaging interview that was published in the *Daily Telegraph,* a British newspaper, in 1908. In the interview, Wilhelm fumbled his attempt to heal the division with Britain and to charm the English people, making a variety of provocative and bizarre statements. In one famous excerpt, he declared:

> You English . . . are mad, mad, mad as March hares. What has come over you that you are so completely given over to suspicions quite unworthy of a great nation? What more can I do than I have done? I declared with all the emphasis at my command, in my speech at Guildhall, that my heart is set upon peace, and that it is one of my dearest wishes to live on the best of terms with England. Have I ever been false to my word? Falsehood and prevarication are alien to my nature. My actions ought to speak for themselves, but you listen not to them but to those who misinterpret and distort them. That is a personal insult which I feel and resent. (Snyder 1958, 296–297)

The effect of Wilhelm's ill-considered remarks was catastrophic, with the interview igniting fierce anti-German sentiment abroad and prompting serious questions about his judgment at home. Deeply embarrassed, Wilhelm removed Chancellor von Bülow from office, hoping to use him as a scapegoat for the debacle, but the damage was done. He appointed a reliable Prussian bureaucrat, Theobald von Bethmann-Hollweg (1856–1921), to the post, but after 1908, Wilhelm's influence within the German government waned.

By 1911, relations between Britain and Germany were strained, owing to Wilhelm's reckless attempts to challenge Britain's control of the sea and the bellicose nationalism exhibited by the two nations' presses. When a rebellion broke out against the Moroccan sultan, Wilhelm seized his chance to avenge the humiliations he had suffered at the Algeciras Conference by using Germany's navy to intervene in the crisis, openly challenging Anglo-French control of the region. When the revolt against the sultan had broken out in Morocco in April 1911, the French and Spanish had rushed troops to the region to quell the rebellion. When a German gunboat, the *Panther,* landed at the Moroccan port of Agadir a month later, however, the French sent troops into Fez and the British readied their Gibraltar fleet to counter the Germans. Faced with the combined forces of Britain and France, whose Entente Cordiale once again held firm, the Germans were forced to seek terms to defuse the crisis. In early July, the German ambassador to France offered to withdraw from Morocco and recognize French administration of the region in exchange for territorial concessions from the French in the Congo. The subsequent Treaty of Fez, signed on November 4, 1911, set these terms, ending the crisis. Again, the episode had the opposite effect from the one the Germans intended: Instead of breaking the Anglo-French alliance, it strengthened their combined opposition to Germany. The Germans' failed use of "gunboat diplomacy" also exacerbated the growing animosity between Britain and Germany and confirmed fears of Wilhelm's growing naval might.

German Society in the Kaiserreich

Despite the stifling, autocratic nature of German politics during the Wilhelmine period, Germany's intellectuals, artists, and scientists gained increasing international prominence in the decades around the turn of the century. In 1902, Theodor Mommsen (1817–1903), a professor at the University of Berlin, was awarded the Nobel Prize in literature for his monumental, five-volume study of the history of Rome. The year before, Thomas Mann (1875–1955) published his celebrated novel *Buddenbrooks*, and he went on to win the Nobel Prize in 1929. German artists associated with the Blaue Reiter art movement, most notably the painters Wassily Kandinsky and Franz Marc, proved extremely influential in the development of modern art, especially the movement known as expressionism. These scholarly and artistic achievements were rivaled by the accomplishments of German scientists and inventors. In Mannheim, Karl Benz (1844–1929) pioneered the development of the gasoline-powered automobile, producing a viable three-wheeled Motorwagen in 1885. Meanwhile, German scientists and engineers were pioneers in the so-called Second Industrial Revolution in the fields of chemicals and electricity.

During this period of rapid change, the German economy continued to expand dramatically, and in the decades before the outbreak of World War I, German steel production gradually outstripped and eventually doubled British output. As Germany's share of industrial production and international trade increased, the population also grew dramatically. Between 1890 and 1913, Germany's population increased by a staggering 40 percent. Germany's burgeoning population was

This print engraving, published in 1888 in the Leipziger Illustrirte Zeitung, is the first illustration of Karl Benz's Patent-Motorwagen, the world's first commercially available automobile using an internal combustion engine. Karl Benz completed the first model in 1885 and patented his new invention, based upon bicycle technology, the following year. (oldtimer-markt)

deeply stratified, and the workers who crowded the tenement blocks of German cities often lived in appalling conditions.

Economic and demographic changes were not the only forces transforming German society at the turn of the century. German women began to agitate for political rights during this period. As middle-class German women entered the workforce in greater numbers, often working as secretaries and schoolteachers, their newfound economic clout prompted them to challenge the legal restrictions they faced and their wholesale exclusion from political life. Consequently, women began to organize, leading to the formation in 1894 of the Bund deutscher Frauenvereine, or BDF, an association that fought for women's rights in the workplace and in the political arena. The BDF grew rapidly, and by 1901, it had 137 chapters with some 70,000 members. In the following decade, its ranks had swelled to include 2,200 chapters and almost half a million members. Other women's organizations flourished during this period as well, drawing women from across the political spectrum.

Thus, socialist women's groups flourished, alongside conservative organizations for nationalist women, such as the female auxiliary of the German Navy League, and religious associations for both Protestant and Catholic women. As women became more vocal within Wilhelmine Germany, they managed to secure new rights. In 1908, for example, a reform bill legalized women's political participation, giving them for the first time the right to join political parties. German women would have to wait for the end of the Kaiserreich in 1918 before they won the right to vote.

Nationalist fervor ran high in Wilhelmine Germany, and in the decades after unification, militant patriotism was often promoted by leading intellectuals. The prominent historian Heinrich von Treitschke (1834–96), for example, a professor at Humboldt University in Berlin, was an aggressive nationalist, who enflamed patriotic passions within Germany. Like Theodor Mommsen, von Treitschke was also a Reichstag delegate, remaining active in national politics throughout his career. In stirring speeches and fiery essays, von Treitschke glorified the Hohenzollerns and enthusiastically supported the German state's efforts to suppress socialism, to acquire a colonial empire, and, above all, to challenge the might of Britain. A more troubling element of von Treitschke's nationalist zeal was its anti-Semitic nature, which helped foster the growing animosity Germany's Jewish citizens endured during the late 1870s.

The rampant nationalism of the Wilhelmine period identified national unity with cultural assimilation, and the German Jews' distinctive religious and cultural identity was viewed as a divisive threat. Ironically, by the time of unification, Germany's Jewish population had become highly assimilated, enthusiastically embracing German patriotism and German culture. For ardent nationalists like von Treitschke, however, the "refusal" of German Jews to assimilate completely was appalling, and in 1879, the prominent intellectual launched a public campaign excoriating Germany's Jewish community. German Jews faced many restrictions during this period and were precluded from important government, military, and university posts. Their association with leftist politics in the public imagination amplified the conservatives' vilification of the Jews. At the same time, German conservatives identified Jews with the modernist cultural forms that were emerging in Germany's cities, challenging new modes of architecture, art, music, and theater that many viewed as a threat to traditional German values. In the 1890s, an anti-Semitic political party emerged, and although it earned just 16 of 399 seats in the 1893 Reichstag elections, it reveals the worsening climate for Jews in Germany at the time.

Germany's colonial experience also indicates that Wilhelmine nationalism harbored a dangerous racist dimension. After Germany acquired the colony of Southwest Africa (modern-day Namibia) in 1884, German settlers began to exploit the indigenous population. These indigenous peoples, cattle-herders known as the Herero and the Nama, rebelled in 1904, killing a number of German settlers. The revolt unleashed brutal reprisals that culminated in what can be regarded as the first genocide of the 20th century. After defeating the Herero at the decisive Battle of Waterberg on August 11, the German commander General Lothar von Trotha (1848–1920) forced the survivors, including women and children, into the Kalahari Desert. Having poisoned the wells in the region, he ordered his men to shoot any of the Herero who tried to leave the desert, condemning an entire people to die of thirst. Only a few managed to survive. Subsequently, the Nama were herded into rudimentary labor camps, where they died by the thousands of exhaustion and malnutrition. While von Trotha was eventually relieved of command owing to the outcry within Germany about his brutal tactics, the shameful episode would provide an ominous blueprint for the Holocaust and would prompt the German government to issue a formal apology in 2004.

Herero prisoners photographed in German Southwest Africa in 1904 (Bundesarchiv, Bild 146-2003-0005)

Despite Bismarck's efforts to suppress leftist political parties since the 1870s, socialism continued to thrive within Wilhelmine Germany. The ideology crafted by the German communist Karl Heinrich Marx proved highly influential in the decades after his death in 1883. As Europe underwent the painful transition from being a traditional agrarian society to an industrial, urban one, Marx's interpretation of history as a series of "class struggles," and his prediction of the ultimate triumph of the working classes, or proletariat, provided succor for the exploited masses. For Germany's socialists, Marx's revolutionary call for the foundation of a stateless, classless, communist society that would erase the inequalities of capitalism provided hope for a better future. For monarchists and conservatives, these visions represented an anarchic nightmare.

Inspired by Marx's teachings, the Social Democratic Party strengthened in the waning years of the Kaiserreich, growing from 100,000 members in 1890 to more than 1 million in 1914. In fact, by 1912, harnessing the voting power of Germany's working classes in the major cities and industrial regions, the SPD had become the largest party in Germany, winning almost a third of the seats in the Reichstag that year. Tied closely to the trade unions and highly organized, the SPD became a central feature of working-class life, with its own newspapers, social clubs, and welfare programs. As the German socialist party gained in strength and influence, SPD leaders increasingly pursued a pragmatic, reformist agenda, subsuming the most revolutionary aspects of Marxist theory to avoid the sort of state repression it had suffered before 1890.

World War I

The tensions that had been building in Europe during Wilhelm II's reign set the stage for war. The estrangement of Britain and Germany and their ensuing naval arms race helped fuel a spirit of bellicosity among Europe's great powers. Worse yet, the entangling obligations imposed by the continent's shifting and often secret alliances, meant to preclude military aggression, actually made the diplomatic situation more precarious. All that was needed to ignite a war that would have global implications was a spark. As Bismarck had predicted, the spark would come from the Balkans, a troubled region that, as he had famously informed the Reichstag in 1875, "was not worth the healthy bones of a single Pomeranian grenadier."

The Balkans

The Balkans, situated between the Adriatic and the Black Sea in Eastern Europe, was peopled by a bewildering array of antagonistic ethnic groups. With a history of conflict, fueled by religious strife, Albanians, Bulgarians, Croats, Macedonians, Romanians, Serbs, and Slovenes had chafed for centuries under Turkish rule. Inspired by the era's ardent nationalism, these diverse peoples were eager to carve out their own nation-states in the region after the Ottoman Turks' loss in the Russo-Turkish War of 1878. These dreams of independence did not suit the Habsburgs, however, who feared that Slavic nationalism would lead to the splintering of their Austro-Hungarian Empire. Hoping to quell a nationalist uprising in the region, Austria occupied the fractious province of Bosnia-Herzegovina after the Turks withdrew in 1878. The Austrians intended to annex the territory but needed Russian support, since the czars (Russian emperors) had long championed Slavic interests in the Balkans. In 1908, the Russians secretly agreed to allow the Austrian annexation, in exchange for Habsburg support for Russian designs in the Mediterranean. The two empires soon had a falling out, however, when the Habsburgs hastily seized the territory without first providing the diplomatic concessions Russia had demanded. Meanwhile, the Serbs, who also had claims in Bosnia-Herzegovina, also protested the annexation. War seemed imminent, until German support for its Austrian ally, promised in the Dual Alliance of 1879, forced the Russians and Serbians reluctantly to acquiesce.

With the Ottoman Empire appearing increasingly moribund, a coalition of Balkan states, including Bulgaria, Montenegro, and Serbia, joined with Greece in 1912 to form the Balkan League, a coalition created to drive the Turks from the region. In the First Balkan War of 1912–13, the league did just that, forcing the Ottomans from the Balkans and creating a dangerous power vacuum in the region. The Great Powers stepped in to arrange the postwar settlement and in the 1913 Treaty of London created a new Slavic nation, Albania, exacerbating the already tense politics of the region. The Serbs had expected to win an outlet to the Adriatic as their spoils of war, but the creation of Albania blocked these designs. Serbia turned once again to its powerful protector, urging Russia to support their demands for Adriatic territorial concessions from Macedonia. Meanwhile, Bulgaria was also eager to acquire Macedonian territory, sparking the Second Balkan War of 1913 that pitted Serbia, and a host of allies, including Greece,

Montenegro, Romania, and even Turkey, against Bulgaria. Bulgaria was crushed by this powerful coalition, and in the postwar settlement, Serbia and Greece partitioned Macedonia, while Bulgarian territory was ceded to Romania. The conflict further destabilized the region and stirred the nationalist aspirations of other Baltic ethnic groups, most notably the Bosnians, tensions that would soon lead Germany and the rest of Europe into war.

Assassination of Franz Ferdinand

On June 28, 1914, the event that plunged Europe into the nightmare of World War I occurred in Sarajevo. There, a young Bosnian nationalist, Gavrilo Princip (1894–1918), angered at the 1908 Austrian annexation of Bosnia-Herzegovina, assassinated the Habsburg archduke Franz Ferdinand (1840–1914), and his wife, Sophie Chotek Ferdinand (1868–1914). Franz Ferdinand, next in line for the Austro-Hungarian throne, had been invited by the Austrian provincial governor to Sarajevo to review a military parade. The visit was conducted under heavy security, given the activities of violent Slavic nationalist groups in the region who were eager to drive the Austrians from their homeland. On the morning of the military review, as the car carrying the royal couple passed along the parade route, several of Princip's coconspirators failed to carry out the planned assassination, although a bomb exploded near the archduke's car. As Archduke Franz Ferdinand made his way to the hospital to visit bystanders wounded in the bomb blast, his driver took a wrong turn, and by a strange coincidence encountered a dejected Gavrilo Princip hiding from the police at a café. Princip approached the car and fired two shots into the car, fatally wounding the archduke and his wife. The Bosnian assassin was arrested and under questioning divulged that he and his coconspirators had received aid from the dreaded Serbian nationalist organization known as the Black Hand.

The July Ultimatum

All of Europe was outraged by the deed, and as the Austrian people clamored for revenge, the Austro-Hungarian government was determined to make Serbia pay. Assured of unqualified German support by Wilhelm II and his chancellor, Bethmann-Hollweg, Austria's government weighed its diplomatic and military options, as French and Russian diplomats scrambled to secure a peaceful settlement to the dispute. On July 23, the Austrians issued the infamous July Ultimatum to the Serbians, a series of humiliating demands they were almost certain to reject, even at the risk of war. The July Ultimatum began an irreversible chain reaction, as Europe's complicated system of entangling alliances embroiled nation after nation in the conflict.

First, on July 24, Russia promised to aid its Serbian ally and warned Austria against any aggression against the Serbs. Russia had long supported Serbia, influenced by Panslavism, a movement that sought the unity of all Slavic peoples under Russian leadership, and seeking to bolster its influence in the Balkans. Next, the Turks, fearing that Russia would exploit the situation to attack them, signed an alliance with Germany in case of war. France honored the Franco-Russian alliance, promising to aid the Romanovs militarily if hostilities began. By now events were moving quickly, and a day later, July 25, Serbia agreed to all of the terms save one. The Serbs refused to acknowledge any culpability in the Sarajevo assassination, and having given Austria the excuse it needed for an invasion, began to mobilize for war. Eager for war, Austria and Germany declined a proposal to resolve the matter through an international conference. Finally, on July 28, Austria declared war on Serbia, starting World War I. The next day, Germany lost its nerve and tried to reach an agreement with Britain ensuring their mutual neutrality in the coming conflict, but it was too late. The Russians had begun to mobilize, and by August 1, the French and Germans were doing the same. Germany declared war on Russia on August 2, and then on France the following day, bringing about the two-front war it had long feared.

Fighting Begins

The coming of war in August 1914 was greeted with almost universal enthusiasm throughout Europe. Nationalistic fervor and romantic sentiments about the glory of fighting for king and country were heard from Moscow to Paris. As millions of troops mobilized for war, cheered by jubilant crowds, everyone was confident that the war would be over by Christmas, with their side celebrating a glorious victory. Throughout Germany, all ranks of society welcomed the coming struggle as a means of demonstrating the superiority of the German people over those they considered the backward Slavs and decadent French. Even the Social Democrats, convinced that Russia was the aggressor, abandoned their pacifist stance and helped harness Germany's working classes to the war effort. Likewise, Germany's Jewish population, despite the latent anti-Semitism of the Wilhelmine period, enthusiastically supported their fatherland, enlisting in the army at the same rate as the rest of their countrymen.

The German General Staff mobilized efficiently, according to a secret prewar strategy known as the Schlieffen Plan, crafted in the early 1890s to deal with the possibility of a future two-front war. Now that such a war had come to pass, the German generals put the plan into action. The Schlieffen Plan called for a rapid invasion of France, through neutral Luxembourg and Belgium, with the intention of taking Paris before lumbering Russia, hampered by its muddy roads and lack of modern railways, could even mobilize its enormous army. Once France was defeated, Germany could turn its full attention to the east, joining their Austrian allies in beating Russia. Meanwhile, the Austrians had their own plan to invade Serbia before turning to face their more powerful adversary, Russia. The first sign that the war would not go according to plan for the Germans was Italy's declaration of neutrality, despite its promises to join the German Empire and the Austro-Hungarian Empire against Russian aggression in the Triple Alliance in 1882. Henceforth, Germany and Austria-Hungary, encircled by their enemies with only the dubious support of the Turkish sultan, would be known as the Central Powers.

Once Germany's massive invasion force of 1.5 million troops began their march on Paris, they immediately experienced costly setbacks. In tiny Belgium, the Germans encountered surprisingly tough resistance, costing them casualties and slowing their advance into France. Worse yet, their violation of Belgium's neutrality, guaranteed by an 1837 treaty, brought England into the war, joining France and Russia in the Triple Entente. Soon the British Expeditionary Force landed in northern France, helping to slow the German advance.

Having stationed most of their troops on the German frontier, hoping to invade Germany through Alsace-Lorraine, the French found it difficult to stop the Germans as they advanced steadily toward Paris from the north. At the Battle of the Marne, waged in the early weeks of September, the French managed to halt the German advance but suffered horrific casualties. Faced with the grim realities of modern warfare—bolt-action rifles, machine guns, high-explosive artillery shells, and barbed wire—both sides soon recognized the futility of offensive operations on the western front. The war bogged down into a bitter stalemate, and for four years the troops endured brutal trench warfare and fruitless suicide assaults on enemy positions, attrition that would ultimately claim millions of lives.

Incapable of making a decisive breakthrough on the western front, the Schlieffen Plan had failed, and Germany was forced to engage in a potentially disastrous two-front war. The Russians had mobilized with unexpected speed, surprising even their allies in the Entente. On the eastern front, the war initially had a completely different character than in the west and was marked by rapid maneuver and decisive, pitched battles. As the Russians invaded East Prussia, a pair of brilliant German generals, Paul von Hindenburg (1847–1934) and Erich Ludendorff (1865–1937), checked their advance. To the jubilation of the German public, reading of their triumphs in fiercely nationalistic newspapers, the aging von Hindenburg, a hero of the Franco-Prussian War lured out of retirement, and his able chief of staff, Ludendorff, smashed the Russians in a pair of battles in August and September 1914, taking almost a quarter of a million prisoners. Once the impetus of the Russian attack on Germany was broken, the Germans and Austrians invaded Russia's Polish territories. These campaigns soon bogged down as well, however, and fighting in the east also assumed a defensive character.

Meanwhile, the Austrians were engaged in their own two-front war and faced stiff opposition in the Balkans. While the Austrians managed to take Belgrade, suffering heavy casualties, by the end of 1914 their forces had retreated from Serbia. Having been expelled by the Serbians, the Austrians spent most of 1915 in a fruitless invasion of Italy, fighting

Emperor Wilhelm II and senior military commanders in April 1915 (Bundesarchiv, Bild 183-R11105)

TRENCH WARFARE

Alfred Dambitsch, a German lieutenant wounded at the Battle of the Somme in 1916, gives readers a harrowing account of the horrors of the new military technologies unleashed in the trench warfare of World War I. Here, he describes the experience of the Germans at the start of the Battle of the Somme:

In respect to new methods and machines, the present French and British offensive is the last word. The aim of any offensive in modern warfare is the destruction of the enemy. This is the object of the present offensive, the idea being to enclose us in a tactical ring by simultaneous bombardment with long-range guns from the front and the rear. Accordingly the greedy beast began eating at the back lines of the German front. First of all our third and second trenches were incessantly bombarded, mostly by heavy artillery, of which the enemy had concentrated unprecedented masses in the sector of attack. It was dugouts that had to be battered down, so that at the moment of assault all the defenders, except a few survivors, and all the machine guns might be buried. Our second and third trenches were bombarded in order to prevent our bringing up reserves. For the same reason all the communication trenches leading from the rear to the front position were kept under incessant fire. On the Somme every one of our columns had a good communication trench that led from the headquarters of the battalion to the front trench. But the attack against our front from the rear extended still further. All the main and side roads and all the crossroads were kept under fire so that approaching troops, munitions, supplies, and provisions had to pass through several lines of fire. Bombarding villages and places behind the

a bitter campaign in the Alps. Hoping to knock Serbia out of the war, the Germans and Austro-Hungarians convinced Bulgaria to participate in a joint invasion of Serbia. Attacked by the Austro-Hungarians from the east and the Bulgarians from the west, the Serbian army faced total annihilation and retreated into Albania before the survivors found refuge in Greece.

The horrors of modern warfare pitted millions of citizen-soldiers against each other in a war of attrition waged with deadly modern weaponry, itself the product of industrial technology. Both sides in World War I sought to break their enemy's resolve through mass infan-

front where the various reserves are supposed to be quartered is an old trick of the British and French, but this time the principle was carried out more consistently and recklessly than ever. All places up to a distance of 10 miles behind the front were brought under incessant heavy artillery bombardment, which often started actual fires, thanks to the incendiary shells used by the enemy.

The battering down of our advanced trenches was almost exclusively left to the heavy artillery and trench mortars, especially the latter. The French have made great improvements in this weapon lately. For the destruction of our trenches they exclusively employed those of the heaviest caliber, and they now throw their shells with greater accuracy and over longer ranges than formerly. Opposite my company no fewer than six mortars were placed. They were worked uninterruptedly, throwing hundreds of aerial torpedoes on our position from the first to the third trenches. They tore up our wire obstacles from the ground, poles and all, and threw them all over the place, crushing the dugouts if they fell on them, and damaging the trenches. In a very short time great portions of our trenches had been flattened out, partly burying their occupants. This fire lasted for seven days, and finally there came a gas attack, also of an improved kind.

The deepest impression left on me was not a feeling of horror and terror in face of these gigantic forces of destruction, but an unceasing admiration for my own men. Young recruits who had just come into the field from home, fresh twenty-year-old boys, behaved in this catastrophic ploughing and thundering as if they had spent all their life in such surroundings, and it is partly thanks to them that the older married men also stood the test so well.

Source: Horne, Charles F., ed. *The Great Events of the Great War.* Vol. IV (n.p.: The National Alumni, 1920), pp. 253–254.

try attacks on entrenched positions, exposing their troops to murderous machine-gun fire and deadly artillery bombardment. In the bloodiest battles of the war, waged in France at Verdun and at the Somme in 1916, Europeans experienced carnage of an unimaginable scale. At the Battle of the Somme, more than 1 million men perished in futile attempts to break the stalemate. As the war dragged on, commanders resorted to employing deadly new military inventions, hoping to gain an edge. Thus, the Germans unleashed the horrors of chemical warfare, using poisonous mustard gas against their enemies, and the British introduced primitive tanks meant to crush enemy troops beneath their steel tracks. Despite these deadly innovations, and the slaughter of millions of soldiers on both sides, the fortified trenches stretching south from Belgium through the Ardennes Forest and into Germany, which marked the front lines in the west, moved barely 10 miles in three years of bloodshed.

The stalemate on the western front and the horrors of Verdun and the Somme shook Emperor Wilhelm's faith in Germany's military leadership. The emperor replaced the aging Helmuth von Moltke (1848–1916), nephew of the hero of the Franco-Prussian War, after the disastrous Battle of the Marne in 1914. The German army's new chief of the general staff, the pragmatic Erich von Falkenhayn (1861–1922), increasingly despaired of achieving a military victory and advocated a negotiated settlement to the conflict, angering Wilhelm. In August 1916, the heroes of the Russian offensive, Paul von Hindenburg and Erich Ludendorff, replaced the cautious von Falkenhayn. These popular generals brought a new confidence to the German military high command, blindly preaching that Germany could win despite her increasingly precarious position. In their unbridled zeal to win the war at all costs, von Hindenburg and Ludendorff ruthlessly silenced internal dissent, and Germany increasingly resembled a military dictatorship.

The German people would ultimately pay the price for their determination to achieve total victory. As the carnage continued on Europe's battlefields, World War I also introduced the concept of total war to an unprepared world, erasing the line between soldiers and civilians and harnessing entire societies to the war effort. Wilhelm II's expensive fleet proved no match for the celebrated Royal Navy and, after an inconclusive naval skirmish off Jutland, remained at anchor for the rest of the war. With total command of the seas, the British took the fight to the German people, blockading Germany's ports in 1914 in an attempt to starve the Germans into submission. In response, Germany introduced submarine warfare, using its tiny fleet of U-boats to torpedo supply ships headed for the British Isles. The German navy's use of "unrestricted submarine warfare" entailed sinking any ships they encountered in the waters off Britain without warning, including the merchant vessels of neutral countries such as the United States. As German chancellor Bethmann-Hollweg had feared, this policy eventually brought the Americans to the brink of war against Germany, with the sinking of the British liner RMS *Lusitania* on May 7, 1915. Among the civilians killed in the sinking of the vessel off the Irish coast were 128 U.S. citizens. Outraged, the American public pressured President Woodrow Wilson (1856–1924), who was reluctant to enter the fray, to declare war on Germany. The Germans promised to halt their submarine attacks on civilian shipping, but von Hindenburg and Ludendorff's decision to resume unrestricted submarine warfare in 1917 finally brought the United States into the war.

Once the United States entered the war, its capacity to bring fresh troops and war matériel to Europe's battlefields overwhelmed a war-weary Germany. As victory slipped from Germany's grasp, the nation's civilian leadership gave way to a new government dominated by the German military. Despite growing pressure on the western front, and mounting economic crisis on the home front, in the east, the Germans still advanced on Russia. As Russian troops retreated in disarray, workers and soldiers at home rioted, and the czarist government toppled. Although Czar Nicholas II soon abdicated, the provisional government that replaced the czarist regime proved short-lived and was itself overturned by the Bolsheviks in November 1917. The leader of this communist party, Vladimir Lenin (1870–1924), had been smuggled from Switzerland to Russia by the German military aboard a sealed train on the heels of the czar's abdication. The German high command had hoped that Lenin's Bolshevik Party would destabilize Russia and lead to its withdrawal from the war. Their calculations proved correct, and once the Bolsheviks took over, Lenin sued for peace with Germany, abandoning the former czar's imperialist war in order to consolidate the revolution in Russia.

The Germans signed the Treaty of Brest-Litovsk with the Bolsheviks in March 1917, gaining valuable territorial concessions in Poland, the Baltic States, Finland, and the Ukraine in exchange for the cessation of hostilities. For the Allies, the punitive nature of the treaty supplied a propaganda bonanza and a justification for dealing harshly with Germany in the war's aftermath. Thus, the leaders of the Entente used the terms of the Treaty of Brest-Litovsk as a demonstration of Germany's ruthless way of dealing with defeated enemies. Worse yet, the punitive treaty shattered the wartime consensus within Germany. Once the territorial concessions demanded in the Treaty of Brest-Litovsk became known, Germany's radical socialists, who had left the SPD over its support for the war, had clear evidence of the "imperialistic" aims of the war. Communist agitators used this to foment a series of crippling strikes among Germany's war-weary workers, strikes that threatened to hamstring Germany's war efforts. Only the swift intervention of Friedrich Ebert (1871–1925), a prominent SPD Reichstag delegate, brought the strikes to an end in time for the German military to gear up for a final offensive in the west.

The situation on the western front was increasingly dire for Germany by the spring of 1918. With U.S. troops and munitions pouring into Europe, General Ludendorff planned a final, massive German offensive along the western front for the spring of 1918, a last-ditch gamble to win the war before U.S. might tipped the balance. The desperate offensive started promisingly in March 1918, and German troops, using innovative hit-and-run tactics, pushed the British forces near Amiens back nearly 40 miles. By late March, the Germans had advanced to within 75 miles of Paris, and heavy railway guns were shelling the French capital, causing jubilation in Berlin. With the end of the war in sight, however, the German assault bogged down once again. By the end of July, the exhausted Germans had been pushed back to their staging areas, having gained nothing from the sacrifice of more than 250,000 of their best troops. For many Germans on the home front, suffering the privations caused by the British naval blockade, this costly defeat was the final straw. Angry crowds throughout Germany, a nation that had lost 6 million war dead, staged antiwar demonstrations as morale plummeted among soldiers and factory workers alike.

As Germany reeled, its allies on the eastern front began to falter as well. After a string of defeats, Germany's Bulgarian and Turkish allies both dropped out of the war in late 1918. Beset by nationalist uprisings among the Czechs and Slavs and faring poorly on the battlefield, the Austro-Hungarian Empire sued for peace as well on November 3, 1918. As 1918 drew to a close, Germany stood alone against the combined Entente powers. The end of the war was near as anxiety mounted within Germany.

American troops and supplies had been flowing into Europe since May, bolstering the Entente powers, and by the late summer of 1918, many German generals advocated suing for peace, including even hard-liners like von Hindenburg and Ludendorff. In early October 1918, with the depleted German army facing annihilation, Germany's new chancellor, the liberal ruler of Baden, Prince Max (1867–1929), was authorized to begin peace negotiations. The German diplomats approached the Americans first, offering to accept President Wilson's Fourteen Points, a liberal postwar settlement based upon the principle of national self-determination and international cooperation. Wilson rebuffed the German diplomats, refusing to open separate peace negotiations with autocratic imperial Germany. Meanwhile, tensions within Germany were rising, as the German navy mutinied, and riotous crowds in Munich toppled the Bavarian monarchy.

After the standoff at Jutland in 1916, the German imperial navy had been trapped in the naval yards at Kiel by the British Royal Navy. Now that the end of the war loomed, the aristocratic officers of the kaiser's fleet sought to salvage the honor of the German navy by engaging the British fleet. Once the German fleet heard of this suicidal plan, the sailors mutinied, refusing to steam against the British. While the naval commanders abandoned the planned attack, given the recalcitrance of the sailors, when the imperial fleet returned to Kiel, the local dockworkers joined the sailors in rebellion. The rebellious sailors and workers repulsed attempts by officers to arrest the mutiny's ringleaders, sparking violence. As the revolt intensified, the sailors commandeered their ships and proclaimed a communist revolution. Inspired by the recent Bolshevik Revolution in Russia, sailors, soldiers, and workers in cities throughout Germany began forming revolutionary councils and taking part in mass demonstrations and strikes. On November 7, 1918, one such insurrection toppled the Wittelsbachs, the dynasty that had ruled Bavaria since the 12th century, and proclaimed the establishment of the Bavarian Republic. In Berlin and other German cities, firebrand revolutionaries called for paralyzing general strikes to force the kaiser's abdication and an immediate armistice to end the war.

With Germany spinning out of control, Emperor Wilhelm II's most trusted advisers began to press him to abdicate. Wilhelm initially resisted these overtures, reluctant to give up his crown. Although Wilhelm offered, somewhat pathetically, to give up the imperial title if he could continue to rule as king of Prussia, it was too late for compromise. On November 9, 1918, Prince Max of Baden, acting as chancellor, announced that Emperor Wilhelm II had finally agreed to abdicate. The last Habsburg emperor of Austria had already stepped down a week earlier, as his empire fragmented into a series of ethnic enclaves. Wilhelm, reduced since early in the war to figurehead status amid the rising popularity and influence of the German military high command—especially the heroes of the eastern front, Generals Paul von Hindenburg and Erich Ludendorff—went into exile in neutral Holland, as growing unrest erupted in Berlin. The Independent Socialists, radical communists who had split from the SPD, were preparing to fill this power vacuum by launching a Bolshevik-style revolution.

In an attempt to preempt the communists, the socialist Philipp Scheidemann (1865–1939) declared the end of the monarchy from the balcony of the Reichstag building, proclaiming all of Germany a republic. While Scheidemann acted without proper authorization from the German government, once the radical leader Karl Liebknecht

(1871–1919) responded by announcing the foundation of a communist regime, the issue was moot. Several hours later, fearing the outbreak of a full-blown communist revolution, Prince Max resigned, handing power to the capable socialist leader Friedrich Ebert. Max hoped that Ebert might be able to build a coalition of moderate socialists and conservatives that could forestall communist revolution, steering a dangerous course between the radicals demonstrating in Germany's streets and the conservatives who controlled the nation's military. Friedrich Ebert delivered immediately, convincing the angry crowds marching in Germany's streets to disperse and putting an end to the crippling general strikes.

On November 10, 1918, under Ebert's leadership, leading German liberals from the Social Democratic Party established a provisional government. The SPD had grown in prestige amid the hardships of total war, as the German people suffered the effects of the British naval blockade and the strict rationing imposed by the nation's military government. As war-weariness set in, increasing numbers of Germans, eager for an end to the carnage, had turned to the parties of the German Left, and especially the SPD, for leadership. Ebert capitalized upon this socialist support to arrange elections for a new German National Assembly in January 1919, an assembly that would draft a constitution for the fledgling republic and negotiate a postwar settlement with the victorious allies. Fleeing the revolutionary turmoil of Berlin, the delegates drafted a constitution that transformed Germany into a republic with an elected president and a chancellor appointed by the Reichstag. A day after establishing the provisional government, Germany's new leaders signed an armistice with the Entente powers: On the 11th hour of the 11th day of the 11th month in 1918, World War I finally ended, having claimed almost 10 million lives.

The Treaty of Versailles

Germany's new government had already promised to cede the territories its forces had gained in the war in exchange for an armistice, erasing the sweeping territorial gains Germany had acquired through the Treaty of Brest-Litovsk. As the provisional government in Berlin would soon learn, this was only the beginning of the heavy indemnities Germany would have to endure in the postwar period. The peace negotiations began in earnest in January 1919 in Paris. Ominously for the Germans, they were not invited to attend the meetings until April, after the victorious allies had hammered out the settlement. So, in the German delegates'

SPD supporters campaigning in Berlin to gain votes for their candidates in the National Assembly elections of January 1919 (Bundesarchiv, Bild 146-1972-001-21 / Gebrüder Haeckel)

absence, the British representative, David Lloyd George (1863–1945), the French leader George Clemenceau (1841–1929), Woodrow Wilson of the United States, and a pair of Italian representatives drafted the settlement, disagreeing almost from the start on how to deal with a defeated Germany.

While all of the victorious powers agreed that Germany should be punished for its prewar belligerence, there was disagreement among the delegates over how punitive the postwar settlement should be. The French, on whose soil most of the war had been fought, sought to cripple their longtime German enemy. Thus, they demanded that Germany should forfeit its industrial heartland, the Saar region, as well as all territory west of the Rhine. While both Britain and the United States thought this too punitive, the Americans likewise disagreed with the British over whether the Germans should repay the victorious allies for the entire cost of the conflict. In the end, the more retaliatory allies carried the day, and Germany suffered a range of costly sanctions. Germany lost many precious territories along its borders, surrendering Alsace-Lorraine to France, a pair of Prussian provinces to Poland, and a trio of cities to Belgium. The Germans were also forced to disarm: Their postwar military was limited to 100,000 men, a puny force without a large surface fleet, submarines, or warplanes that posed no threat to Germany's neighbors. Worse yet for the Germans, they were forced to accept total responsibility for starting the war and to pay crushing war reparations, amounting to more than $32 billion. French troops would occupy the Rhineland, at German expense, until these crushing debts were paid in full.

Once they learned of the provisions of the Treaty of Versailles, the German populace was shocked and outraged. Having been fed a constant stream of misleading propaganda that boasted of German battlefield victories, Germany was shaken by the sudden collapse of the imperial military. Article 231, the war guilt clause of the treaty, was particularly shocking, since Germany did not acknowledge any particular role in provoking hostilities. Furthermore, Germany had never been invaded by its enemies, and its frontline troops had retreated in good order in 1918, causing many within Germany to cling to the fantasy that their country had not really been defeated but rather was the victim of a "stab in the back" delivered by defeatist elements at home. Thus, many of the German people felt betrayed by their government, which seemed weak and perhaps even traitorous, in letting the victorious allies impose such draconian terms.

The settlement also had dire economic ramifications that eroded support for the provisional government. The German economy was still in shambles from the war, and the British blockade, which continued after the armistice, inflicted hunger on millions of Germans during the terrible winter of 1918–19. Thus, most Germans viewed the crushing reparations demanded by the Versailles settlement to be rapacious and cruel. Despite these misgivings, Germany's provisional government had no choice but to agree to the victors' terms.

Establishment of the Weimar Republic

Germany's new democratic government, formed under the shadow of the humiliating Versailles capitulation, inherited a host of daunting problems. In January 1919, as the German people seethed with resentment over the postwar settlement, a radical communist group, the Spartacists, staged a futile coup in Berlin, inspired by the Bolsheviks in Russia. The leaders of the Spartacist movement, Rosa Luxemburg (1871–1919) and Karl Liebknecht, had split from the SPD when the socialist party's leader, Friedrich Ebert, chose to support the war effort at the outbreak of World War I. Outraged by this apparent repudiation of Marxist doctrine regarding the unity of the world's working classes, these former SPD members founded a new, radical party known as the Communist Party of Germany (KPD) that sought to bring communism to Germany in 1919 through violent revolution.

Desperate to restore order, the fledgling provisional government turned to the army to put down the rebellion, and the military responded with a brutal crackdown. The right-wing paramilitary units known as the Freikorps rounded up and summarily executed communist leaders and activists, and the movement's most prominent leaders, Rosa Luxemburg and Karl Liebknecht, were murdered while in police custody. Luxemburg's lifeless body was found months later in Berlin's Landwehr Canal. On the heels of these tumultuous events, general elections proceeded in Germany, with the moderate socialists of the SPD taking the majority of seats in the Reichstag, the national assembly that would draft Germany's new constitution. A host of competing parties, including the more radical socialists of the USPD, the Catholic Center Party, as well as several militant conservative and nationalist factions, also won seats, presaging the fractious political situation that would afflict interwar Germany.

As violence raged in the streets of Berlin, these newly elected delegates retreated to Weimar to hammer out a new German constitution. As they shaped the government that would come to be known as the Weimar Republic, Germany tore itself apart. Communist uprisings flared in Munich and Berlin, and communists battled in the streets with the Freikorps. Meanwhile, the French attempted to establish a separatist republic in the Rhineland. Amid the growing chaos, the Weimar delegates elected the SPD statesman, Friedrich Ebert, as Germany's new president. Ebert, leading a defeated and disunited Germany, isolated and impoverished by the war, was forced to accept the harsh terms of the Treaty of Versailles. On July 7, 1919, the treaty was ratified.

The Weimar constitution, ratified soon afterward, was a remarkably progressive document that guaranteed democratic participation for all. The president would be elected to a seven-year term, Reichstag delegates to four-year terms, with seats in the assembly allocated to each party according to the percentage of votes they won in national elections. The republic's president would appoint a chancellor from the majority party, and the chancellor would in turn form a cabinet to help him govern. While this liberal constitution provided the German people with true representative government, for many Germans the fragile Weimar Republic, having signed the hated Versailles Treaty, would forever be associated with the stigma of humiliation and defeat. Moreover, the Weimar constitution contained an emergency provision,

Article 48. According to Article 48, in a crisis, Germany's president could temporarily suspend the constitution and rule without consulting the Reichstag. The sweeping powers granted by this emergency provision, a provision born amid the unrest of 1919, would ultimately doom the Weimar Republic.

The Weimar Republic was plagued by instability from the very start, and during the early 1920s, the fledgling government endured attacks from radicals from the right and the left of the political spectrum. Right-wing extremists castigated the Weimar government for the "betrayal" of the Versailles Treaty and launched a series of dangerous uprisings. In March 1920, an ardent nationalist named Wolfgang Kapp (1868–1922) marched on Berlin at the head of a brigade of Freikorps soldiers and occupied the city, hoping to overthrow the republic. Ominously, the conservative German military stood silent during the attempted coup, which was only thwarted by a massive general strike, which brought the city to a halt and aroused public outrage against the Kapp Putsch's leaders. In Bavaria, right-wing extremism was more successful, and Munich soon became a hotbed of radical nationalism. Despite his socialist background, Ebert's government also came under fire from communists intent on fomenting a Bolshevik-style revolution within Germany. In the Ruhr, Marxist agitators sparked a workers' rebellion that was only suppressed with the aid of the German military, suppression that in turn invited French military intervention in the volatile region. French occupation of the Ruhr in 1923 enflamed German patriotism and encountered widespread passive resistance, but the unrest also hindered Germany's economic recovery.

Germany suffered from serious economic problems during the early 1920s, exacerbating the political instability that plagued the country in the early years of the decade. Desperate deficit spending during the First World War and devastating reparations payments in its aftermath had caused a dangerous devaluation of the nation's currency. As runaway hyperinflation erased the life savings of millions of German citizens, it exacerbated the anxiety afflicting the country. Hampered by the crushing schedule of reparations payments owed to its neighbors, and hamstrung by factional infighting within the Reichstag and political strife on Germany's streets, Ebert's government proved powerless to halt the decline of the German currency. Throughout Germany, the anxious populace was plagued by images of pensioners hauling wheelbarrows of near-worthless currency to the bakery to buy bread as the Weimar government printed billions of new bills in a desperate attempt to keep pace with inflation. The economic crisis and the anxiety it produced prompted radical political actions, including a communist uprising in Thuringia, a state in central Germany. Another failed coup, the Munich Beer Hall Putsch of 1923, was inspired by Mussolini's fascist takeover of Italy the year before, and was led by an ambitious nationalist politician and military veteran named Adolf Hitler (1889–1945). As Germany careened into chaos, Ebert's new chancellor, the capable Gustav Stresemann (1878–1929), managed to stave off the total collapse of the German economy by issuing a new currency. As the economy slowly recovered, the political situation also became less volatile and less violent. By 1924, the Weimar Republic had entered the calm before the storm.

The second half of the 1920s proved to be a period of political, economic, and cultural renewal in Germany. Under Stresemann's able direction, Germany's diplomatic isolation ended. Stresemann reestablished diplomatic ties with the leading victors of World War I—Britain, France, and the United States—and even managed to persuade them to soften the sanctions against Germany. In a major triumph in 1924, the Weimar government succeeded in convincing Britain and France to accept the Dawes Plan, which reduced German reparations payments and provided Germany with American loans to help rebuild its economy. Rejuvenated by these loans, the German economy began a rapid recovery, as production rose and drove both profits and wages higher. The following year, Stresemann negotiated the Locarno Treaties, in which Germany promised to respect the territorial borders of France and Belgium and to submit to arbitration to resolve border disputes with Poland and Czechoslovakia. In 1926, Germany was even welcomed to join the League of Nations and seemed to be shedding its pariah status. As the nation's diplomatic standing improved and its economic prospects brightened, violent political unrest began to die down. Weimar culture, centered on Berlin's glittering nightlife and artistic scene, flourished. It appeared that good times had returned to Germany.

Even before the onset of the Great Depression, however, storm clouds were gathering over Germany. In 1925, after the death of the socialist statesman Ebert, the German people elected the aging war hero Paul von Hindenburg as president, a sign of lingering nostalgia for the strident militarism of the Kaiserreich. Furthermore, despite Stresemann's conciliatory policies toward the victorious allies, resentment of the stringent terms of the Versailles settlement was also evident within the German military. In 1922, the German government had signed the Rapallo Treaty with the Union of Soviet Socialist Republics, or USSR, whereby the two outcast nations promised each other mutual diplomatic and economic support. These obligations were renewed in 1926 in the Berlin Treaty, a settlement between Germany and the Soviet Union that masked ominous developments. Unbeknownst to the western powers eagerly welcoming Germany back into the international order, the German military was busy training for a new war on the remote plains of Russia, in defiance of the restrictions set by the Versailles Treaty.

The fragile stability within the Weimar Republic was shattered in 1929 as the world succumbed to the economic catastrophe that would come to be known as the Great Depression. With the collapse of the U.S. stock market, American banks stopped issuing new loans to Germany and even called in loans they had already issued. Without this infusion of capital, the German economy faltered, and the nation's major banks began to fail. By early 1930, the ripple effects had devastated major sectors of the German economy: factory production ground to a halt, businesses went bankrupt, and unemployment rates soared. Starved of revenue, the Weimar government was hard-pressed to offer adequate unemployment benefits, spreading fear and anger throughout German society. Paralyzed by internal dissension, President von Hindenburg and the Reichstag proved powerless to avert the looming disaster.

The spreading anxiety fostered radical politics, and in the elections of September 1930, Germany's frustrated citizens gave unprecedented support to extremist parties. While the moderate socialists of the SPD managed to hold the largest proportion of seats, with just over 24 percent of the vote, the militant nationalists of the National Socialist, or Nazi, party won around 18 percent of the vote, followed closely by the radical communists of the KPD, which gained 13 percent. The radicalization and fragmentation of the Reichstag precluded compromise, and legislative deadlock quickly ensued. The conflict on the floor of the Reichstag was matched in the streets, as Germany's major cities once again endured bloody street fighting, this time between the Nazis and the communists, who shared a disdain for parliamentary democracy. As the situation spiraled out of control, President von Hindenburg invoked the sweeping emergency powers permitted him by Article 48 of the republic's constitution, an ominous portent of the Weimar Republic's coming demise. Germany's troubles grew worse between 1930 and 1932, as the Weimar Republic, wracked by economic collapse, tore itself apart. In the April 1932 presidential elections, the beloved old warhorse Hindenburg barely won the required majority, earning just over 53

Adolf Hitler appearing before his supporters in Weimar in 1930 (Bundesarchiv, Bild 102-10541)

percent of the vote. Ominously, the rising Nazi leader, Adolf Hitler, claimed almost 37 percent of the vote, despite the violence of his henchmen and the radical ideology he espoused. The KPD candidate, Ernst Thälmann (1866–1944), trailed his Nazi nemesis, earning just more than 10 percent of the total votes.

Adolf Hitler was an obscure Austrian who had immigrated to Bavaria shortly before World War I. A failed artist, he enlisted in the German army when the war began and found a sense of purpose in the trenches. A rabid German nationalist, Hitler had worked for the army in Bavaria after the armistice, spying on the radical parties emerging in Munich in the aftermath of the war. Bitter about Germany's defeat in World War I and humiliation in the Versailles Treaty, Hitler blamed socialists and Jews for the catastrophe. Despite the fact that thousands of Jewish soldiers died fighting for Germany during the war, Hitler espoused the scurrilous myth that Jews were alien traitors who had stabbed the German military in the back, sabotaging the war effort. Attracted to the radical political scene in postwar Munich, Hitler joined the German Workers' Party in 1919, rapidly climbing to leadership within the organization. Having changed the name of

177

the party to the National Socialist German Workers' Party (NSDAP), or Nazis, Hitler enthralled growing crowds as he railed against the Weimar Republic. Jailed for nine months in the wake of the failed Beer Hall Putsch in 1923, Hitler wrote his twisted manifesto, *Mein Kampf*, chronicling his paranoid delusions about the superiority of the German race and the grave threat posed by Jews and socialists to its destiny. By 1932, Adolf Hitler had built the Nazi party into a political force, harnessing the German people's lingering dissatisfaction with the Versailles settlement and growing disillusionment with the seeming ineptitude of democratic government in the face of the Great Depression. The Nazis appealed to a broad swath of the German population, attracting fervent nationalists and radical conservatives, as well as those who hated the Versailles settlement, feared the communists, or despised the Jews.

The growing popularity of Germany's radical parties was reaffirmed in the Reichstag elections of 1932, when the Nazis supplanted the SPD as the dominant party, winning almost 38 percent of the votes and doubling the number of seats they held. The SPD's share of the vote had dwindled to just 21 percent, and the KPD trailed with 14 percent of the vote. These voting trends suggest that the majority of Germany's voters had abandoned the Weimar Republic by 1932, throwing their lot with the antidemocratic fringe parties of the radical left and the extremist right. Despite the ascendancy of the Nazi Party, Hindenburg refused to appoint the dangerous radical Adolf Hitler to be chancellor. Disregarding the Weimar constitution, von Hindenburg named the conservative former military officer Franz von Papen (1879–1969) chancellor instead. Von Papen's cabinet proved unpopular with the delegates of the Reichstag, and he called for new elections in November 1932, hoping to gain a majority for his party, the conservative DNVP. The chancellor proved unable to contain the Nazis' growing popularity, however, and the NSDAP managed to win almost 200 seats, while the Communists won 100. Unable to bring Hitler to heel, von Papen was forced to resign and was replaced as chancellor by his old friend and cabinet appointee, the former minister of defense, Kurt von Schleicher. Jealous of Schleicher's power, von Papen worked to arrange his former associate's ouster, negotiating with Hitler about forming a new coalition between the DNVP and the NSDAP. Promising Hitler the chancellorship if he agreed to support the coalition, von Papen convinced President von Hindenburg to oust Schleicher. Von Hindenburg had long resisted making Hitler chancellor, but the aging president reluctantly agreed, relying on von Papen's promise that he could control the Nazis. On January 30, 1933, von Hindenburg made Hitler chancellor of Germany, with von Papen as vice chancellor. Hitler would assume the title führer, or "leader," the following year. The ill-fated Weimar Republic, Germany's brief experiment in democracy, was at an end.

10

NAZISM AND WORLD WAR II

In the autumn of 1934, the new German führer, Adolf Hitler, addressed thousands of adoring Nazi Party members at the Sixth Party Congress held in Nuremberg. These annual convocations of the Nazi Party, which had been held in the Franconian city since 1926, provided the fascist dictator with a valuable propaganda opportunity. For the 1934 Nuremberg rally, Hitler enlisted the services of a brilliant young filmmaker, Leni Riefenstahl (1902–2003), to commemorate the event and to create a vision of Aryan power and unity. Using innovative shots of the carefully choreographed masses at the party rally, she created *Triumph of the Will,* one of the most striking, and dangerous, films in history.

The film records Hitler delivering a maniacal speech, raging at the mesmerized throng about the pride and the purity of the German people. Hitler believed Germany could only realize its glorious destiny once it became unified and purified itself of alien, non-Aryan elements. While Riefenstahl's cameras capture the pride swelling in the breasts of the cheering crowds applauding their führer's oration, the film obscured the Nazis' true aims. For Hitler, the German race could only be purified in the crucible of war and through the extermination of those he deemed "non-Aryan" or "weak," including Jews, communists, and the mentally and physically handicapped. Accordingly, he believed that until Germany purified itself through conquest and extermination, it could not claim its rightful place atop the world order. Riefenstahl's film proved to be a smashing success, and along with almost 1 million Germans who took part in the festivities in Nuremburg, millions more were afforded an opportunity to hear the words of their führer in German theaters.

The Nazi Takeover

Adolf Hitler, having been imprisoned after his failed 1923 coup, was careful to use the machinery of democratic politics to subvert the Weimar democracy as the Nazis grew in power. After President von Hindenburg appointed Hitler chancellor, in late January 1933, Hitler immediately began to lay the groundwork for his dictatorship. He delivered a radio address to the German people, promising to save Germany from the scourge of communist revolution and foreign domination. He also demanded that President von Hindenburg dissolve the Reichstag and schedule a new election for March 5, 1933. Shortly before the upcoming election, on the night of February 27, 1933, the Reichstag building burned, and the Nazis blamed the communists for the fire, warning that it signaled the start of a leftist revolution. Using this excuse, Hitler passed a series of emergency decrees that suspended a wide range of constitutional liberties. The Nazi chancellor also ordered the KPD's offices to be raided and had communist leaders jailed: Ernst Thälmann, Hitler's rival in the recent Reichstag election, was sent to a concentration camp.

With communist opposition crushed, in the March 1932 Reichstag elections, Weimar's last democratic election, the Nazis and their nationalist allies gained a slim majority, as the SPD's share of the electorate dwindled to just 18 percent. Tragically, this prevented the left from having the votes necessary to preclude Hitler from enacting the Enabling Act on March 23, 1933. This legislation, which passed easily with the support of Germany's other mainstream political parties, gave Hitler sweeping emergency powers, powers he used to dismantle the democratic government. The Enabling Act gave the cabinet, dominated by Hitler, legislative authority for four years, permitting the Nazis to control Germany without having to consult the Reichstag. Furthermore, their control of the police allowed the Nazi Brown Shirts, the Sturmabteilung (Assault Division), or SA, the party's paramilitary force, to operate in Germany's streets with impunity. Using these auxiliary police powers, the Nazis were free to arrest their political opponents and detain them in concentration camps.

Despite the brutality of the SA, Hitler gained widespread support throughout the country through his passionate public speeches, exploiting the anxious populace's fear of communism, mistrust of Jews, and anger over the Versailles settlement. Hitler's crude and violent rhetoric attracted adherents from throughout German society. The Nazi platform appealed not only to violent thugs and Freikorps veterans but also to anxious middle-class Germans traumatized by the Great Depression, who were attracted to Hitler's ardent nationalism and charismatic personality in a time of unsettling crisis and instability. Students and intellectuals were enchanted by the Nazis' aura of confident modernity, embracing the party's fascination with mass media, technological efficiency, and racial pseudoscience. For Germans disenchanted with the Weimar Republic, the carefully staged mass rallies put on by the Nazis presented an idealized image of German unity and national pride that provided a striking contrast with the divisive parliamentary politics of the Weimar era.

Using the Enabling Act's sweeping emergency powers, on July 14, 1933, the Nazi government outlawed the SPD, thereby stamping out the last vestiges of open dissent within Germany. Having crushed all opposition from Germany's socialists, Hitler had thousands of leftists arrested. Hitler did not stop at suppressing leftists, however. Although he had relied upon a coalition of parties opposed to the Weimar government to come to power, once he controlled Germany he turned on his erstwhile allies, eliminating right-wing challengers as well. By the summer of 1933, the Nazi Party was Germany's sole legal political organization. Likewise, Hitler outlawed all independent trade unions, as well as the country's state governments, gradually bringing Germany under his control. Also in 1933, Germany's Jewish population began to feel the first effects of Hitler's rabid anti-Semitism, as Jewish civil servants, jurists, and educators were removed from their posts by government decree. Finally, the Nazis took over the German media, banning all opposition newspapers and radio stations and placing the others under the control of the Party's propaganda minister, Joseph Goebbels (1897–1945).

The Nazi takeover was accompanied by a bloody purge of Hitler's earliest and most ardent followers, the Brown Shirts of the SA, as he sought to rid the party of its most unruly and radical elements. On the "Night of the Long Knives"—June 30, 1934—Hitler's personal bodyguard, under the command of Heinrich Himmler (1900–45), assassinated hundreds of Nazi Party members, including Ernst Röhm, the head of the SA. Having consolidated his control over Germany, Hitler used this brutal purge to establish total mastery over the ruling Nazi Party and to appease the German military and business community, uneasy with the Brown Shirts' excesses and the Nazis' revolutionary past. Once President Paul von Hindenburg died, on August 2, 1934, Hitler proclaimed himself führer, or leader, of Germany, a move subsequently legitimized through a national plebiscite that overwhelmingly approved his new authority.

Nazi Germany: The Third Reich

Once Hitler had gained total power over Germany, he set about reviving the German economy and rebuilding the German military. Having excoriated the former Weimar government for its ineptitude in handling the economic crisis brought on by the Great Depression and for its weakness in dismantling Germany's armed forces, Hitler needed quick results. He turned to the famous World War I pilot Hermann Göring (1893–1946), to make Germany into a European powerhouse once again. Göring, who along with Goebbels and Himmler was part of Hitler's inner circle, harnessed German production to the creation of the war machine the dictator would use in his attempts to fulfill the dark designs he laid out in *Mein Kampf*. As military production skyrocketed after 1934, Germany's unemployment rate declined and manufacturing output increased, to the delight of the country's workers and industrialists. Despite the curtailment of political freedoms, for many Germans the depredations of the depression—against which liberal democracies proved powerless—seemed to justify Hitler's dictatorship.

Ultimately, however, Nazi power was based upon terror and violence. Already in 1933, the formation of a ruthless secret police force, known as the Gestapo, and the creation of a system of concentration camps where tens of thousands of political prisoners and criminals labored and died, showed the true character of Hitler's fascist leadership. As he had promised in *Mein Kampf*, Adolf Hitler also launched a repressive program based upon dubious racial science that depicted the Germans as an "Aryan" master race destined to rule over supposedly inferior peoples such as the Jews and Slavs. Following these twisted tenets, the Nazis sought to purify Germany by ridding it of the biological pollution of so-called "non-Aryans," namely the Jews. Beginning in 1935, with the appearance of the Nuremberg Laws, which officially excluded Jews from German citizenship and defined whom the Nazis considered legally to be a Jew, the Nazis began to erode the rights of Germany's Jewish population. The legislation derived its name from the city of Nuremberg, where Hitler announced the laws at the annual party rally on September 15, 1935. The Nazis claimed that the laws were necessary to protect "German Blood and German Honor." By the end of the 1930s, the regime had stripped Germans with even a single maternal or paternal Jewish grandparent of their citizenship rights, outlawed their marriage with non-Jews, barred them from a variety of occupations, and even established exclusionary ghettos where they forced Jews to live. On November 9, 1938, Germany's Jews endured the Kristallnacht, or Night of Broken Glass, a Nazi-sponsored wave of anti-Semitic violence that swept the country. Fueled by Goebbels's virulent anti-Semitic propaganda, the pogrom left thousands of Jewish synagogues and businesses damaged or destroyed and tens of thousands of Jewish people attacked, killed, or deported to concentration camps. Around half of Germany's Jewish population, which numbered more than 500,000 in the 1930s, emigrated to avoid further persecution. The rest stayed to look after aged family members or businesses built over generations, hoping for a return to sanity in Germany.

As his Nazi henchmen unleashed this outbreak of anti-Semitic discrimination and violence, Hitler began a series of aggressive diplomatic moves aimed at rebuilding German military might. Hitler sought not only to redress the humiliation Germany suffered through the Versailles settlement but also to realize another aspect of the master plan he laid out in *Mein Kampf:* conquering territory within Europe in order to provide lebensraum, or living space, for his supposed Aryan master race. First, Hitler set out to repudiate the Versailles Treaty. In the fall of 1933, he declared that Germany would withdraw immediately from the League of Nations. Having taken this confrontational stance in relation to the western powers, Hitler turned to the strategic industrial region of the Saarland, occupied by the French since the end of World War I, in January 1935. Encouraged by the January 1935 plebiscite conducted by the League of Nations in which 90 percent of the local population chose to rejoin with Germany, rather than become part of France, Hitler demanded the restitution of the important region, a move that prompted a vigorous French diplomatic response. Using France's reaction as pretext, Hitler declared that Germany would abandon the military restrictions of the Versailles Treaty and embark upon a rapid rearmament. Alarmed, the western allies met in order to discuss how they would respond, but the British, French, and Italian delegates could not reach a mutually satisfactory resolution, and Hitler's military buildup continued unopposed. On January 15, the Saar rejoined Germany.

The following year, 1936, as the Spanish civil war raged, an anxious Europe, still haunted by the horrors of World War I, had to deal with an even more provocative move from Hitler. When the Nazi leader announced that Germany would no longer honor the promises made in the Stresemann-negotiated Locarno Treaty of 1925 regarding Germany's postwar territorial boundaries in the west, a dangerous threat to France, the western allies again hesitated. Fearing war, the British refused to place a vote for sanctions against Germany in the League of Nations. Pouncing on this divide among his western adversaries, Hitler boldly sent troops into the Rhineland, which had been demilitarized in the Versailles Treaty. Although this was a serious violation of the Versailles settlement, and a direct military provocation of the French, France and its allies did not send troops. Thus, they missed the opportunity to deal with the Nazi menace, allowing Hitler's rejuvenated military—and the führer's megalomania—to grow unchecked.

Having backed down the Western powers, Hitler spent 1936 building his own coalition, readying the Reich for the war of conquest he would soon unleash upon Europe. Hitler began, in July of that year, by signing an alliance with his native land, Austria, which he planned to absorb into Nazi Germany. Next, in October of the same year, the Nazi leader signed an alliance, to the condemnation of the Western powers, with Benito Mussolini, the fascist strongman of Italy who was poised for an invasion of Ethiopia. Seeking his own battlefield proving ground for the reinvigorated German military, Hitler also pledged support for General Franco, the fascist ruler of Spain, sending troops to support the Spanish generalissimo's overthrow of his country's republican government. Finally, at the end of 1936, in November, the Japanese—engaged in their own conquest of China—joined with Italy and Germany, forming a coalition of aggressive, expansionist states known as the Axis.

Facing the threat of armed aggression from Nazi Germany and its Axis allies, the Western powers increasingly sought to appease Hitler by caving in to his diplomatic demands. Thus, when the Nazi dictator, emboldened by his success in remilitarizing the Rhineland, demanded that ethnic Germans living in surrounding countries be brought into his Third Reich, the Western powers acquiesced. (*Reich* is the name given to three German imperial states. The Nazi Party under Hitler called their state the Third Reich, since it followed the first, the Holy Roman Empire, and the second, the German empire [1871–1918] of Wilhelm I and Wilhelm II.) In February 1938, Hitler pressured the Austrian government to accept a Nazi takeover of their country. Hitler had forced the Austrians to place Nazi puppets in several key government posts and had even supported an abortive Nazi coup in Vienna in July 1934. Now he moved openly to force an *Anschluss,* a German word for "joining together" or "union," with Austria. German troops crossed the Austrian border on March 9, 1938, and Hitler entered Vienna four days later, to the jubilation of pro-Nazi crowds, proclaiming that Austria was now part of the Third Reich. Horrified at these brazen provocations, and afraid of Hitler's growing might, the hapless Western allies again complained to no avail. Showing a similar disregard for international law, Hitler immediately manufactured another crisis, this time in Czechoslovakia.

Playing upon simmering tensions within this multiethnic republic, Hitler presented himself as the champion of ethnic Germans living in Czechoslovakia's Sudetenland, a strategic industrial region located on the frontier with Germany. The Nazi leader had long funded German separatist agitators within the region, and with the Nazi takeover of Austria, Germany seemed poised to envelop the Sudetenland. Supported by Hitler, the Sudeten-German Party staged demonstrations in September 1938, demanding autonomy from the beleaguered Czech government. Meanwhile, German troops massed along the frontier, as Hitler publicly backed the Sudeten Germans. Hoping to resolve the issue peacefully, the British prime minister Neville Chamberlain (1869–1940) flew to Germany to meet with the Nazi leader. Seeking to intimidate the Western allies, Hitler threatened military action, warning Chamberlain that he would go to war over the Sudetenland. Once again, the allies balked. France and Britain agreed to allow the Nazis to annex the Sudetenland but promised to defend the rest of Czechoslovakia. Even this humiliating concession failed to satisfy Hitler. Raising the ante, he now demanded the rest of Czechoslovakia as well.

Appalled, Chamberlain, and his French counterpart, Premier Édouard Daladier (1884–1970), rejected Hitler's new demands. As the Czechs mobilized and world leaders held their breath, the Nazi leader finally agreed to negotiate. On September 29, 1938, the leaders of Germany, Britain, France, and Italy reached the Munich Agreement, which allowed Germany to annex the Sudetenland immediately. Other Czechoslovakian regions with a German minority would determine whether they would join Germany through voting. Britain and France guaranteed to safeguard what was left of Czechoslovakia. After the Munich conference, Chamberlain got off the plane in London promising the public that he had secured "peace in our time." Events would soon prove this policy of appeasement to be tragically misguided. In March 1939, the Nazis overran the rest of Czechoslovakia. As Hitler reviewed his triumphant troops in Prague, the Western powers did nothing to stop him, despite their earlier promise to protect Czechoslovakia.

The Nazi dictator next set his sights on Poland, ignoring similar promises by Britain and France to defend the Poles in case of German aggression. By April 1939, Hitler's generals were planning for a full-scale invasion of Poland, while the Nazis roused the German population in the Polish city of Danzig (called Gdańsk in Polish) to agitate for self-determination in order to provide a justification for an attack. To pave the way for an invasion, Hitler entered negotiations with Joseph Stalin (1879–1953), the Soviet leader. The Non-Aggression Pact of August 1939, signed between Nazi Germany and Soviet Russia, was a cynical agreement that allowed these ideological enemies to carve up Poland between them. Now that Hitler was sure that the Soviet Union would not interfere, he was free to invade Poland, confident that the Western powers would back down yet again. This time he was wrong. German troops poured into Poland on September 1, 1939, and Britain and France declared war two days later. This was the beginning of World War II.

World War II

Hitler's blitzkrieg tactics, spearheaded by columns of speeding tanks and supported by relentless air attacks, quickly overran Poland. *Blitzkrieg,* a German word meaning "lightning war," is the tactic of rapid attack with massive numbers of mechanized infantry and tank divisions covered by close air support. The strategy was designed to overawe defenders with a fast, violent, and highly mobile attack while special units interrupted their communication and supply, furthering confusion. Blitzkrieg tactics robbed Poland of time to mobilize its forces and resources. The rapid German victory was not purely the result of these startling new blitzkrieg tactics, however. The cynical collusion of Hitler and Stalin, the Soviet dictator, also worked against the unfortunate Poles. On September 1, 1939, 50 divisions of the German army—almost 2 million troops—poured over the Polish border and raced toward Warsaw. With the Polish army diverted to its western border to deal with the German onslaught, Soviet troops invaded eastern Poland on September 17. Caught between two powerful enemies, the Poles could not hold out for long. After the fall of Warsaw, on September 27, 1939, the German and Russian dictators divided defeated Poland between themselves.

As France and Britain, caught unprepared for fighting a modern war, struggled to mobilize, the Nazis set to work remaking Poland as an eastern outpost of an Aryan empire. In the wake of the Wehrmacht—the name applied to all of Germany's armed forces, including the army (Heer), navy (Kriegsmarine), and air force (Luftwaffe) from 1935 to 1945—Nazi officials carried out a sort of grim dress rehearsal for what Hitler termed "the final solution of the Jewish question," the extermination of Europe's Jews. This Final Solution began with German troops rounding up Poland's large Jewish population and herding them into overcrowded ghettos in the country's major cities. Polish Jews were registered, forced to wear a yellow Star of David, and stripped of their property and belongings. In the squalid conditions of the Jewish ghettos, Poland's Jewish community, which numbered some 3 million before the war, slowly succumbed to starvation and disease. Meanwhile, the Western Allies stood by, seemingly powerless to stop Hitler.

After consolidating his gains in Poland, Hitler set his sights on Scandinavia, as the Soviets invaded the Baltic states of Estonia, Latvia, and Lithuania and struggled to bring Finland to heel. In March 1940, the Germans quickly overran Denmark and also conquered Norway, overwhelming the Norwegian military, despite the presence of a British and French expeditionary force. In the aftermath of their victory, the Germans installed a Nazi puppet government. By the spring of 1940, the Wehrmacht had also conquered the Low Countries—the low-lying region of Northwest Europe occupied by Belgium, the Netherlands, and Luxembourg—paving the way for an invasion of France. The blitzkrieg unleashed on France proved unstoppable, and the Germans easily advanced on Paris. The rapidly advancing German columns drove a wedge between the French forces and the British Expeditionary Force, trapping the latter on the coast of the North Sea at Dunkirk in late May 1940. The British troops, stranded on the beaches, were at the mercy of German aerial attacks as a flotilla of small English vessels, including fishing boats and pleasure yachts, struggled to rescue them from the slaughter. While more than 300,000 British and French soldiers escaped to England, tens of thousands perished in the humiliating defeat. By June, the Germans, seemingly invincible, were marching along the boulevards of a conquered Paris, as the French government collapsed. After the French surrender, on June 22, 1940, the Germans occupied northern France, turning the south over to a compliant puppet regime, the Vichy government led by the collaborator Henri-Philippe Pétain (1856–1951).

Having conquered France in just two weeks, Hitler began preparing for an amphibious invasion of England. Before the Germans could land on British soil, however, they had to destroy the Royal Air Force and establish air superiority over the English Channel. Hitler turned to his trusted follower, the Luftwaffe's flamboyant commander, Hermann Göring, to crush the British air force. The ensuing air war, known as the Battle of Britain, proved to be one of the key turning points of the war. The campaign also provided a bitter taste of the suffering that civilian populations would endure during the world's first true total war, as German and British bomber fleets pounded their enemy's airfields, industrial cities, and transportation networks. In addition to the air war, the German submarine force blockaded Britain, attempting to cut the island nation off from its colonies and allies, including the United States, which, although it remained neutral, supplied crucial aid to the British. While the German Luftwaffe devastated London, Hitler proved incapable of knocking out the Royal Air Force or stop-

Wehrmacht troops marching in the streets of Paris, 1940 (Bundesarchiv, Bild 1011-126-0347-09A)

ping the flow of American supplies into British ports. By the early summer of 1941, Hitler had called off the fruitless air war, abandoning his plan to invade England. Instead, he began preparations for a massive

189

invasion of the Soviet Union, a betrayal of Stalin, his former partner in the Polish campaign.

Relations between Hitler and Stalin had deteriorated the year before, amid rising diplomatic tension and ideological animosity. In addition, the two dictators both laid claim to the strategic oil fields of the Balkans. While Germany had been attacking England, Stalin had annexed the Baltic states of Lithuania, Latvia, and Estonia. He then seized Bessarabia, which had been under Romanian control. As the Soviets pressured Romania, coveting its strategic Ploesti oil fields, the Germans and Italians sent troops that brought the oil-rich country, as well as Hungary, Yugoslavia, and Greece, into the Axis fold by April 1941. By positioning troops in the Balkans and southeastern Europe, as well as by concluding secret agreements with neutral Sweden and Finland to facilitate the transit of German troops stationed in occupied Norway eastward to the Russian border, Hitler was setting the stage for an invasion of the Soviet Union. Hitler's desire to conquer the USSR was driven by his racist ideology, as the Nazi leader had long proclaimed his intention to seize land and resources in the east to provide "living space" for the Aryan master race by conquering the "inferior" Slavic peoples of Russia and dismantling the "Jewish Bolshevik" government that ruled them. Accordingly, Hitler ordered his generals to begin planning a surprise attack on the USSR.

The German invasion of Russia, code-named Operation Barbarossa, began on June 22, 1941. Attacking without warning, the massive invasion force of more than 3 million soldiers advanced across the Soviet border from Finland in the north, from occupied Poland in the center, and from Romania in the south, driving deep into Russia. Unleashing the sort of blitzkrieg attack that had overwhelmed France the previous year, the Germans and their allies pounded Stalin's Red Army, capturing almost 2.5 million Soviet troops by December 1941. By early December, the Germans had advanced to within 15 miles of Moscow and seemed poised to conquer the Soviet Union. However, the savage Russian winter did something Stalin's Red Army could not: It stopped the German advance just outside Moscow. Despite its early success, the largest military campaign in human history had ground to a halt. As Hitler's troops, ill-equipped for the deadly Russian winter, froze in their field positions, the battered Red Army regrouped, preparing for a counterattack that would drive the Germans from Russia.

The stalemate on the eastern front was compounded by reverses elsewhere. After the attack on Pearl Harbor on December 7, 1941, the United States, heretofore reluctant to enter the fray, had declared war on Japan. In turn, Hitler and Mussolini backed their Japanese ally by declaring war on the United States. While the United States was not yet prepared for war, its ability to mobilize unmatched resources in manpower and matériel would soon prove decisive. In the spring of 1941, German forces under the command of the "Desert Fox," Erwin Rommel (1891–1944), landed in North Africa, ordered to reinforce the hapless Italians who were reeling from a failed invasion of British-held Egypt. After a series of daring German victories engineered by Rommel, a brilliant tank commander, the tide of war changed in October 1942, when combined British and American attacks drove the Germans from North Africa. Despite these setbacks, in the autumn of 1942, Germany still held sway over Europe from the English Channel to the gates of Moscow. Meanwhile, Japan, Germany's Axis ally, had suffered its own reversal at the hands of the Americans at the Battle of Midway in June 1942, but it still dominated the Pacific. The nightmare of World War II had only begun.

The Holocaust

Once Hitler had unleashed his assault on the Soviet Union, he redoubled his efforts to eradicate Europe's Jews. As his troops fought the Red Army on the front lines of Russia, special paramilitary detachments known as Einsatzgruppen operated behind the lines, rounding up and executing gypsies, Communist leaders, and Jews. These death squads were commanded by Himmler's Schutzstaffel, commonly known as the SS, The word *Schutzstaffel* means "protection squadron," and its members—selected for their racial purity and fanatical devotion to Nazi ideology—acted as the muscle behind the Nazi Party's tactics of terror and intimidation. The Einsatzgruppen, often assisted by the local population in occupied territories, claimed hundreds of thousands of victims, but this was only a prelude to the horrors of the Holocaust to come. Concerned at the inefficiency of the Einsatzgruppen's murderous activities, leading SS officers met at a secret conference in a villa on Lake Wannsee in southwestern Berlin in January 1942, a conference intended to provide a "final solution to the Jewish question," a Nazi euphemism for the extermination of Europe's Jews. Harnessing the full capacity of a modern, mechanized society to genocide, the Nazis laid out plans for a massive system of concentration camps, labor camps, and extermination camps that would be established in the occupied territories of the east. Trains would roll around the clock, bringing victims to the gas chambers and ovens of sprawling death camps such as Auschwitz and Treblinka. Aided by collaborators throughout occupied

ANNE FRANK

Among the most evocative and heartrending accounts of the Holocaust is the diary left behind by a young German girl named Anne Frank, who died in the Bergen-Belsen concentration camp in northwestern Germany in the spring of 1945. Anne Frank was born in Frankfurt am Main in 1929, the daughter of Otto Frank, a liberal Jewish businessman. As Hitler came to power, the rising atmosphere of anti-Semitism within Germany prompted the Franks to immigrate to Amsterdam, joining hundreds of thousands of Jews who fled Germany in the early years of the Nazi regime. After Germany invaded the Netherlands in May 1940, the occupation authorities began to persecute the country's Jews. As the Germans mandated increasingly harsh restrictions on Dutch Jews, Anne began keeping a diary recording her daily experiences, dreams, and fears. Facing increasing discrimination, the family went into hiding in July 1942 after Anne's sister, Margot, was ordered to report to the occupation authorities for deportation to a work camp. The family, joined by other Jewish fugitives, resided for the next several years in a secret set of rooms behind one of Otto Frank's former office buildings, its entrance hidden behind a bookcase. A handful of Otto's former business associates were the only people who knew about the family's hiding place, and they supplied the Franks with food and news of the outside world, risking punishment if they were caught aiding Jewish fugitives. In August 1944, German police raided the Franks' hideout, on information delivered by an unknown informant. Taken into custody, the family was interrogated by the Gestapo, the dreaded Nazi secret police, and sent to a Dutch penal camp. A month later, the family was transported in crowded cattle cars to Auschwitz, the infamous Nazi extermination camp in occupied Poland. When the trains arrived at Auschwitz, the camp guards, members of Himmler's ruthless SS, separated Otto Frank from his wife and daughters. He would never see any of them again.

Upon arrival at Auschwitz, the bewildered prisoners endured an initial selection, ruthlessly sorted into two groups. The aged, young

Europe, and the acquiescence of the German people, the Nazis arrested Jews, confined them in ghettos, and herded them into cattle cars routed to the death camps. So central was this mass extermination to the Nazi ideology that the Germans even diverted resources needed for combat children, and the feeble were immediately sent to the gas chambers for extermination. Those who appeared fit for hard labor were stripped, deloused, had their heads shaven, and were marked with tattoos on their arms, their names replaced with numbers, their identities in the outside world eradicated. The Franks survived this initial selection, and 15-year-old Anne, along with her mother and sister, spent the next several months enduring inhumane treatment as they hauled rocks on starvation rations. Confined in squalid, overcrowded barracks, prisoners contracted diseases and fell ill. In October 1944, the SS guards at Auschwitz selected women to be transported to the forced labor camp at Bergen-Belsen, in Niedersachsen. Anne and her sister were selected for transportation, but their mother was deemed unfit and later died in Auschwitz.

While Bergen-Belsen was not technically an extermination camp and did not have the machinery of genocidal murder, the gas chambers and ovens of death camps in the east like Auschwitz, Sobibor, or Treblinka, it had been taken over by the SS in August 1942 and was still deadly. Prisoners were engaged in forced labor, and the fetid and crowded conditions fostered the spread of diseases. In March 1945, a deadly typhus outbreak swept the camp, claiming thousands of victims among the inmates, including both Margot and Anne Frank. The British army liberated Bergen-Belsen a few weeks after Anne's death, on April 15, 1945, and burned the camp to halt the spread of the epidemic.

Otto Frank was among the handful of Jewish prisoners to survive the horrors of Auschwitz. After the war, he returned to Amsterdam and reunited with the Dutch friends who had risked their lives sheltering his family during the war. After attempting to locate his wife and children, he learned they had died in the camps. Otto discovered that Anne's diary, which recorded her experiences while her family hid out in Amsterdam, had been saved by his Dutch friends after the family's arrest, and he had it published in 1947. Translated into a dozen languages, *Anne Frank: The Diary of a Young Girl* has become an enduring symbol of the horrors of the Holocaust and the ultimate survival of Germany's Jews.

operations to keep the trains running to the death camps in the waning days of the war. By war's end, the Holocaust had claimed the lives of more than 6 million Jews. Most of Europe's Jewish population was lost. The Nazis' victims included not only Jews but also gypsies, Soviet prisoners of war, religious and political dissidents, and Germans the Nazis considered to be degenerate, such as homosexuals and the mentally disabled.

Fall of the Third Reich

The turning point of World War II came in the winter of 1942, in the smoldering ruins of the Soviet city known as Stalingrad. Named after the Soviet dictator Joseph Stalin, the city had both strategic importance and symbolic value, and Hitler gambled Nazi Germany's future on taking the city. Fighting in horrific winter conditions, the stubborn Soviets turned back the German onslaught at Stalingrad, winning a stunning victory in February 1943 and taking more than 90,000 Axis prisoners. The battle was the costliest in human history, and the combined casualties suffered by the Soviet and the Axis armies likely numbered around 2 million. To Hitler's disgust, the Wehrmacht had failed to conquer Russia, and German forces on the eastern front began a slow and inexorable retreat. Meanwhile, on the heels of the Allied defeat of the Germans in North Africa, an Anglo-American invasion force landed in Sicily in July 1943. Germany's Italian allies crumbled, but the Wehrmacht stood fast, slowing the Allied advance on Rome. On June 4, 1944, American troops entered Rome, and several days later, a massive Allied invasion force landed in Normandy during the famous D-day landings. The Normandy landings were the largest amphibious operation in history, and almost 200,000 Allied troops landed on the beaches of northern France on D-day. These soldiers overwhelmed the German troops defending the beaches and established an invaluable foothold on French soil. Soon Allied tanks and infantry columns were fighting their way across occupied France, advancing on Germany.

Having brought the war to the European mainland, the Western Allies began a steady advance toward the German frontier, overwhelming the Germans with fresh troops and war matériel shipped over from the United States. The Germans were now on the defensive on both the eastern front, where they faced the resurgent Soviets, and the western front, where they faced the Allies. Running short of men and supplies, by 1944, the Germans were fighting a losing battle on both fronts as massive fleets of Allied bombers demolished Germany's cities. By the beginning of 1945, the Soviet Red Army was poised to invade Germany from the east and British and American forces from the west. In his fortified command post, Hitler, shaken by the defeats of the previous year and increasingly delusional about the reality of

Victims of the Nazi concentration camp at Buchenwald after its liberation by the U.S. Army in April 1945 (Bundesarchiv, Bild 183-35011-0004)

Germany's dire situation, railed at his officers with insane plans to turn the tide of war and dreamed of a wonder weapon that would bring ultimate victory. It never came, and by late February 1945, the Soviets were closing in on Berlin, as British and American forces approached the Rhine. Germany's leader, Adolf Hitler, committed suicide with his new bride, Eva Braun, on April 30, 1945, in his subterranean bunker beneath the ruins of Berlin. The dead führer's thousand-year Reich had barely lasted a decade. The German capital fell to the Russians two days later, and the tattered remains of the once-proud German Wehrmacht began to surrender on both the eastern and western fronts. Hitler's successor, Admiral Karl Dönitz (1891–1980), offered an unconditional surrender to the American commander General Dwight Eisenhower (1890–1969) on May 7 and surrendered to the Soviets the following day.

World War II, the product of Adolf Hitler's megalomania and racial paranoia combined with the unresolved issues of World War I, had devastated Europe. Once-glittering European cities had been reduced to smoldering ruins; rail yards, ports, and factories had been destroyed; and entire peoples had been uprooted and made refugees. More than 35 million Europeans had died in the course of the war. For Germany, the Nazi years had proved an unmitigated disaster. Defeated and disgraced, Germany had lost more than 4.5 million soldiers and an unknown number of civilians, perhaps as many as 2 million, during the conflict. Hundreds of thousands of ethnic Germans residing outside of Germany died as well. Traumatized and hungry, German civilians in eastern Germany suffered under a brutal Soviet occupation marked by pillaging, rape, and murder. In the wake of this catastrophe, the shocked German people, deluded by wartime propaganda, also had to confront the atrocities their nation had committed during the war, including the extermination of more than 6 million of Europe's Jews.

11

THE COLD WAR: DIVISION AND REUNIFICATION

In the aftermath of World War II, a conquered and devastated Germany became the first flashpoint in the cold war. At the Potsdam Conference in 1945, the victorious Allies had divided Germany into four occupation zones, and each zone was administered by one of the Allied military commands. The three Western zones, occupied by the United States, Britain, and France, coordinated their activities relatively closely, but a dangerous rift was developing between these Allies and the Soviets, who occupied eastern Germany. The former Nazi capital, Berlin, had also been divided among the Allies, but it lay deep within the Soviet zone. The Russians had pledged to allow the Western Allies to cross their territory to supply their enclave, West Berlin, but by 1948, tensions were at a boiling point.

As the Soviets tightened their grip on Eastern Europe, the Western Allies issued a shared currency for use in their zones, hoping to stabilize Germany's devastated economy. The move angered the Soviets, who responded by cutting off all surface traffic into West Berlin on June 27, 1948. Diplomatic entreaties had no effect, and the beleaguered people of West Berlin, cut off from shipments of food, fuel, and medicine, faced the grim prospect of starvation. The Western Allies immediately began preparing to supply the city through a massive airlift, in what would become the largest aerial supply operation in human history. Turning the massive air flotillas of World War II into a humanitarian relief force, American, British, and French pilots delivered more than 2 million tons of needed supplies. During a harsh German winter, which would have caused the death of thousands of West Berliners, the Allies flew more than 270,000 relief flights. The Soviet blockade was finally lifted on May 12, 1949, as the frustrated Red Army commanders realized that the Allies had the resources and resolve to supply the city indefinitely.

The Berlin Airlift had demonstrated the growing animosity between East and West during the cold war and presaged the eventual triumph of the Western democracies in the ideological struggle. It would take another four decades, however, before a divided Germany was finally reunified.

The Potsdam Conference and Postwar Germany

In the aftermath of World War II, a shattered Germany was divided into a series of occupied zones by the victorious Allies. The four-way partition of Germany was carried out according to an agreement, reached in February 1945 at Yalta in the Soviet Union among the Allies, that gave the United States, Britain, the USSR, and France each an occupation zone to administer. Berlin, the fallen Nazi capital, was also partitioned by the four Allies and administered by a joint Allied council. Although it lay deep within the Soviet zone, Stalin promised to provide free access to the city to his wartime allies. These divisions became official on June 5, 1945. Having subdivided Germany, the Allies began the arduous process of feeding and housing the inhabitants of the ruined German nation. Hampering the Allies' efforts to provide housing, sustenance, and medical care for the German people, millions of ethnic German refugees poured into Germany from the east, expelled from their former homes in Czechoslovakia, Poland, and the Baltic countries. Meanwhile, millions of displaced persons, as well as former inmates of German forced labor camps and concentration camps, also had to be provided for by the Allies. Amid the chaos and dearth of the immediate postwar period, the population of Germany went hungry as the Allies worked to rebuild the country.

In July 1945, the leaders of the United States, the Soviet Union, and Great Britain met in the Berlin suburb of Potsdam to discuss the future of occupied Germany. At the Potsdam Conference, the Soviet leader Joseph Stalin met with Harry Truman (1884–1972), who had become the president of the United States with the death of President Franklin Delano Roosevelt two months earlier, and Clement Attlee (1883–1967), who had succeeded Winston Churchill (1874–1965) as British prime minister after winning the election of July 1945. These leaders met to decide how to deal with occupied Germany, including how to punish the defeated nation, how to administer its occupation, and how to establish a new postwar order. One sticking point was the issue of what would become of Eastern Europe, which under Soviet occupation had installed a series of communist puppet regimes. Facing these divisive

A photograph of the Brandenburg Gate in 1945, showing the ruins of postwar Berlin
(Bundesarchiv, B 145 Bild-P054320 / photo: Carl Weinrother)

issues, the inexperienced Western leaders proved no match for Stalin, and the conference ended by reaffirming the Soviet grip on Eastern Europe. In Germany, the four occupying powers agreed to administer the country jointly, authorizing each to proceed independently with disarming, denazifying, and rebuilding their respective zone. Even before they set about reconstructing the shattered country, the occupying powers began denazification efforts, arresting former Nazi leaders and interviewing German citizens about their wartime activities. Former Nazi officials were barred from posts in the new German administration, and the Allies established war crimes tribunals to try wartime atrocities and human rights violations.

While the occupying powers had agreed to cooperate in the administration of Germany, stark differences soon emerged between the Soviets and the Western Allies in how they administered their zones. By the time of the Potsdam Conference, Britain, France, and the United States were more concerned with the reconstruction and economic recovery of Germany than its punishment. In the Soviet zone, east of the Elbe River, however, the Russians moved forcibly to wrest reparations from Germany and to remake their zone into a communist puppet-state. The Soviet occupation authorities, headed by wartime hero Marshal Georgii

Zhukov (1896–1974), dismantled what was left of German industry in the east, sending raw materials and heavy equipment, and even entire factories painstakingly taken apart piece by piece, to the Soviet Union by rail. The new occupation government, constructed by the Soviets and composed only of socialist and communist parties, nationalized all banks and remaining factories in the eastern zone. By the 1950s, the government also began to take private agricultural land to be redistributed as Soviet-style collective farms. German communists, trained in the Soviet Union, returned to East Germany to rebuild and administer the Russian zone. The first postwar political party to emerge in East Germany was the Soviet-sanctioned Communist Party, chartered in June 1945. A Social Democratic Party formed later in the same month, but it then merged with the communists to form a single, dominant party, known as the Socialist Unity Party, or SED, the acronym derived from its German name.

Within East Germany, the ardent German communists who worked with the Soviets to administer the occupation zone dreamed of creating a utopian state based upon Marxist-Leninist tenets. Cheering the triumph of the Red Army over Nazism, these German communists drew much of their political legitimacy from the persecution of communist and socialist dissidents under the Nazis, and denazification efforts proved brutally effective in the Soviet zone. Former Nazis were rooted out from government posts and sent to reeducation camps or executed. Meanwhile, a new curriculum adopted in the compulsory schools of the Soviet zone inculcated Marxist-Leninist norms in the students, preparing them for life in a communist state. After 1946, East German youths were pressured to join the Free German Youth organization, where they were indoctrinated through their participation in state-planned social and educational activities. Likewise, the East German proletariat was managed through the Free German Trade Union Federation, a compulsory, SED-run union that harnessed labor to the centrally planned economy. Finally, East German women were organized by the Democratic Women's League, which advocated female equality and supported women's activities at the university, in the workplace, and in government.

As the East Germans worked to build their workers' and farmers' utopia, the Western Allies also sought to rebuild West Germany in their own image, establishing fledgling democratic governments and rebuilding capitalist enterprise in their occupation zones. In the American zone, administered by the U.S. military authorities, rebuilding proceeded more quickly than in the east, but denazification efforts got off to a shaky start. Fearing the spread of communism, the Western Allies proved somewhat reluctant to remove German officials with Nazi ties if they proved able administrators. Like the Soviets, the Western Allies permitted the formation of political parties within their zones in the summer of 1945. In West Germany, however, a more diverse array of parties formed. The first political organization to emerge was the Christian Democratic Union (CDU), a conservative alliance of Catholics and Protestants that first appeared in Cologne in July 1945. The party's dynamic leader, Konrad Adenauer (1876–1967), a leading figure in the postwar political arena, advocated capitalist economics tempered with expansive social welfare programs. Another conservative Protestant-Catholic religious party, Bavaria's Christian Social Union (CSU), formed in October 1945. Among the first liberal political parties to form in the Western zones were the German People's Party (DVP) and the Free Democratic Party (FDP), both founded in the late summer of 1945. A rejuvenated Social Democratic Party (SPD) became the voice of socialism in the West, led by the fiery Kurt Schumacher (1895–1952), who had spent the war in the Nazi concentration camp at Dachau, 12 miles northwest of Munich.

Before the Allies could forge a new Germany, they had to clear away the vestiges of the Nazi past and punish the surviving Nazi leaders responsible for World War II. Thus, they arranged for a war crimes tribunal that would meet in Nuremburg to try leading Nazis who had been apprehended in the wake of the conflict. Charged with wartime atrocities and crimes against humanity, 22 leading Nazis, including former Luftwaffe commander Hermann Göring, faced an international military court that convened in November 1945. When the trials concluded a year later, the tribunal handed down death sentences to a dozen Nazi ringleaders. Göring, the most notorious Nazi defendant, committed suicide in prison before his sentence could be carried out. Aside from a pair of acquittals, the remaining Nazi leaders received long incarceration sentences, including Rudolf Hess (1894–1987), a confidant of Hitler, who received a life sentence and died in Spandau prison after spending 41 years there as its only inmate.

By the spring of 1949, the Western Allies—the United States, Great Britain, and France—had unified their occupation zones under a single administration. Increasingly, the Western Allies found themselves at odds with the Russians over the issue of transferring German reparations between zones. These disagreements signaled the start of the cold war, a political and ideological struggle between the Soviet Union and its communist client states and the United States and its Western

201

Allies. While open conflict never broke out between the Soviets and the Americans, the cold war dominated the rest of the 20th century, waged through propaganda, espionage, and proxy wars in Africa, Asia, and Latin America. At the beginning of the cold war, Britain's wartime prime minister, Winston Churchill, had delivered a watershed speech on an American college campus in the winter of 1946. Warning of the appearance of an expansive Soviet sphere of influence in Eastern Europe, Churchill coined the term "Iron Curtain" to describe the totalitarian communist control that had descended upon East Europe, closing it off from the democratic nations of the capitalist West. The growing tension between the Soviets and the Western powers in the wake of the war was exacerbated by Russian support for Communist uprisings in Greece, Turkey, and Iran after 1947. In response, the United States issued the Truman Doctrine, promising aid to any democratic state threatened by Communist insurrection, and began funneling military aid to Greece and Turkey. Increasingly, Churchill's picture of a Europe—and a Germany—divided by an iron curtain seemed to become a reality.

The cold war standoff between the former wartime Allies reached a crisis point when the United States announced its plans for an economic recovery program for Europe in June 1947. The program, known as the Marshall Plan, would offer the devastated countries of Europe billions of dollars of U.S. aid as they sought to rebuild the European economy (and provide a rejuvenated market for American exports). In 1947, much of Europe was still marred by war damage, and prewar production levels had still not been reached. Germany was particularly hard hit, its industry and transport networks destroyed by Allied strategic bombing, and its people malnourished and impoverished. Fearful that American aid would undermine their control over Eastern Europe, the Soviets forbade their satellites from participating in the Marshall Plan, widening the gap between East and West. The Marshall Plan went into effect in 1948, boosting the economic recovery of Western Europe. Powered by American loans, the countries of Western Europe experienced unprecedented economic growth and began to forge closer economic and military ties with the United States. The Marshall Plan fostered European economic integration, and Western leaders even began to discuss the future formation of a European Union. The areas of Germany administered by the Western Allies received more than $1 billion U.S. aid and increasingly diverged from the eastern part controlled by the Soviets. Angered at the United States's unilateral implementation of the Marshall Plan, the Soviets charged the Western Allies with repudiating the Potsdam agreement, which called for the Allies to cooperate in administering occupied Germany, and on this basis, Stalin withdrew entirely from the joint administration of the country.

The Berlin Blockade and Cold War Division

In an attempt to thwart the Allies' attempts to carry out the Marshall Plan in western Germany, the Soviets announced in June 1948 that they would interdict all road and rail transport from the western zone into Berlin. This provocation cut off the Allied-controlled sectors of the city, which lay deep within the Soviet occupation zone, and threatened its inhabitants with starvation. The Soviets hoped that the Western powers would have to appeal to the Russians to supply West Berlin with food and fuel, giving them de facto control over the city. Refusing to give in to the Russians, the Western Allies resorted instead to undertaking the largest aerial operation in human history, known as the Berlin Airlift. During the Berlin Airlift, which lasted from June 1948 until May 1949, the Americans, British, and French logged a total of 277,569 flights, bringing an astounding 2.3 million tons of food, fuel, and essential supplies to the beleaguered people of West Berlin. The success of the airlift was a humiliating defeat for the Soviets and a demonstration of the power and resolve of the Western Allies. Smarting, the Russians lifted the failed blockade in May 1949, reopening the road and rail lines into Berlin.

The Western Allies, having cooperated so effectively during the Berlin Airlift, worked together in its aftermath to create a new German state in their occupation zone. On July 1, 1948, the Western powers declared that the individual states of western Germany should work together to draft a constitution for a federal state. Meeting in Bonn, south of Cologne on the Rhine River, delegates from the German states (Länder) drew up a federal constitution for West Germany, which would be known as the Federal Republic of Germany or BRD (Bundesrepublik Deutschland). The Basic Law (Grundgesetz), a provisional constitution that was intended to govern the nation until it was ultimately reunified, was enacted on May 23, 1949. The Basic Law guaranteed a range of civil rights, established a federal government, and set up a national judiciary. Under this republican constitution, a federal president, a chancellor, and a pair of legislative bodies—the Bundestag and the Bundesrat— would govern West Germany. The German president would serve as the head of state, carrying out largely ceremonial functions, and the chancellor would head the federal cabinet that administered the country. A national vote would select delegates for the Bundestag, while delegates drawn from the Länder staffed the Bundesrat.

In the first elections for the West German Bundestag, in August 1949, the SPD was confident of victory, but the conservative CDU edged out the socialists by a handful of seats. The CDU leader, Konrad Adenauer, was elected chancellor, beating out the SPD candidate, Kurt Schumacher. By 1948, the cold war had aroused widespread anti-Soviet sentiment in West Germany. Furthermore, the United States threw its resources behind Adenauer, fearing socialist influence in the fledgling Federal Republic. Enraged, the fearsome socialist leader, Shumacher, denounced the CDU as a tool of capitalists and imperialists, positioning himself as Adenauer's most ardent critic until his death in 1952. Theodor Heuss (1884–1963), of the Free Democrats, was elected federal president. A respected liberal, he helped to rehabilitate Germany's reputation on the international scene.

As the Federal Republic of Germany was founded, the Russians oversaw the creation of a competing state in their former occupation zone. Already during the Berlin Blockade, the Soviets had begun moving toward the creation of a communist satellite state in eastern Germany. On October 7, 1949, this new state—the German Democratic Republic (GDR)—was born. The GDR's constitution called for the formation of the Volkskammer, a legislative body that would elect an executive council known as the Council of State. The West German government and the Western Allies refused to recognize the GDR as a sovereign state, denigrating it as an illegitimate Soviet puppet regime. With the establishment of these two mutually antagonistic states, the Federal Republic of Germany and the German Democratic Republic, the division of Germany was now set in stone.

The Two Germanies

During the 1950s, the two states that constituted this divided Germany made enormous strides, emerging from the trauma of World War II. In the coming decades, the ideological and territorial boundary between West Germany and East Germany was the front line of the cold war in Europe. In the Federal Republic, the Western Allies ended their military occupation of Germany in 1949, transferring oversight of German affairs to a civilian commission. West Germany's first chancellor, the CDU leader Konrad Adenauer, worked tirelessly to rebuild his homeland's tattered economy as well as its tarnished reputation abroad. Liberal democracy had failed in Germany in the wake of World War I, giving way to the horrors of Nazism, and Adenauer had to earn the loyalty of the German people and the trust of Western powers.

Germany Divided: The Federal Republic and German Democratic Republic, 1960

Through the forcefulness of his political leadership and his long tenure as chancellor—he served five terms, holding the office from 1949 until 1963—Adenauer provided the continuity and stability that West Germany needed.

In the GDR, the fledgling communist government also benefited from the leadership of a determined statesman during the 1950s, namely Wilhelm Pieck (1876–1960). Pieck, trained as a carpenter, had been a prominent KPD leader during the Weimar period and had fled to Moscow after the Nazi takeover. A trusted associate of Joseph Stalin, Pieck was elected by the Volkskammer to lead the new communist regime in East Germany, becoming the GDR's first president in 1949. Along with Otto Grotewohl (1884–1964), East Germany's first prime minister, Pieck set to work building a new communist state in central Europe, one featuring a Soviet-style state-run economy and a totalitarian political structure based upon a populist rhetoric of the empowerment of workers and farmers. While Pieck and Grotewohl held important positions within the new East German state, the real power broker in the postwar GDR was the German communist leader Walter Ulbricht (1893–1973), especially after Pieck's death in 1960. Ulbricht, who had spent the Nazi years as an exile in the Soviet Union producing wartime propaganda for Stalin, headed the dominant Socialist Unity Party. Selected by the Russians for his Stalinist loyalties, he fostered close cooperation with the Soviet Union and cultivated a triumphant civic identity based upon the German and Russian communists' shared resistance to fascism.

Having eschewed Marshall Plan aid, Ulbricht constructed a Stalin-style centrally planned economy to rebuild and industrialize the East German economy, a predominantly agricultural region ravaged by the war and impoverished by crushing Soviet reparation exactions. In answer to the Marshall Plan, the Soviets created the Council of Mutual Economic Assistance (COMECON), an organization that would coordinate central economic planning among their satellite states. Under Soviet direction, the GDR issued an ambitious Five-Year Plan in 1949, one that called for major industries to be nationalized and for massive redistribution of agricultural land. Modeled on the four Five-Year Plans that had been assigned in the Soviet Union since 1928, which set rigid production quotas on Russian factories to foster rapid industrialization, the GDR's first Five-Year Plan focused on rebuilding and expanding East Germany's economic sector. Despite the unyielding pressure that the communist government placed upon East Germany's workers and bureaucrats, the nation's first experiment with central economic planning proved a dismal failure.

The pressures to meet the rigid production quotas called for by the East German government's Five-Year Plans fell heavily upon the GDR's industrial workers, sparking widespread discontent. When the Ulbricht government raised factory production quotas in 1953, disgruntled workers throughout the GDR took to the streets. Staging strikes and mass demonstrations, the protesters denounced the government's economic policies and demanded change. Backed by Soviet tanks, East German security forces used violence to quell the demonstrations. Hundreds of East German workers were killed before the street clashes of the Uprising of 1953 ended, providing a blueprint for the violent suppression of the Czech uprisings of 1968. The East German government forced the workers back to their factories. Despite the failure of East Germany's workers and farmers to reach the production quotas mandated by the first Five-Year Plan, in 1956 the Ulbricht regime issued the even more ambitious second

A propaganda poster from the GDR, encouraging workers to support the Five-Year Plan (Bundesarchiv, Plak 103-020-010)

Five-Year Plan. This central economic program increased production quotas dramatically and emphasized the modernization of heavy industry and the collectivization of agriculture, two areas of glaring failure in the first Five-Year Plan, By this time, however, it was painfully obvious that, while the GDR's planned economy adhered to Marxist-Leninist principles and afforded its workers stable employment, it was incapable of producing the rapid economic recovery and increasing prosperity enjoyed in West Germany. The East German economy never rivaled that of West Germany, but it grew into a leader among the nations in the Soviet orbit, providing export goods for Eastern Europe.

In West Germany, on the other hand, the 1950s proved to be a period of remarkable economic expansion and growing prosperity known as the "economic miracle." After 1949, the Federal Republic used Marshall Plan funds to rebuild the economy, integrate the millions of refugees produced by the war, and foster capitalist investment. In stark contrast to East Germany, the government at Bonn, the provisional capital of the new Federal Republic until 1991, let the economy function according to free-market principles, without extensive direction or regulation. To provide social security amid this rapid economic transformation, the West German government also established an expansive social welfare system, guaranteeing workers and retirees a generous range of benefits and entitlements. The results of this "economic miracle" are staggering: By the mid-1950s, the West German economy had been transformed from the devastation of the postwar crisis into one of the world's leading economies. Unhampered by military expenditures, the West Germans invested in their own corporations and developed lucrative export markets throughout Europe and the United States. The rapid accumulation of affluence in West Germany was a source of pride in the West and a scandal in the East.

West Germany's remarkable economic recovery during the 1950s was mirrored by its diplomatic reintegration. Under Adenauer and his able president, Theodore Heuss, Germany shed its pariah status imposed in the wake of World War II. Eager to regain a place among the West's democratic governments, the West Germans quickly sought to make amends with the survivors of the Nazi genocide. Accordingly, in 1951, the Bonn government agreed to pay billions of dollars of reparations to Israel as compensation for the Holocaust. Meanwhile, Adenauer also sought to repair Germany's relationship with France, whose suffering under the Nazis still provoked considerable hostility among the French, who remained wary of Germany's resurgence. In 1949, Adenauer announced that economic administration of the industries of the Ruhr region, a borderland that had been a bone of contention between France and Germany since the 1920s, would be controlled jointly by France, Germany, Belgium, Luxembourg, the Netherlands, and the United States. This diplomatic move not only helped to appease the French but also fostered greater economic cooperation among the nations of Western Europe, laying important groundwork for Europe's later economic integration.

West Germany's reintegration into the postwar diplomatic order was confirmed in 1950, when it was permitted to rearm itself and join the North Atlantic Treaty Organization (NATO). Formed in April 1949, this mutual defense alliance joined the United States, Canada, and 10 Western European nations together to provide for collective security. In the 1950s, amid the rising tensions of the cold war standoff, the United States gradually convinced an anxious France to consider allowing West Germany to rearm, on a limited basis, and to join NATO. The culmination of Adenauer's attempt to normalize Germany's diplomatic status came in 1952 with the Bonn-Paris conventions, a series of agreements finally ratified by the three Western Allies on May 5,

1955, which granted the Federal Republic of Germany full sovereignty and ended the Allies' occupation authority. Interestingly, according to one of the provisions in the settlement, the Western Allies retained the right to administer West Berlin and exercise control over the issue of any future reunification of Germany. With cold war tensions rising, the United States became deeply concerned with the security situation in Western Europe and sought to bolster NATO's strength by convincing their European allies to accept a rearmed West Germany. Accordingly, soon after proclaiming its full sovereignty, on May 9, 1955, the Federal Republic of Germany joined NATO and began rearming. In recognition of Germany's aggressive past, the Federal Republic's constitution stipulated that its army, known as the Bundeswehr, was permitted to operate only if the Federal Republic or one of its allies was attacked by an outside enemy. By the end of the decade, the West German "miracle" had been accomplished. Just a decade and a half after the collapse of the Nazi regime, a new democratic Germany had rebuilt a shattered country, regained its place in international diplomacy, and become an economic powerhouse in the heart of Europe.

Just as the Soviet Union had responded to the announcement of the Marshall Plan with the formation of its own economic program for Eastern Europe, the inclusion of West Germany in NATO prompted Moscow to form the Warsaw Treaty Organization (WTO), also known as the Warsaw pact. The pact was founded on May 14, 1955, with the signing of a Treaty of Friendship, Cooperation, and Mutual Assistance. This military alliance of communist states—Albania, Bulgaria, Czechoslovakia, Hungary, Poland, Romania, and the Soviet Union—included a remilitarized East Germany and signaled a growing rift between the divided Germanies. Early hopes for reunification in West Germany gradually withered in the face of this cold war standoff. A flashpoint in the troubled relations between East and West Germany arrived in September 1955 when the Adenauer government issued the Hallstein Doctrine, which sought to prevent international acknowledgment of the GDR by refusing to uphold diplomatic relations with countries that established relations with it. When the Soviets had announced, in 1954, that East Germany had full sovereignty, Adenauer was outraged. The Bonn government maintained that the only sovereign state in Germany was West Germany and, with the Hallstein Doctrine, warned that it would not engage in diplomacy with any nation that recognized East Germany's sovereignty. In response, Ulbricht, staunch in his support for the Soviet Union and opposed to any détente with the West, issued his own declaration. This Ulbricht

Doctrine called for forging closer ties among the Warsaw Pact nations and ensured that their governments would not recognize West German sovereignty until the Adenauer government recognized the sovereignty of the GDR. These hostile declarations drove a wedge between the Federal Republic and the Warsaw Pact. More important, it deepened the division between the two states of Germany.

Facing this diplomatic impasse, the conservative Adenauer government sought to strengthen West Germany. Adenauer actively pursued rearmament in the face of protests from the West German left and, in 1956, persuaded the Bundestag to authorize universal military conscription. Meanwhile, West Germany also played a leading role in Europe's increasing economic integration, signing the Treaty of Rome in 1957 with France, Italy, Belgium, Luxembourg, and the Netherlands. This groundbreaking agreement established a joint commission to manage the development of nuclear power plants and founded the European Economic Community (EEC), which created a common market within Europe, fostering unimpeded trade among its nations. Having accomplished these diplomatic coups, and with West Germany prospering economically, Adenauer's CDU triumphed in the 1957 elections, gaining more than 43 percent of the vote and forming a solid majority within the Bundestag through a coalition with its allies in the CSU. On the heels of his victory, however, Adenauer faced a grave challenge that brought the two Germanies to the brink of war.

The Berlin Crisis

In November 1958, the fiery new Soviet premier, Nikita Khrushchev (1894–1971), ordered the Western Allies to leave Berlin, threatening that if they did not agree to the establishment of a free city in Berlin, the Russians would seize the city on behalf of the GDR. In December, NATO refused the Soviet demands, setting the stage for the Berlin Crisis. In response, Khrushchev offered an alternative solution: a permanent division of Germany with Berlin as a demilitarized free city. The West also refused this proposal, and the Berlin issue remained a simmering point of contention. By 1961, the GDR was becoming increasingly irritated by the flow of defectors from East Berlin into West Berlin. While the frontier between East and West Germany was a fortified military frontier, impeding the flow of defectors, the boundary between the two halves of Berlin had been porous, and more than 2 million enterprising East Germans had fled to the prosperity and opportunity of the West during the 1950s. In 1953 alone, as many as 400,000 East Germans flowed into the West, escaping economic stagnation, ideological indoctrination, and political oppression. The oppressive nature of East Germany's communist regime is exemplified by the activities of the Ministry for State Security, the secret police force known as the Stasi. Founded in 1950, the Stasi was led initially by Wilhelm Zaisser, before he was ousted in favor of his subordinate, Erich Mielke (1909–2000) in 1957. Mielke would run the Stasi until the fall of the Berlin Wall, building it into a dreaded instrument of repression and intimidation. Under Mielke, the Stasi recruited an extensive network of agents, with tens of thousands of informants reporting on the speech and activities of their coworkers, neighbors, and associates. In the early 1960s, as cold war tensions mounted and the GDR clamped down on dissent, the activities of the Stasi became more repressive and the flow of defectors increased dramatically, embarrassing the East German government and draining the country of many of its most promising young citizens. In response, Khrushchev authorized the East Germans to build the Berlin Wall, a barrier that would separate East and West Berlin for almost three decades. The Berlin Wall, symbol of the oppressive nature of East German communism, separated families. More than 100 people, mostly young men trying to find opportunity by escaping to West Berlin, were killed by the East German border police guarding the Berlin Wall. When the East Germans also fortified the frontier around West Berlin, the mayor of the surrounded western enclave, Willy Brandt (1913–92), fearing that his city would be cut off from the outside world, appealed to the United States for help. After the Soviets delivered an aggressive ultimatum, ordering the Western Allies to leave Berlin, tense Soviet and U.S. soldiers confronted each other across the barrier for 22 months, on the brink of war. The American president John F. Kennedy (1917–63) flew to Berlin, and on June 23, 1963, delivered a famous speech, declaring "Ich bin ein Berliner," or "I am a Berliner," a moving promise of support for West Berlin. While the Soviets, convinced that the United States was determined fight to remain in West Berlin and guarantee the freedom of the West Berliners, chose not to send their tanks into the western enclave, the crisis accentuated the increasing rift between East and West Germany and doomed any plans for the immediate reunification of Germany.

Konrad Adenauer retired the same year as Kennedy's speech in Berlin, on the heels of the *Spiegel* Affair, which split the coalition that had reelected him in 1961. To win the 1961 election, Adenauer had consolidated his power by negotiating an uneasy alliance of the conservatives of the Christian Democratic Union and the Christian Social Union with the liberals of the Free Democratic Party. Soon after his reelection, however, the Adenauer government was rocked by a major scandal involving the German magazine, *Der Spiegel*. In October 1962, with cold war fears rampant, the magazine exposed weaknesses within the German military, criticizing Adenauer's security policies. The government response was heavy-handed. The West German police raided the magazine's offices, and the publisher, media tycoon Axel Springer (1912–85), was charged with treason. The public was outraged by the Adenauer government's lack of restraint and its disregard for constitutional protections of the press. Shocked, the liberal FDP ministers on Adenauer's cabinet abruptly resigned, which threatened to break the coalition that secured the chancellor's power. In the face of rising criticism, the chancellor later apologized for breaching the freedom of the press, but the damage was done. While Adenauer's long tenure as chancellor would end with an important diplomatic coup, by the time he left office, his public support was waning. In January 1963, Adenauer's government signed a historic accord, the Élysée Treaty, with France. The agreement brought the two nations, once the bitterest of enemies, into close cooperation in matters of diplomacy, trade, and security. Strongly linking Western Europe's two largest states—serving as a counterweight to both the Atlantic and Soviet powers—the treaty aimed to tie West Germany securely to its European neighbors and strengthen German democracy, which would in turn enhance the economic and military power of Western Europe. While it helped pave the way for Europe's future integration, the alliance between West Germany and France was soon threatened by France's withdrawal from NATO in 1966. The aged Adenauer retired on October 15, 1963, having dominated the West German political scene since the new nation's inception.

With the East German economy faltering, and failing to meet the production quotas stipulated by the government's Five-Year Plans, the Ulbricht regime changed course in 1963. As in the Soviet Union, East German economic planners abandoned the rigid Five-Year Plan structure and adopted a less centralized system. Based upon more flexible annual production quotas, the implementation of the government's economic plans was to be carried out at the regional level with production incentives for local managers. By the end of the decade, however, the East German economy's performance was still anemic by Western standards, and the SED reversed its policies once again, reverting to more centralized planning.

In the Federal Republic, Adenauer's retirement left a political void that the Christian Democratic Union's coalition government filled with the former chancellor's trusted economic advisor, Ludwig Erhard

(1897–1977), whom they tapped to be his successor. Erhard immediately began working to thaw relations with the eastern bloc. While he was able to gain some concessions in Berlin, namely easing restrictions on border crossings for West Berliners, he proved incapable of repairing the damage done by the Adenauer government's Hallstein Doctrine of the 1950s. Erhard's tenure was also complicated in February 1966 by a growing rift within the ranks of the Western powers when President Charles de Gaulle (1890–1970) pulled France out of NATO, forcing West Germany to choose between fulfilling its obligations to its alliance partners or to pursue its burgeoning partnership with France. Erhard resigned in November 1966, amid a worsening economic recession that led to the dissolution of the CDU/CSU/FDP coalition when the FDP finally withdrew from the political alliance. By the beginning of December, West Germany had a new chancellor, Kurt Georg Kiesinger (1904–88), the leader of an unlikely "Grand Coalition" between his own Christian Democratic Union and the SPD.

Kiesinger was a former Nazi Party member who had worked in the radio propaganda division of the German foreign ministry during World War II. Detained by the occupation authorities after the war, he had been released and acquitted of war crimes charges. A staunch Catholic, Kiesinger rose quickly through the ranks of the CDU during the postwar period, but when he was appointed chancellor, his Nazi past came back to haunt him. His political allies in the SPD were branded traitors for associating with him, and leftist intellectuals demanded his ouster throughout his tenure. Meanwhile, his chancellorship provided a propaganda bonanza for the East Germans, who had long excoriated West Germany for abandoning stringent denazification and for the influence of former Nazis in West German politics and industry. Despite the enduring controversy, Kiesinger proved an able administrator, and he managed to reduce tensions with several Warsaw Pact countries, including Czechoslovakia, Romania, and Yugoslavia, despite the lingering impasse with East Germany. On the economic front, his cabinet ministers enacted a series of measures

A 1969 political poster for the Christian Democratic Union in support of the party's candidate, Kurt Kiesinger (Library of Congress)

that brought West Germany out of its recession by 1968. Later that year, however, West Germany was wracked by waves of radical revolt, protests that began on the nation's university campuses.

The radical student protest movement that erupted in 1968 had its origins in earlier outbursts of campus unrest in the United States and France. These student protests were sparked by outrage at the United States's increasing military involvement in Vietnam and its carpet-bombing campaign, code-named "Operation Rolling Thunder," that pounded communist North Vietnam between 1965 and 1968. In West Germany, however, leftist discontent with the perceived oppression and hypocrisy of West German society also fueled the movement. Outraged by events such as the *Speigel* Affair and the election of the former Nazi, Kiesinger, leftist student organizations organized violent demonstrations throughout West Germany, raging against what they perceived to be the defects of German society. For the protesters, these included its hidebound, authoritarian nature, its failure to confront and atone for its Nazi past, and its smug faith in a capitalist economic system they saw as morally bankrupt. The students demanded democratic reforms in the political system and on university campuses, arguing for a greater say in policy making in both arenas. As in France and the United States, German student demonstrators and police often met in increasingly violent clashes during the late 1960s, horrifying the public. Hoping to quell the disturbance, in May 1968, the government passed the Emergency Acts, an amendment to the West German constitution that permitted the executive branch to operate without legislative approval, to suspend certain constitutional rights, and even to use the military to restore order during periods of crisis. Evoking memories of Hitler's use of Article 48 and realizing the left's worst fears about the seemingly "fascist" nature of Germany's conservative government, the amendment was fiercely resisted to no avail by the FDP, the student movement, and the trade unions and went into effect in June.

Amid the rising unrest in West Germany, the leftist outrage fostered by the student movement spawned other reactions, both violent and peaceful. The first was domestic terrorism. Elements of the student movement had been radicalized in June 1967, when an unarmed 26-year-old graduate student protester, Benno Ohnesorg, was shot and killed by police. This act of brutal violence—interpreted from an ideological perspective informed by the writings of radical dissidents and intellectuals like Karl Marx, Vladimir Lenin, the Chinese communist Mao Zedong (1893–1976), the Italian communist Antonio Gramsci (1891–1937), and the German-Jewish Marxist philosopher

214

Herbert Marcuse (1898–1979)—helped spark the formation in 1970 of an "urban guerrilla" organization known as the Red Army Faction (RAF), or the Baader-Meinhof Gang, after its two cofounders, the leftist activists Andreas Baader (1943–77) and Ulrike Meinhof (1943–76). Garnering significant support from West German liberals and students, the Red Army Faction staged a series of bank robberies, arson attacks, bombings, and assassinations in the 1970s and 1980s, claiming 34 lives in the name of the armed struggle against "fascist imperialism."

A more peaceful, and lasting, manifestation of the leftist agitation of the late 1960s was the foundation of the Green Party, an organization committed to environmental causes. The Greens gained seats in West Germany's state governments and even formed a national party in the late 1970s, as Germany's increasing investment in nuclear power raised environmental concerns. As environmental issues gained prominence in West Germany in the decades after its formation, the party gained supporters and drew attention to the perils of destroying the ecosystem.

The growing influence of the left in West Germany at the close of the 1960s helped to bring an end to the CDU/CSU monopoly on political power in Bonn. In the September 1969 Bundestag elections, the SPD ran a close second behind the conservative coalition, but the liberals of the FDP joined with the Social Democrats in a new coalition that gave the chancellorship to the SPD leader Willy Brandt. Brandt, the former mayor of West Berlin, had become a socialist as a young man and escaped Nazi persecution in 1933 by fleeing to Norway and later Sweden. Returning to Germany in 1946, Brandt settled in West Berlin, serving as that city's mayor from 1957 until 1966. Brandt had served as head of the SPD since 1964 and had been appointed foreign minister and vice chancellor in 1966, after a failed bid for the chancellorship. Under Brandt's leadership, West Germany abandoned the Hallstein Doctrine and instead vigorously pursued the policy of Ostpolitik, seeking to engage the GDR and its Warsaw Pact allies in fruitful dialogue and diplomacy.

Ostpolitik was a controversial reversal of the conservative policies of the Adenauer era, when the West German government refused even to recognize the sovereignty of East Germany. Brandt's first move came in early 1970 when he met with the GDR's minister president in the first direct diplomatic talks between the two German states since the late 1940s, talks that helped pave the way for the two Germanies to reestablish formal relations. By August 1970, Brandt had also forged an agreement with the Soviets, the Moscow Treaty, which stated the partners' intention to avoid military conflict and to respect Europe's existing territorial borders. In a second treaty, known as the Warsaw Treaty, signed in December 1970, Brandt and the leader of Poland resolved the postwar dispute over the German-Polish border, eschewed the use of military force between the signatories, and established ongoing diplomatic relations in an effort to work past the painful legacy of World War II. On the heels of this dramatic rapprochement, Brandt negotiated a settlement with the Soviets that guaranteed free access between West Germany and West Berlin but maintained the four-power administration of the city. When Walter Ulbricht opposed these accommodations, the Soviets arranged for his ouster. Ulbricht's Stalinist policies were no longer acceptable, and in May 1971, Erich Honecker (1912–94) replaced him as SED chairman.

Erich Honecker came from a humble background: His father was a coal miner, and he trained as a roofer. From his early teens, Honecker was an ardent communist, joining the youth wing of the KPD when he was just 14 years old. Once he joined the KPD, in 1929, his ardor impressed party officials, and he was sent to Moscow for a socialist education at the International Lenin School. After returning to Germany in 1931, Honecker was arrested by the Nazis and spent a decade in prison for resisting Hitler's takeover. After the war, Honecker entered the East German government as an early member of the SED and was appointed for a seat on the Council of State in 1971. Honecker's economic policies were driven by his staunch ideological beliefs, but he ameliorated the GDR's centrally planned economy—based upon state ownership of the means of production and rigid industrial production quotas—with expanded social welfare programs to benefit the East German proletariat. Furthermore, Honecker refocused much of the GDR's industrial capacity to the production of consumer goods. Soon, the citizens of East Germany enjoyed the highest standard of living in the Warsaw Pact, although they still lagged behind the West in both material luxury and political liberty. Honecker's foreign policy was based upon his unflinching support for the Soviet Union and the principle of *Abgrenzung,* which repudiated the goal of unification with West Germany and sought to slow the process of détente with the West by accentuating the ideological and political distinctiveness of the GDR.

Despite this chilling in the East German government's relationship with the West, and the widespread criticism Willy Brandt's Ostpolitik evoked among West German conservatives, the chancellor was awarded the Nobel Peace Prize in 1971 in recognition for the stunning success of his diplomacy in fostering understanding across the cold war ideological divide. However, his most important diplomatic coup was still to come. In December 1972, the Federal Republic of Germany and the

German Democratic Republic signed the Basic Treaty, recognizing each other's sovereignty and guaranteeing to maintain peaceful relations. This was the start of an era of fruitful dialogue and exchange between the two German states, including diplomatic visits, trading relations, and cultural exchange, that went on uninterrupted despite their ideological differences and the rising cold war tensions of the era.

In 1972, Brandt's attempt to draw the Warsaw Pact countries into peaceful dialogue instigated a political crisis that almost lead to the chancellor's ouster. Early in 1972, several prominent members of the SPD and others from the FDP joined with the CDU in protest of Brandt's Ostpolitik, branding him a traitor for collaborating with the GDR, thus threatening his parliamentary majority. On April 24, 1972, the opposition authorized a vote of no confidence, which would have removed Brandt from office, but it failed by just two votes. In the wake of this bitter political dispute, West Germany prepared to celebrate its status as host country of the Games of the XX Olympiad. These summer games, scheduled to be held from August 26 to September 11, 1972, would be the first in Germany since the Nazi games of 1936. Having constructed a fabulous Olympic venue on the outskirts of Munich, known as the Olympiapark, the West German government was eager to showcase the prosperity and the prestige of the new Germany.

Unfortunately, the Munich games are remembered today as the site of a terrible tragedy. On September 5, 1972, eight Palestinian members of the Black September group (which derived its name from events following the 1967 war involving Israel and its Arab neighbors) stormed the Olympic Village at the summer games in Munich and took 11 Israeli athletes and coaches hostage, killing two immediately for resisting in the initial chaos of the attack. The terrorists demanded the release of more than 200 Palestinian militants being held in Israel, as well as Red Army Faction leaders Andreas Baader and Ulrike Meinhof, incarcerated in West Germany. After a botched rescue attempt, the terrorists murdered all nine of the surviving hostages, further eroding Brandt's reputation.

Despite these scandals and crises, two months later, Brandt's SPD managed to secure a narrow victory over the CDU in the Bundestag elections of November 1972. Having won reelection, Brandt continued his conciliatory policies toward the Warsaw Pact nations, and in 1973, West Germany forged diplomatic ties with Bulgaria, Czechoslovakia, and Hungary. Both of the Germanies joined the United Nations that same year. These diplomatic milestones were overshadowed in 1973, however, when the German economic miracle came to a grinding halt as oil prices soared amid unrest in the Middle East, causing a global recession. The Social Democrats' costly social programs came under increasing scrutiny as the German economy faltered and the ranks of the unemployed swelled. By 1975, more than 1 million West Germans were jobless, a number that would double by the mid-1980s.

It was not West Germany's economic problems that toppled Brandt, but rather a scandal that erupted the following year, one that called Brandt's Ostpolitik into question and toppled him from power. In 1973, as the German economy faltered in the face of an international oil crisis, West German intelligence learned that one of Brandt's personal assistants, Günter Guillaume (1927–95), was a spy with ties to the East German secret police, the Stasi. After Guillaume's arrest for espionage, in April 1974, the West German government compelled an embarrassed Brandt to tender his resignation. Brandt was succeeded as chancellor by another Social Democrat, Helmut Schmidt (1918–   ), but he retained a seat on the Bundestag and the leadership of the SPD.

Helmut Schmidt was well placed to replace Brandt, having served as defense minister and finance minister in the former chancellor's cabinet. Conscripted into the German army during World War II, Schmidt had joined the SPD in 1946, as a university student in Hamburg, and risen in the party owing to his reputation for competence. The new chancellor took office as the 1973 oil crisis brought crippling inflation to Germany and took decisive action, pursuing nuclear energy in the face of attacks from environmentalists. Schmidt also showed his resolve in taking tough action during the "German Autumn" of 1977, when a wave of Red Army Faction violence terrorized Germany.

The wave of terrorist violence began on July 30, 1977, when members of the Red Army Faction murdered Jürgen Ponto, the head of the Dresdner Bank, in a botched kidnapping attempt. The RAF followed up on this violent murder with an audacious attack on a police convoy in Cologne transporting Hanns-Martin Schleyer, a prominent industrialist. The terrorists killed Schleyer's driver and three police officers, abducting the businessman. The kidnappers demanded that the Schmidt government release several early RAF leaders in police custody in exchange for Schleyer, including one of the group's original founders, Andreas Baader. When the Schmidt government refused to cooperate, the RAF escalated their terrorist campaign by hijacking a Lufthansa flight with the aid of Palestinian terrorists and diverting it to Mogadishu, Somalia. Helmut Schmidt authorized a daring rescue, using the elite West German antiterrorist unit, known as GSG 9, a unit formed after the 1972 Olympic tragedy. The GSG 9 assault team stormed the plane on the night of October 18, rescuing the hostages and killing or capturing the hijackers. The same night, the imprisoned RAF leaders, including original members Andreas Baader and Gudrun Ensslin, were found dead in their cells, victims of apparent suicide. In retaliation, the RAF kidnappers holding Schleyer murdered him and left his body in the trunk of a car in rural France. The violent autumn of 1977 had finally come to an end.

The SPD had maintained a slim majority in the Bundestag elections of 1976, as Schmidt beat out Helmut Kohl (1930–) of the CSU for the chancellorship, but during his second term, he faced a range of daunting challenges, including the continued stagnation of the West German economy, soaring unemployment, and growing unrest among the nation's workers. Meanwhile, the SPD's conciliatory policy toward the Warsaw Pact was called into question by the Soviet Union's increasingly aggressive stance, culminating in its invasion of Afghanistan in 1980. As German conservatives called for increased defense spending and a tougher policy toward the Warsaw Pact, Schmidt's support began to erode. In October 1982, Schmidt was ousted when the opposition delegates in the Bundestag called for a no-confidence vote. The vote passed, and Schmidt was deposed as chancellor. His replacement was the moderate CSU head who had ran against Schmidt in the last Bundestag election, Helmut Kohl, elected with the help of the FDP.

Helmut Kohl was born in 1930, the son of a Catholic civil servant. He was conscripted into the German army in the waning days of the war, never saw combat, and continued his schooling after the conflict ended. As a student, in 1946, he joined the newly formed Christian Democratic Union and after graduation entered local politics. By 1973, he had risen to become federal chairman of the CDU and served on the Bundestag. Once Kohl became chancellor, after the ouster of Helmut Schmidt in October 1982, he worked to shore up his support, and in the federal elections of March 1983, he won a crushing reelection victory. After forming his second cabinet, Kohl's conservative supporters in the Bundestag authorized his plan to allow the stationing of NATO nuclear missiles on German soil, to the consternation of the left. He also worked to form closer diplomatic ties with Western allies, a reversal in the SPD's earlier policy of seeking détente with the Warsaw Pact nations. Most important, in 1984, Kohl met with French president François Mitterrand (1916–96) at Verdun, where the two statesmen offered reconciliation for the bloodshed between their two nations in World War I and World War II. The ceremony was the beginning of a close relationship between Kohl and Mitterrand and helped lay the foundations for Europe's future integration. Meanwhile, the chancellor also shored up

West Germany's relationship with the United States and its NATO allies. In 1985, Kohl and U.S. president Ronald Reagan (1911–2004) visited the Bergen-Belsen concentration camp and a German military cemetery at Bitburg, ceremonial visits intended to commemorate the end of World War II in Europe and the close postwar relationship of the two former combatants. The visit to the military cemetery proved controversial, however, when it was discovered that members of the Waffen SS, an elite Nazi military unit, were buried there. The episode caused embarrassment for the Kohl government, as did certain corruption scandals involving high-ranking members of his cabinet.

Despite these scandals, and the left's outrage at the deployment of nuclear weapons within Germany, Kohl won reelection in Bundestag elections of 1987. Soon after his electoral victory, Kohl reversed his hard-line policy toward the eastern bloc, inviting the East German leader, Erich Honecker, to visit West Germany, making him the first leader of the GDR to do so. By the late 1980s, the communist regimes of Eastern Europe were under immense pressure, as their citizens began to agitate for democratic reform. In Poland, for example, an illegal, nongovernment-controlled trade union, known as Solidarity, emerged in the Gdansk shipyards in 1980. In the face of brutal repression, the movement's leader Lech Wałesa (1943–   ) exposed the corruption and violence of the communist government and, by the late 1980s, had forced the government to negotiate. The news of these events spread through the eastern bloc like wildfire, reaching the GDR as the nation was grappling with a serious economic recession. In 1984, as the East German economy faltered, and government quotas and shortages eroded workers' living conditions, disgruntled East Germans began to seek asylum in foreign embassies. By January 15, 1986, a state holiday, the official communist commemorations were disrupted by outbursts of angry protest, as demonstrators demanded democratic freedoms. Honecker denounced the movement as traitorous, and the protesters were sentenced to lengthy prison sentences. In 1989, when a new Soviet leader, Mikhail Gorbachev (1931–   ), took power and began to authorize startling reforms that shook the Soviet Union to its core, the communist regimes in Eastern Europe began to falter. German reunification suddenly seemed possible.

Reunification

Soviet premier Mikhail Gorbachev took over as head of Russia's Communist Party in March 1985, after a series of ineffectual leaders.

Part of a new generation of Soviet leaders born after the 1917 Bolshevik revolution, Gorbachev launched a sweeping program of reforms at the Communist Party Congress of February 1986, reforms guided by the principles of glasnost, or transparency, and perestroika, or economic and political reform. The refreshing spirit of reform emanating from Moscow swept through the Warsaw Pact nations, and people took to the streets demanding similar reforms in their own countries. When Gorbachev announced in June 1988 that the Soviet Union would abandon the 20-year-old Brezhnev Doctrine, which had guaranteed Soviet military intervention to uphold communism in the Warsaw Pact countries, and would instead allow these nations to determine their own political futures, it ignited a firestorm of demonstrations in the eastern bloc. In the course of 1989, these mass protests toppled one communist regime after another.

By the spring of 1989, hundreds of East Germans were flocking to the West German embassies in neighboring Warsaw Pact countries, requesting asylum. This trickle turned into a torrent in August when the Hungarians opened the border with Austria, and thousands of East Germans escaped the GDR. During a state visit to East Germany by

German chancellor Helmut Kohl meeting with Soviet leader Mikhail Gorbachev in Bonn on November 9, 1990 (Bundesregierung, B 145 Bild-00010809 / Arne Schambeck)

221

FALL OF THE BERLIN WALL

A round midnight on November 9, 1989, an amazing spectacle unfolded in Berlin, as cheering crowds gathered on both sides of the Berlin Wall, celebrating the opening of the border crossings between East and West Berlin. The Berlin Wall, constructed in August 1961, was a symbol of the repression and brutality of the GDR's communist regime. The wall was intended to stop the flow of defectors to the west, a growing source of embarrassment for the GDR. Dividing the city, and separating family and friends, the Berlin Wall was guarded by border police instructed to kill anyone trying to scale it in an attempt to reach the freedom and opportunity of the west. Since September, the people of East Berlin had staged peaceful demonstrations forcing the communist dictatorship to allow them to breach the barrier that divided their city for nearly 30 years. The dramatic opening of the Berlin Wall symbolized the coming end of the cold war division of Germany and showed the world the remarkable possibilities of peaceful protest.

The opening of the Berlin Wall checkpoints was the culmination of a wave of rapid changes within the communist dictatorships of Europe. On August 23, 1989, Hungary—its own communist regime teetering—had opened its own borders with Austria. Once word got out, thousands of East Germans flocked into Hungary, hoping to make their way into Austria to escape the oppression of the GDR. When the overwhelmed Hungarian border guards turned them away, the East Germans packed into the West German embassy in Budapest, seeking asylum. The GDR forbade further travel to Hungary, sparking a similar situation in nearby Czechoslovakia and mass demonstrations in East Germany. Amid the growing unrest, the GDR's hard-line leader, Erich Honecker, abruptly resigned on October 18. His replacement, Egon Krenz (1937–), faced a growing protest movement. By November 4, 1989, around 500,000 demonstrators had taken to the streets of East Berlin, engaged in peaceful protests and calling for freedom and reform. In an attempt to appease the protesters, Krenz decided to allow East Germans to travel to the west, with government approval, using border checkpoints between East and West Germany, including those in Berlin. The changes were supposed to go into effect on November 17, 1989, but at a press conference on November 9, a government spokesperson mistakenly announced that the opening of the borders was to go into effect immediately.

An enthusiastic crowd watches as a section of the Berlin Wall is dismantled to create a new border crossing between East and West Berlin on November 11, 1989. (Bundesarchiv, Bild 183-1989-1111-005 / Robert Roeske)

On the heels of this announcement, which was broadcast in the GDR and on West German television, East Germans began to congregate at the Berlin Wall and ordered the border guards to open the checkpoints and allow them to cross into West Berlin. Overwhelmed, and lacking clear instructions from their superiors, the border police opened the gates. Huge crowds of jubilant East Germans began to surge through the checkpoints, met by cheering West Berliners on the other side. The two peoples, separated by the Berlin Wall and cold war animosities, celebrated together throughout the night as a stunned world watched. A week later, the Krenz regime opened 10 new border crossings, using bulldozers to break through the barrier as crowds cheered them on from both sides of the wall. By July 1, 1990, border controls between East and West Germany ended: The era of the Berlin Wall had come to an end.

Gorbachev, crowds of demonstrators greeted the Soviet leader, shouting for change. The hard-line Honecker government responded with repression, using violence in an attempt to suppress the demonstrations, drawing worldwide criticism. The East German government's tactics only inflamed the crowds, spurring continuing demonstrations throughout the country. On October 18, with the situation spiraling out of control, the East German government ousted Erich Honecker. A massive demonstration took place in East Berlin on November 4, prompting the East German government to declare that its citizens were free to travel abroad. In response, on November 9, 1989, large East German crowds massed at the Berlin Wall, and the overwhelmed border police opened the crossings. East Germans flowed through the checkpoints, greeted enthusiastically by cheering crowds of West Berliners on the other side. The scene of East and West Berliners celebrating together in the shadow of the Berlin Wall, a symbol of division and repression, enthralled a watching world.

As the communist government of East Germany disintegrated, and free elections were being planned in the GDR, Helmut Kohl began working toward the reunification of Germany. In November, the East German Volkskammer elected the moderate communist Hans Modrow (1928–) to serve as the country's interim leader, opening the door to meaningful dialogue with the Federal Republic. Kohl reached out to the East German people at the end of November with his Ten-Point Plan, which offered generous economic aid to East Germany, encouraged cultural and social exchange, promised mutual disarmament, and laid the groundwork for the creation of a German federation. Meanwhile, the SED's stranglehold on East German politics was rapidly slipping. In early December, Erich Honecker and other top SED leaders were expelled from the party amid mass party resignations. As the SED's monopoly on power unraveled, new democratic parties emerged in East Germany, including New Forum, Democracy Now, and Democratic Awakening. These new opposition parties worked with the Modrow government to arrange free elections and constitutional reforms. In a remarkably nonviolent revolution, East Germany was moving toward democracy.

In December 1989, on the heels of these rapid political changes in the GDR and growing enthusiasm for reunification among the German people, Helmut Kohl met with Hans Modrow in the city of Dresden to discuss building closer relations between East and West Germany. In February 1990, Kohl traveled to the Soviet Union to meet with Gorbachev to discuss the possible reunification of Germany. Owing to Kohl's guarantees that a reunited Germany would pose no threat to the Soviet Union, Gorbachev informed the chancellor that he would not oppose reunification. Kohl also secured the acquiescence of the Western Allies for unification, despite lingering fears in some European nations about the threat of a reinvigorated Germany.

The momentum toward unification was now unstoppable, and on May 18, 1990, the two German governments signed an agreement to unify their economies. On October 3, 1990, the Unification Treaty went into effect, joining East and West Germany into a single nation under the federal constitution with its capital at Berlin. The new German nation would remain part of the EEC and of NATO. The powers that had occupied postwar Germany, the Soviet Union, the United States, Great Britain, and France signed the Treaty on the Final Settlement with Respect to Germany on March 15, 1991. The treaty, signed by both East and West Germany and ratified by the unified German state, removed the final limitations on German sovereignty remaining from the aftermath of World War II. The new Germany was born.

12

CONTEMPORARY GERMANY

On November 9, 2009, German chancellor Angela Merkel (1954–   ) marked the 20th anniversary of the fall of the Berlin Wall along with the leaders of Russia, France, and Britain. Merkel, Germany's first female chancellor, was raised in the former East Germany and as a young prodemocracy activist had played an active role in the communist dictatorship's demise. She led the assembled world leaders, including U.S. Secretary of State Hillary Clinton, through the Brandenburg Gate before delivering a historic address. Speaking before tens of thousands of spectators in a rainy Berlin, Chancellor Merkel commemorated the victims who died trying to escape communist tyranny. She also joined the other world leaders in celebrating the memory of German reunification and the end of the cold war. However, her speech also demonstrated Germany's growing prominence on the world stage in the 21st century.

Asserting Germany's determination to help tackle the daunting problems facing the contemporary world, including global poverty and climate change, Merkel used the fall of the Berlin Wall as a metaphor of the power of hope and collective action. Speaking to the gathering, the German chancellor reminded the assembled crowd that the same determination that brought down the Berlin Wall could serve as a source of strength in the 21st century. In a speech before the U.S. Congress a week before, Merkel had made a similar point, urging her audience that the world needs to demonstrate that it can meet the challenges of the 21st century and that it can tear down these "walls" as surely as the Berlin Wall was dismantled 20 years before. After fireworks and a festive concert, Angela Merkel returned to the checkpoint she had used two decades before to cross over into the west. Having escaped the oppression of her childhood, Merkel has risen against the odds to become the leader of the Federal Republic,

Contemporary Germany: *Länder*

Baltic Sea

North Sea

Kiel

Schleswig-Holstein

Mecklenburg-Vorpommern

Schwerin

Hamburg

Elbe R.

Bremen

Niedersachsen (Lower Saxony)

Brandenburg

Oder R.

POLAND

Berlin

THE NETHERLANDS

Hannover

Magdeburg

Potsdam

Nordrhein-Westfalen (North Rhine–Westphalia)

Sachsen-Anhalt (Saxony-Anhalt)

Düsseldorf

Erfurt

Sachsen (Saxony)

Dresden

Hessen

Thüringen

BELGIUM

Rheinland-Pfalz (Rhineland-Palatinate)

Wiesbaden

LUX.

Mainz

CZECH REPUBLIC

Saarland

Saarbrücken

Bayern (Bavaria)

Stuttgart

FRANCE

Baden-Württemberg

Rhine R.

Danube R.

N

München (Munich)

0   50 miles
0   50 km

SWITZERLAND

© Infobase Publishing

LIECH.

AUSTRIA

a democratic nation that is a leader within the European Union and a prominent member of NATO and the G8, an influential forum of the world's eight most industrialized democracies. With her nation, Chancellor Merkel now faces the challenges and uncertainties of the 21st century.

Building a New Germany

On December 1, 1990, national elections determined the composition of the new German Bundestag. Helmut Kohl's coalition, the conservative alliance of the CDU/CSU, won 319 of the 662 seats, giving it a clear majority in coalition with the moderates of the FDP, which won 79 seats. The SPD failed to gain many new seats in the former East Germany and claimed just 239 seats. East Germany's former ruling party, the SED, which had changed its name to the Party of Democratic Socialism in 1989, also ran in the election. However, hampered by widespread outrage at the activities of the former regime's security service, it won just eight seats.

Among the first controversies in the newly reunited Germany was where its capital should be located. While Berlin had been designated the Federal Republic's capital, and huge sums of money had been budgeted for the construction of state buildings, many former West Germans proved reluctant to abandon their former capital at Bonn. After a contentious debate in the Bundestag in June 1991, the delegates voted to locate Germany's capital in Berlin, a city whose history reflected the legacy of both of the former German states.

The controversy surrounding the symbolic choice of Germany's new capital proved trivial compared with the massive problems associated

The renovation of the Reichstag building in Berlin was completed in 1999, and the historic building is now the meeting place of Germany's parliament, the Bundestag. (Bundesregierung, B 145 Bild-00208054 / Bernd Kühler)

with integrating the former East Germany into the Federal Republic's capitalist economic system. The two German states had signed an economic treaty on July 1, 1990, prior to unification, one that consolidated their economies and established the deutsche mark as the sole currency. However, bringing the dilapidated East German economy up to the production and profitability levels of the former West Germany proved a daunting task. Factories and transport networks in the former East Germany had fallen into disrepair, and the state-owned industries, crippled by debt and hampered by ineffective management, proved unable to compete with Western companies. Meanwhile, German workers in the east were unused to the rough-and-tumble competition of the capitalist system, having been raised in a society that promised universal employment and extensive social welfare entitlements. Recognizing the enormous gulf between the economic capacity of the former East Germany and West Germany, the Kohl government scrambled to revitalize the inefficient state industries of the East. Kohl formed the Trust Agency (Treuhandanstalt) and charged it with privatizing some 8,500 state-owned industrial concerns and agricultural holdings in the former East Germany, huge enterprises that had more than 4 million total employees. In restructuring, closing, and dismantling these failing, debt-ridden concerns, the German government found few enthusiastic buyers and soon wracked up an enormous debt. By 1994, when its activities ceased, it had borrowed almost 270 billion deutsche marks to finance its operations. Worse yet, the activities of the Trust Agency caused more than 2 million workers in the former East Germany to be laid off in the early 1990s, more than half of the total workforce of the former state-owned industries, sparking mass protests in Berlin and other German cities. The controversy turned deadly in April 1991 when the Trust Agency's director, Detlev Rohwedder (1932–91), was assassinated by terrorists, perhaps affiliated with the Red Army Faction.

The former East Germany's state-run industries were not the only expensive problem facing the newly unified Germany. The east's transportation and communication networks also required costly modernization. The federal government poured more than 800 billion deutsche marks into the former East Germany during the 1990s to upgrade its obsolete transportation systems, communication infrastructure, and energy networks, to fund unemployment payments and vocational training for laid-off workers, and to finance costly environmental cleanup projects.

Despite the massive infusion of money into the former GDR, many of its former citizens seethed with resentment as candidates from the west claimed top positions in government, business, and education. Educated in a capitalist system and untainted by any past association with the GDR's repressive communist regime, immigrants from western Germany seemed to be getting the best jobs as the ranks of the jobless swelled in the east. For many former citizens of the GDR, the reality of unification, expressed in economic uncertainty and lost social security benefits, failed to live up to their expectations. In the decade after the fall of the Berlin Wall, older East Germans pined for the security afforded by the old socialist state. As anger mounted in eastern Germany, the Kohl government organized a series of talks that led to the 1992 Solidarity Pact. This agreement provided for nationwide tax hikes to help fund the rejuvenation of eastern Germany without continuing to rely on uncontrolled deficit spending that might trigger runaway inflation.

Dealing with the excesses of the former East German communist regime also proved divisive in the aftermath of German reunification. The most pressing issue concerned the activities of the Ministry of State Security, known as the Stasi. The Stasi, the SED's secret police, monitored the activities of East German citizens, using wiretaps and thousands of paid informants to compile damaging files on enemies of the state, real and imagined. The Kohl government formed a commission in the fall of 1990 to review the millions of secret files amassed by the Stasi and to prosecute the ministry's former agents. By January 1992, the government commission agreed to give former East German citizens access to their Stasi files, unleashing a torrent of anger and dismay at their contents. The legacy of surveillance and suppression revealed by the opening of the Stasi files rent eastern Germany, pitting victims of communist repression against former Stasi operatives as well as neighbors, coworkers, and family members who collaborated with the regime.

As controversy over the GDR's past swirled, the Federal Republic's judiciary also prosecuted leading SED figures for atrocities committed under their authority. Thus, the former director of the Stasi Erich Mielke faced charges in 1993. Mielke's political career had begun in the 1930s, when he fought for the KPD in street battles against the Nazis. After orchestrating the murder of a pair of Berlin police officers who had broken up KPD meetings, Mielke fled to the Soviet Union and was tried in absentia for the killings. He spent World War II as a political officer in the Red Army and returned to Germany after the war to head the GDR's secret police, coordinating the nefarious activities of the Stasi. In December 1989, as the SED regime crumbled, the reviled

Stasi head was expelled from the party and arrested by GDR authorities. After unification, in October 1990, Mielke was arrested and tried by the federal court for the 1931 murders of the two Berlin police officers. Found guilty in 1993, he was sentenced to six years' imprisonment but released after just two years, owing to his poor health. A broken man, he died in a Berlin nursing home in obscurity in 2000.

Mielke's former boss, the East German dictator Erich Honecker also faced charges in the wake of reunification. In the face of massive demonstrations in October 1989, an aging Honecker had been ousted as SED leader. A year later, when the GDR was dissolved, Honecker and his family took refuge in a Soviet military hospital outside Berlin before fleeing to the USSR to avoid arrest for his regime's atrocities. After the collapse of the communist regime in Russia in December 1991, Honecker was extradited to Germany to answer for his crimes. By the time he was brought to trial, however, in 1993, he was so ill that the court released him. After this controversial decision, Honecker sought refuge in Chile, dying there a year later of liver cancer.

Germany and European Integration

Since its inception, the Federal Republic of Germany has been a leading force in European integration, working with its neighbors to forge strong economic and political ties. West Germany's interest in European integration had been apparent since the 1950s. It was a key partner in the organizations that laid the foundations for the European Union, signing the Treaty of Paris in 1951, which founded the European Coal and Steel Community in 1951 and the Treaty of Rome in 1957, which established the European Economic Community (EEC), the forerunner of the European Community (EC). Ironically, Germany's troubled past played a role in fostering European integration, since France and Germany initially envisioned economic coordination as a mechanism to preclude future wars between the two former enemies. The cooperation among EC nations had intensified during the 1980s, and the reunification of Germany had been conceived within the context of European integration. Accordingly, on the heels of German reunification, the Federal Republic signed the Maastricht Treaty, which went into effect on November 1, 1993. This groundbreaking agreement formed the European Union (EU), joining the original members of the EC, France, Germany, Italy, Belgium, Luxembourg, and the Netherlands, with newer members Denmark, Ireland, the United Kingdom, Greece, Spain, and Portugal in an economic, political, and security partnership. Member

231

states were not just bound together economically, as in the EC, but also coordinated European diplomacy, defense, and even justice and immigration policy.

The foundation of a common market within Europe fostered trade, and new members, particularly the former communist nations of the Warsaw Pact, rushed to join the EU. These applicants had to meet the stringent requirements of the Copenhagen criteria established in 1993: democratic government, the rule of law, the protection of human rights, a stable market economy, and the acceptance of EU responsibilities and obligations. In 1995, Austria, Sweden, and Finland joined the European Union, and in 2002, the individual currencies of the EU's member nations were replaced by a single currency, the euro. This sparked a dramatic increase in membership, and in 2004, Cyprus and Malta joined along with the Baltic states of Estonia, Latvia, and Lithuania and the Eastern European nations of the Czech Republic, Hungary, Poland, Slovakia, and Slovenia. With the addition of Bulgaria and Romania in 2007, the European Union has grown to its current total of 27 member nations. As a founding member of the EU, with the largest economy among the member nations, Germany has enjoyed tremendous influence within the newly integrated Europe.

In the 1990s, Germany also began to play a more active—and controversial—role in international affairs. An important member of NATO, Germany provided substantial funds to help pay for United Nations military operations in Iraq during the Persian Gulf War (1990–91) but did not send troops. In 1993, however, Germany participated in the UN peacekeeping mission in Somalia, sending a transportation unit. Although the Kohl government stopped short of committing combat troops, the operation in Somalia elicited controversy among the German people. In light of Germany's belligerent history, the Federal Republic's military had been founded as a self-defense force, prohibited from operating outside Germany. The issue was finally resolved in the federal courts, and in the summer of 1994, the justices hearing the case ruled that the German military was allowed to serve abroad, but only in the context of UN, NATO, or EU operations. As a result of this landmark decision, Germany's involvement in international peacekeeping has increased dramatically. In December 1995, for example, Chancellor Kohl sent troops to Bosnia as part of a multinational NATO peacekeeping force operating to enforce the Dayton Peace Accords, the 1995 peace agreement brokered by the United States to bring peace to Bosnia and Herzegovina. German involvement in the Balkans intensified in 1999, however, when German aircraft participated in the NATO

232

GERMANY'S ROLE
AS AN EU MEMBER

The European Union (EU), with its origins in the 1950s, has brought political stability and economic prosperity to its member nations. It has brought Europe a single market and a single currency, and it has allowed its member nations to coordinate their political action. The EU is one of the world's most important economic powers and provides more foreign aid to developing nations than any other polity. Having expanded from six original members to 27, the European Union now has a population of nearly 500 million. Germany is situated at the heart of the European Union, not only geographically, but also in the areas of politics, economics, and diplomacy. A founding member, Germany has become the most prominent of the European Union's 27 member nations, with the EU's largest population and most productive economy. In the 21st century, Germany's economic and diplomatic policies, its future prosperity and security, are tied to its membership in the European Union.

Germany's leadership role within the European Union has given the country renewed international prestige and respect. In 1957, the Treaty of Rome established the European Economic Community, the forerunner of the European Union, one that fostered the creation of a common market and eventually the introduction of a common currency, the euro. In 2007, the 50th anniversary of the Treaty of Rome, German chancellor Angela Merkel helped to negotiate the Lisbon Treaty, an agreement that continues the process of economic integration inaugurated by the 1957 agreement and also strengthens political coordination among EU members.

Germany's leadership within the European Union has fostered not only the enhanced cooperation of the original EU member nations, but also the introduction of new members. Germany has been careful to maintain a close relationship with France, and the friendship between these two nations is the linchpin of the European Union. At the same time, Germany has been instrumental in helping new nations, particularly the formerly communist states of Eastern Europe, to move toward EU membership.

bombing of Yugoslavia during the Kosovo conflict, the first time the Luftwaffe had engaged in combat operations since the end of World War II.

Germany's increasing prominence in international affairs is apparent in the significant role it has played in efforts to provide stability in Afghanistan after the U.S. invasion of 2001. In December 2001, after the ouster of the Taliban by the U.S. military, Germany hosted a meeting of Afghan leaders that led to the Bonn Agreement. The Bonn Agreement established a provisional Afghan government and laid the groundwork for drafting a new constitution and holding democratic elections. It also mandated a NATO-led International Security Assistance Force (ISAF) to help stabilize the country, controlling looting and retaliation in the capital region. Germany provided a substantial contribution to this peacekeeping force, sending more than 4,000 troops to serve in northern Afghanistan, making it the third-largest contributor of soldiers to the ISAF. The German troops serving in Afghanistan have been engaged in combat with Taliban insurgents and have suffered casualties as a result. Despite continuing controversy over the deployment within Germany, the Federal Republic's steady support for the Afghan operation has been essential in persuading other EU nations to retain a role in the country.

Immigration and Diversity

As Germany strengthened its bonds with other European states and honored its peacekeeping obligations in the 1990s, immigration into Germany after reunification caused increasing social strain. As the communist regimes of Eastern Europe collapsed in the early 1990s, some 200,000 ethnic Germans residing there sought a new home in the Federal Republic, applying for citizenship according to the provisions of the German constitution. According to the Basic Law, foreign nationals of German descent, known as Volksdeutsche, could claim citizenship in the Federal Republic, along with non-Germans suffering from persecution at home. As Yugoslavia exploded in ethnic conflict in the early 1990s, 200,000 such asylum seekers flooded into Germany as well. Troubled by widespread unemployment and suffering from soaring budget deficits related to the costs of reunification, the German government struggled to provide the influx of impoverished immigrants with social security benefits.

These new Germans also brought cultural and linguistic diversity to the country, troubling many of Germany's native-born citizens. These tensions compounded the xenophobic reactions remaining from the influx of workers into West Germany during the "economic miracle" of the 1950s and 1960s. Chronic labor shortages during that era prompted the German government to recruit guest workers (Gastarbeiter) from various nations, first Italy and Greece in the 1950s, then Turkey and Portugal after 1960, and finally Yugoslavia at the end of the 1960s.

With the erection of the Berlin Wall in 1961, the flow of industrial laborers from East Germany into the Federal Republic had ended, causing an intense labor shortage. The German government recruited guest workers from Turkey to fill the void. These workers, mostly young males, were supposed to remain in Germany for only a few years before returning home with their wages, but German employers pressured the government to extend the time limits. No longer required to leave, many chose to stay and, in the 1970s, began bringing their families to Germany to live with them. The children of Turkish parents born in Germany were excluded from citizenship, which was reserved for ethnic Germans and asylum seekers, but the Turks were granted the right to reside in the country.

The number of Turkish nationals residing in Germany increased dramatically in the decades to come, climbing from around 7,000 in 1961 to more than 650,000 in 1971, to more than 1.5 million in 1981, to almost 1.8 million in 1991, inflaming right-wing extremism in the country. Since Turkish guest workers had intended to stay in Germany only temporarily, neither the workers nor the government promoted their assimilation. As a result, Germany's Turkish population usually remained separate from their German neighbors, and cultural differences abounded. German reunification exacerbated these tensions between Germany's growing Turkish population and their German hosts. Xenophobic rhetoric was often accompanied by racist violence, particularly in the states of the former East Germany, hard hit by rising unemployment and economic anxiety. Neo-Nazi groups flourished, and violence against foreigners tripled between 1991 and 1993, prompting German liberals to confront Germany's racist past, calling for the nation to reimagine itself as a multicultural society.

These efforts resulted in a major change in German citizenship laws in 2000, one that granted citizenship to the children of foreign nationals born in Germany, regardless of their ethnicity. This change finally broke the link between German citizenship and German blood, turning Germany into a truly multinational society in the face of considerable conservative resistance.

Post-Unification Politics

Helmut Kohl was reelected in a landslide victory in December 1990, the first free democratic election conducted in a united Germany since the collapse of the Weimar Republic in 1933. He was swept into office in 1990 by the enthusiasm of reunification, but by 1994 the mounting economic and social problems associated with merging East and West Germany were eroding the longtime chancellor's popularity. Thus, the federal election of October 1994 was a much closer race, and Kohl barely held on to his office. In fact, the SPD gained the largest percentage of votes, with 37 percent, narrowly beating Kohl's CDU, which claimed 36 percent. While the CDU's coalition with the CSU and the FDP allowed Kohl to retain his seat, the SPD won a plurality of seats in the Bundestag, allowing them to effectively oppose the chancellor's policies. While Kohl managed to achieve many of his foreign policy aims during the rest of his term, the tenor of German politics was clearly shifting to the left.

In the historic federal election held on September 27, 1998, Kohl was ousted by an SPD candidate, Gerhard Schröder (1944–   ), the minister-president of Niedersachsen (Lower Saxony). Schröder's party, the SPD, had run an effective campaign, highlighting Germany's massive economic problems since reunification and their effects on the German people. By the time of the 1998 election, unemployment in Germany stood at more than 9 percent, and more than 4 million workers were unemployed. Most blamed Kohl's government for the crisis. Meanwhile, dissatisfaction in the former East Germany, where the unemployment rate stood at a staggering 20 percent, was rife, and on the eve of the election, angry protests in eastern Germany denounced the ruling party as well.

In the election, Schröder's "Red-Green" coalition, an alliance of the SPD and the Green Party, won a crushing victory, earning slightly more than 47 percent of the votes. The SPD earned a stunning majority in the Bundesrat, with almost 41 percent of the votes, compared with just 28 percent for Kohl's CDU. Humbled by the defeat, Kohl resigned from his post as CDU chief and largely retired from politics. Schröder's victory not only ended Kohl's five-term tenure as chancellor but also signaled the end of the conservative parties' domination of domestic politics in Germany. For the first time in the history of postwar Germany, a center-left party was in control of the government.

Gerhard Schröder was born in Nordrhein-Westfalen during World War II, and his father, Fritz Schröder, was killed in military action shortly after his son's birth. Schröder's mother, Erika, struggled to provide for her family after the war, and he was raised in poverty. The future chancellor held a series of low-paying jobs as he worked his way through high school by attending night school. Schröder eventually attended university and earned a law degree from prestigious Göttingen University in 1971. Schröder was a longtime member of the SPD and, in 1978, took a position heading the party's youth organization. In his legal practice, Schröder supported a variety of controversial leftist and environmentalist causes throughout the 1970s and 1980s. Elected to the Bundestag as an SPD delegate in 1980, Schröder was then elected in 1986 to the parliament of Niedersachsen. Once the SPD won the state elections in 1990, Schröder became minister-president of Niedersachsen and formed the Red-Green coalition that would sweep him into the chancellorship in 1998.

As chancellor, Schröder pursued a variety of ambitious domestic policies that reflected the concerns of the socialist-environmentalist coalition that brought him to power and of his own background. Following the Greens' platform, Schröder's government moved toward ending Germany's reliance on nuclear power and began working on finding renewable energy sources. Schröder also oversaw the liberalization of Germany's citizenship laws, making it easier for foreign nationals residing in the country to naturalize. While conservatives were alarmed at Schröder's stance on German citizenship, during his second term, his economic policies angered many on the German left.

Having narrowly won reelection in 2002, Schröder set out to tackle Germany's lingering economic recession and troubling unemployment rates. Accordingly, in 2003, Schröder announced to the Bundestag his plans to reform Germany's social welfare system in order to stimulate the economy and provide jobs. These reforms, known as Agenda 2010, called for deep tax cuts and reductions in social security programs, aimed at making Germany more competitive in the global economy. Hailed by the conservative opposition parties in the Bundestag, Agenda 2010 caused a near-revolt in Schröder's own party, the SPD. The German left warned of the policy's social effects and threatened to block its passage in the Bundestag. Schröder called their bluff, announcing that he would resign as chancellor if the proposal did not pass. Recognizing that this move would cripple the party, the Social Democrats relented, and the plan was approved in the Bundestag, although the controversial reforms dangerously undermined the chancellor's popularity and prompted public protests, including angry demonstrations in Berlin and Leipzig the summer of 2004. The social welfare cuts associated with Agenda 2010 proved painful for Germany's most vulnerable citizens, particularly in the east, and helped increase the gap between the country's rich and poor. Stubborn unemployment problems also proved hard to rectify, and by 2005, Germany reached 5 million unemployed for the first time. By 2007, however, the German unemployment rate had fallen to a five-year low. Despite this eventual success, the controversy surrounding Agenda 2010 eroded support for the SPD among Germany's workers and the unemployed, eventually helping to drive Schröder from office in 2005.

Born in 1944, Gerhard Schröder was the first German chancellor whose early life was not directly shaped by World War II, and this allowed him to chart a bolder course in foreign policy than his predecessors. During his chancellorship, Schröder pursued an active foreign policy, authorizing German troops to participate in NATO operations in Kosovo, the first time the Wehrmacht had been engaged in combat since the end of World War II. In the wake of the September 11 terrorist attacks on the United States, Germany proved itself a staunch ally of America, as Schröder contributed thousands of German soldiers to the war effort in Afghanistan. In 2003, with the U.S. invasion of Iraq, however, the German-U.S. relationship became tense. During the 2002 federal elections, Schröder's opposition to the planned invasion of Iraq by President George W. Bush (1946–) was central to his successful reelection campaign. Once the war began, he joined the SPD in denouncing the preemptive nature of the planned invasion and refused to contribute troops. As the Schröder government distanced itself from the United States, the chancellor forged key strategic partnerships with France's president Jacques Chirac (1932–) and Russia's president Vladimir Putin (1952–). Like his welfare reforms, Schröder's relationship with the Russian president would also prove controversial in 2004. Critics have questioned Schröder's vocal support for Putin, even in the midst of widespread condemnation of Russia's role in the disputed Ukrainian election of 2004, in light of the former German chancellor's subsequent appointment to the board of a lucrative natural gas cooperative between Germany and Russia soon after he left office.

In the September 2005 federal elections, Schröder's Red-Green coalition failed to win a parliamentary majority. However, his opponent, Angela Merkel, backed by the CDU-CSU-FDP, also failed to win a majority of Bundestag seats, although she won the popular vote by a single percentage point. With the election deadlocked, the parties entered negotiations to form a "grand coalition" between the Christian Democrats and the Social Democrats, Germany's largest, usually antagonistic, political parties. Schröder finally agreed, on October 11, to step down and allow Merkel to become chancellor, with the SPD holding most major offices within the new government. Angela Merkel became the Federal Republic of Germany's first female chancellor on November

Germany's chancellor, Angela Merkel, in April 2006 (Bundesregierung / Sebastian Bolesch)

22, 2005. She was also the first chancellor raised in communist East Germany.

Angela Merkel was born in Hamburg in 1954, daughter of a Lutheran pastor, but soon after Merkel's birth, her father was assigned to a rural parish outside Berlin, and the family settled in East Germany. During her childhood in the GDR, Merkel was a member of the state-sponsored socialist youth organization, the Free German Youth (FDJ), before enrolling at the University of Leipzig, where she studied physics. By 1990, Merkel had earned a doctorate in chemistry at the Academy of Sciences in Berlin.

During her time as a scientific researcher, Angela Merkel became embroiled in the exciting political transformation sweeping East Germany in 1989. After the fall of the Berlin Wall, she joined a fledgling pro-democracy party, Democratic Awakening, formed from existing Christian political groups. Merkel quickly rose to prominence in the democracy movement, and after the GDR's first democratic election, she served in Lothar de Maiziére's provisional government. After reunification, in the federal elections of December 1990, Merkel earned a seat in the new Bundestag. Once her party merged with the West German CDU in August 1990, Merkel joined Helmut Kohl's third cabinet, serving as minister for women and youth. By 1994, she had been named minister for environment and nuclear safety, a more prominent position that afforded her considerable public exposure.

With Helmut Kohl's ouster in the 1998 federal elections, Angela Merkel became secretary-general of the CDU, now Germany's leading opposition party. Under Merkel's direction, the Christian Democrats engineered a run of state election wins in 1999, rebounding from the party's disappointing performance in the federal elections the year before. On the heels of this triumph in the Bundesrat elections, however, Merkel's party became embroiled in a devastating scandal involving her former mentor, Helmut Kohl.

In 1999, Germany was rocked by revelations that under Kohl, its powerful former leader, the CDU had engaged in illegal party financing. Embarrassing disclosures involving CDU revenues, funds generated through illegal kickbacks from foreign governments and deposited in secret Swiss bank accounts, were made public after an official government investigation. The scandal, involving millions of deutsche marks, led to the ouster of the party chairman, Wolfgang Schäuble (1942–). Merkel, having publicly criticized Kohl and his associates for their behavior, replaced Schäuble in April 2000 as CDU leader. Despite her growing prominence in the conservative coalition and popularity within Germany, Merkel was not chosen to run against Gerhard Schröder in the 2002 federal elections. The CSU candidate Edmund Stoiber (1941–) was chosen instead, but he suffered a narrow defeat. In the aftermath of the election, CDU chairwoman Merkel became the leader of the conservative opposition to Schröder's government in the Bundestag.

During Gerhard Schröder's second term, Merkel offered increasingly vocal opposition to his policies, positioning herself to run against the SPD chancellor. An economic conservative, Merkel advocated more radical free market reforms than Schröder, arguing that Germany could not compete globally due to the array of restrictive regulations and taxes that hobbled economic activity. Merkel, former minister for environment and nuclear safety under Kohl, also opposed the Red-Green coalition's plans to deactivate Germany's nuclear power plants. She departed most strikingly from Schröder in terms of foreign policy, however. Drawing comparisons with Britain's former hard-line prime minister, Margaret Thatcher (1925–), Merkel favored rebuilding Germany's strategic partnership with the United States. Accusing the SPD chancellor of pandering to anti-American sentiments in the previous federal elections, Merkel was ardent in her support of the U.S.-led invasion of Iraq in 2003. Finally, she also departed from Schröder over the issue of Turkey's admission to the European Union, contending that that nation should be linked to the EU through partnership treaties, rather than admitted to full membership.

In May 2005, it was announced that Angela Merkel had earned the CDU/CSU nomination to run against Gerhard Schröder in the upcoming federal election for chancellor. Going into the election, the conservative coalition enjoyed a considerable lead, but this lead dwindled as the public grew wary of the CDU's proposed tax policies and as Merkel found it difficult to match the charismatic Schröder's personal appeal. When polls closed after the national election, held on September 18, 2005, the result proved too close to call. Neither Schröder's Red-Green coalition nor Merkel's CDU/CSU coalition had won a clear victory, since neither gained a majority in the Bundestag. As both Schröder and Merkel proclaimed victory, CDU and SPD leaders met to discuss forming a grand coalition to govern Germany. After several weeks of tense negotiations, Schröder finally agreed to concede, making Merkel chancellor. In return, the SPD would hold half of the positions in Merkel's cabinet, retaining a prominent place for the Social Democrats in German politics. The grand coalition plan was approved by both major parties, and on November 22, 2005, the newly constituted Bundestag elected Angela Merkel chancellor of Germany.

As chancellor, Merkel has taken an active role in international diplomacy and has strengthened Germany's ties with the United States, while maintaining close relationships with the European Union, NATO, and the G8. Merkel has been staunch in her support for Israel and, in March 2007, spoke before the Israeli parliament to mark the Jewish state's 60th anniversary. The same year, Merkel also served as president of the European Council and chaired the G8, an indication of Germany's prominent place on the world stage at the dawn of the 21st century.

As president of the European Council, Angela Merkel has been instrumental in the reform of the European Union, taking a leading role in the creation and ratification of the Treaty of Lisbon. The product of efforts to reform the European Union that had been in negotiations since 2000, the Treaty of Lisbon was signed by all of the European Union's member nations in December 2007 and went into effect in December 2009. An attempt to centralize the operation of the EU, the Lisbon treaty amended earlier EU agreements signed at Rome in 1957 and Maastricht in 1992, and included many of the provisions from the failed European Constitution rejected by French and Danish voters in 2005. Serving as a constitution for the European Union, the Lisbon agreement strengthens the political and diplomatic coherence of the EU

GERMANY AND THE EUROPEAN DEBT CRISIS

The European Union (EU) was able to weather the economic downturn caused by the crisis in the U.S. sub-prime mortgage market that began in 2008, as the European Central Bank shored up Europe's banking institutions, keeping the euro sound. In 2010, however, a new crisis emerged in Europe that has dire implications for the European Union and for Germany. Despite the stipulations of the 1992 Maastricht Treaty, which imposes strict borrowing limits on eurozone governments, Greece, facing rising entitlement expenditures and declining revenues, quietly took on an unsustainable debt load. In November 2009, Greece's new socialist government shocked the world by announcing that the country's national debt stood at 12.7 percent of GDP, more than double what the previous government had admitted. The new government of Greece promised to save the country from bankruptcy and announced drastic cuts in spending to help balance the budget, prompting protests in the streets of Athens. By December, investment services began downgrading Greek government bonds, eventually reducing them to junk bond status. As the Greek economy faltered, governments in other troubled eurozone countries facing soaring deficits, including Portugal, Italy, and Spain, announced similar austerity plans, sparking mass protests at home and anxiety abroad.

By March 2010, the looming crisis had prompted the EU and the International Monetary Fund (IMF) to agree to provide a financial safety net to keep the Greek economy, crippled by rising interest rates, from collapsing. On May 2, the Greek government announced that it had reached a deal with the EU and IMF, agreeing to painful and unpopular austerity measures in exchange for a massive three-year bailout package amounting to 110 billion euros. Germany, the leading economy in the EU, agreed to provide more than 22 billion euros toward the planned bailout. The announcement of the austerity measures proved unpopular in Greece, sparking two days of deadly riots in Athens. Germany's contribution to the bailout fund also proved unpopular with the German electorate, and as a result, Chancellor

by expanding the authority of the European Parliament and the president of the European Council. It also authorizes a representative of the EU to speak for the member nations in matters of foreign affairs and security policy. Finally, it confirmed the European Union's human rights

Merkel's party lost a critical state election in North-Rhine Westphalia on May 9, costing her coalition its majority in the Bundesrat. A day later, as concern over the collapse of the euro spread, the EU and the IMF pledged to provide a staggering 750-billion-euro safety net to buttress the European economy and to insulate the declining euro from the financial shockwaves generated by the growing debt crisis. Chancellor Merkel's cabinet approved the single largest contribution of any EU nation to this fund: 123 billion euros in loan guarantees.

Taking a prominent leadership role in the crisis, on May 18, the German chancellor announced a controversial ban within Germany on the speculative practices she blamed for exacerbating the Greek debt crisis, especially the naked short selling of EU government bonds. A day later, she called upon the European Union to move to regulate these practices within the eurozone as a whole. Warning of the grave threat posed by the debt crisis, Merkel reminded the EU that drastic measures were required to save the euro, because if the currency failed it could have grave implications for the European Union and the very idea of European unity. According to the German chancellor, the looming crisis could cause not only the disintegration of the European currency but also that of the EU itself. However, Merkel's efforts to shore up the euro by making German capital available to guarantee loans for debt-ridden countries of southern Europe have proven dangerously unpopular within Germany. Many Germans, remembering their own country's painful experience with hyperinflation and political instability during the Great Depression, disapproved of their government bailing out seemingly spendthrift governments in Greece, Portugal, Italy, and Spain. Painfully aware of this public anger, but fearing the potential devaluation of the euro and a lingering recession, the German government is now faced with a hard choice. Merkel's government must choose between protecting Germany's own economic future by refusing further bailouts to troubled eurozone countries, even if that means the collapse of the European currency and the disintegration of the European Union, or investing more German capital in the costly effort to preserve European unity. Regardless of which of these difficult paths Germany chooses, there is no doubt that the central European nation will continue to play a leading role in the future of Europe.

charter by giving it the force of law within the EU. For her contribution to the reform of the European Union, Angela Merkel was awarded the Charlemagne Prize (Karlspreis) in 2008. Awarded by the German city of Aachen since 1950 to recognize contributions to the unity of Europe, past awards have honored prominent world leaders such as Konrad Adenauer, Winston Churchill, François Mitterrand, Helmut Kohl, Tony Blair (1953–), and Bill Clinton (1946–). Merkel's award was presented by French president Nicolas Sarkozy (1955–), an indication of the enduring partnership between France and Germany that provides the foundation for the European Union.

Chancellor Merkel's domestic policies have centered on making Germany a global economic power. Upon taking office, Merkel announced that the most important aspect of her domestic agenda was dealing with the unemployment that has plagued Germany for decades. In September 2008, however, Germany suffered major setbacks associated with the worldwide economic recession, and the Merkel government has struggled to insulate the German economy from its effects. These concerns shaped the campaign leading up to the federal election of 2009, as Angela Merkel sought reelection as chancellor.

On September 27, 2009, Angela Merkel won reelection, heading a center-right government controlled by the conservative alliance of the CDU, CSU, and FDP. Freed from having to share power with the SPD, her grand coalition partners during her first term, Merkel is now free to pursue a more aggressive agenda that reflects her own ideals. Thus, in her address before the U.S. Congress in November 2009, Chancellor Merkel took a firm stand on the issue of Iran's nuclear ambitions. Reversing Germany's earlier passivity on the issue, she stated clearly that she opposed any attempt by the Tehran government to acquire nuclear weapons. At the same time, Chancellor Merkel has promised to commit Germany to work toward solving the global problems of the 21st century, including climate change and poverty. Emerging from its troubled history as a democratic, multicultural, and innovative nation, Germany is poised to meet these challenges.

APPENDIX 1

BASIC FACTS ABOUT GERMANY

Official Name
Federal Republic of Germany (Bundesrepublik Deutschland)

Geography

Area	137,847 square miles (357,022 sq. km). Germany is slightly smaller than the state of Montana in the United States.
Land Borders	Austria, Belgium, Czech Republic, Denmark, France, Luxembourg, Netherlands, Poland, Switzerland
Coastal Borders	North Sea
Elevations	Germany's highest point is the Zugspitze at 9,721 feet (2,963 m); its lowest point is Neuendorf bei Wilster at 11.6 feet (3.54 m) below sea level.
Terrain	Northern lowlands, central uplands, and southern alpine region (Bavarian Alps)

Government
Germany is a federal parliamentary representative democratic republic founded on May 23, 1949. Germany's political system was established by the Basic Law (Grundgesetzt), as the 1949 constitution is called, and modified slightly during reunification in 1990. The chancellor, elected by the Federal Assembly (Bundestag), serves a four-year term and is the head of the government, and the president, elected by delegates from the Federal Assembly and the state governments, serves a five-

year term as the chief of state. A cabinet of government ministers is appointed by the president on the recommendation of the chancellor. Legislative power is held by the Bundestag, whose delegates are elected by the citizenry, and the Federal Council (Bundesrat), which represents Germany's 16 regional states. Delegates elected to the Bundestag, Germany's principal legislative organ, serve four-year terms. Germany's judiciary is an independent branch of the government, including a powerful Constitutional Court (Bundesverfassungsgericht), which serves as an appellate court that protects the constitutional and human rights of German citizens. All German citizens more than 18 years old are eligible to vote in federal elections.

Political Divisions

Capital	Berlin
Major Cities	Bonn, Bremen, Cologne, Dresden, Düsseldorf, Essen, Frankfurt, Hannover, Karlsruhe, Kassel, Kiel, Leipzig, Lübeck, Magdeburg, Mannheim, Munich, Nürnberg, Rostock, Saarbrücken, Stuttgart, Wiesbaden
Administrative Division (*Länder*)	Baden-Württemberg, Bayern (Bavaria), Berlin, Brandenburg, Bremen, Hamburg, Hessen, Mecklenburg-Vorpommern (Mecklenburg–West Pomerania), Niedersachsen (Lower Saxony), Nordrhein-Westfalen (North Rhine–Westphalia), Rheinland-Pfalz (Rhineland-Palatinate), Saarland, Sachsen (Saxony), Sachsen-Anhalt (Saxony-Anhalt), Schleswig-Holstein, Thüringen (Thuringia)

People

Population	82,282,988 (July 2010 estimate)
Growth Rate	–4.9% (2009 estimate)
Ethnic Groups	German (91.5%); Turkish (2.4%); Other (mostly Greek, Italian, Polish, Russian, Serbo-Croatian, Spanish) (6.1%)
Official Language	German
Religions	Protestant (34%); Roman Catholic (34%); Muslim (3.7%); Unaffiliated/Other (28.3%)
Literacy	(Ability to read and write at age 15) 99% of total population (2003 estimate)

Age Structure	0–14 years: 13.7% (5,768,366 males and 5,470,516 females) 15–64 years: 66.1% (27,707,761 males and 26,676,759 females) 65 years and over: 20.3% (7,004,805 males and 9,701,551 females) (2010 estimate)
Median Age	Total Populaion: 44.3 years Male: 43 years Female: 45.6 years (2010 estimate)
Birth Rate	8.21 births/1,000 population (2010 estimate)
Death Rate	11 deaths/1,000 population (July 2010 estimate)
Infant Mortality	Total: 3.98 deaths/1,000 live births Male: 4.36 deaths/1,000 live births Female: 3.51 deaths/1,000 live births (2010 estimate)
Life Expectancy at Birth	Total Population: 79.41 years Male: 76.41 years Female: 82.57 years (2010 estimate)
Fertility Rate	1.42 children born/woman (2010 estimate)

Economy

Germany's export-dependent economy is the world's fifth largest and the largest in Europe, despite contraction that began in late 2008 and continued into 2009. Contemporary Germany faces several economic challenges, including high unemployment (especially in the former East Germany) and an aging population. These two problems place a substantial burden on Germany's extensive social security system and have necessitated government deficit spending to fund entitlements. The Federal Republic has also been forced to spend sums—around $80 billion annually—on modernizing the economy of the former GDR, which still lags behind the western part of Germany.

Gross Domestic Product (GDP)	$2.81 trillion purchasing power parity (2009 estimate)
Gross Domestic Product Real Growth Rate	–4.9% (2009 estimate)
Gross Domestic Product per Capita	$35,100 purchasing power parity (2009 estimate)

Contribution to GDP by Economic Sector	agriculture: 0.9% industry: 26.8% services: 72.3% (2009 estimate)
Natural Resources	coal, lignite, natural gas, iron ore, copper, nickel, uranium, potash, salt, construction materials, timber, arable land
Land Use	arable land: 33.13% permanent crops: 0.6% other: 66.27% (2005)
Irrigated Land	1,873 square miles (4,850 sq km) (2003)
Agriculture	potatoes, wheat, barley, sugar beets, fruit, cabbages; cattle, pigs, and poultry
Industries	iron, steel, coal, cement, chemicals, machinery, vehicles, machine tools, electronics, food and beverages, shipbuilding, and textiles
Annual Exports	$1.159 trillion (2009 estimate)
Major Exports	machinery, vehicles, chemicals, metals, foodstuffs, and textiles
Total Labor Force	43.5 million (2009 estimate)
Labor Force by Occupation	agriculture: 2.4% industry: 29.7% services: 67.8% (2005)
Unemployment Rate	7.5% (2009 estimate)

Source: The World Factbook 2010. Washington, D.C.: Central Intelligence Agency, 2010.

Appendix 2

A Brief Chronology of German History

Prehistory

130,000 years ago	Neanderthals inhabit area that is present-day Germany.
35,000–40,000 years ago	*Homo sapiens* migrate to Germany; Hohe Fels site inhabited.
5000–3500 B.C.E.	Neolithic revolution in Germany
1200–700 B.C.E.	Urnfeld peoples inhabit Germany.
800–450 B.C.E.	Hallstatt culture thrives in Germany. Celtic tribes inhabit Germany.

Antiquity

First millennium B.C.E.	Germanic tribes migrate into Germany.
58 B.C.E.	Julius Caesar campaigns against Celtic and Germanic tribes in Germany.
9 B.C.E.	Germanic tribes led by Arminius defeat Varus's Roman legions in Teutoburg Forest.
9 B.C.E.–ca. 100 C.E.	Roman frontier established along Rhine and Danube.
98 C.E.	Tacitus writes *Germania*, describing Germanic tribes.
300s–400s C.E.	Germanic tribes migrate across Roman frontier.
410 C.E.	Visigoths under Alaric sack Rome.

Early Middle Ages

431–751	Merovingian dynasty rules Franks.
496	Baptism of Clovis, king of the Franks

732	Charles Martel's victory at Battle of Poitiers
752–911	Carolingian dynasty
768–814	Reign of Charlemagne
800	Charlemagne crowned emperor of the West by Pope Leo III.
814–840	Reign of Emperor Louis the Pious
843	Treaty of Verdun divides Carolingian Empire.
843–876	Western Frankish Kingdom ruled by King Louis the German
876–887	Reign of Emperor Charles III
881	Charles III crowned emperor.
911–918	King Conrad I of Franconia elected king of Germany.
919–936	King Henry I the Fowler, duke of Saxony, elected king of Germany.
936–973	Reign of Emperor Otto I the Great
955	Otto the Great defeats Hungarians at the Battle of Lechfeld.
962	Otto the Great crowned emperor.

High Middle Ages

1056–1106	Reign of Emperor Henry IV
1076	Emperor Henry IV meets Pope Gregory VII at Canossa during the Investiture Controversy.
1122	Concordat of Worms resolves Investiture Controversy.
1138–1250	Hohenstaufen dynasty
1152–1190	Reign of Emperor Frederick I Barbarossa
1212–1250	Reign of Emperor Frederick II
1273–1806	Habsburg Dynasty
1347–1378	Reign of Emperor Charles IV
1356	Charles IV issues Golden Bull, an imperial constitution.
1415	Frederick of Hohenzollern made margrave and elector of Brandenburg.

Early Modern Period

1493–1519	Reign of Emperor Maximilian I
1517	Luther issues Ninety-five Theses at Wittenberg, launching Protestant Reformation.

1519–1556	Reign of Charles V as Holy Roman Emperor
1556–1564	Reign of Emperor Ferdinand I
1564–1576	Reign of Emperor Maximilian II
1576–1612	Reign of Emperor Rudolf II
1612–1619	Reign of Emperor Matthias
1618–1648	Thirty Years' War
1619–1637	Reign of Emperor Ferdinand II
1637–1657	Reign of Emperor Ferdinand III
1640	Frederick William of Hohenzollern crowned elector of Brandenburg-Prussia.
1648	Peace of Westphalia ends Thirty Years' War.
1658–1705	Reign of Emperor Leopold I
1688–1713	Reign of elector Frederick III of Brandenburg-Prussia

The Modern Period

1705–1711	Reign of Emperor Joseph I
1711–1740	Reign of Emperor Charles VI
1740–1786	Reign of King Friedrich the Great in Prussia.
1741–1763	Prussia defeats Austria in three Silesian conflicts.
1742–1745	A non-Habsburg, Emperor Charles VII of Bavaria, reigns as Holy Roman Emperor.
1745	Maria Theresa elected empress of Austria
1745–1765	Reign as emperor of Maria Theresa's husband, Francis I of the house of Habsburg-Lorraine
1765–1790	Reign of Emperor Joseph II, son of Francis and Maria Theresa
1786–1797	King Frederick William II rules Prussia.
1792–1806	Reign of last Holy Roman Emperor, Francis II
1797–1840	King Frederick William III takes the throne in Prussia.
1804–1835	Reign of Francis I as emperor of Austria
1806	Napoléon dissolves Holy Roman Empire and founds Confederation of the Rhine.
1814–1815	Congress of Vienna and establishment of the Austrian-led German Confederation
1821–1848	Metternich serves as Austrian foreign minister.
1834	Prussia organizes the Zollverein.
1840–1861	Reign of Friedrich Wilhelm IV in Prussia

1848–1850	Revolutions sweep Europe; in Germany, failed attempt to found Prussian-led constitutional monarchy by Frankfurt Parliament.
1848–1916	Reign of Francis Joseph I as emperor of Austria
1861–1888	Wilhelm I rules Prussia.
1864	Austro-Prussian victory over Denmark in Schleswig-Holstein
1866	Prussia defeats Austria in Austro-Prussian War.
1867	North German Confederation founded under Prussian leadership.
1870–1871	Prussian victory in Franco-Prussian War
1871	German Empire proclaimed at Versailles, ruled by Emperor Wilhelm I, with Otto von Bismarck as chancellor.
1879	Dual Alliance concluded between Germany and Austria.
1881–1887	Duration of the Three Emperors' League between Austria, Germany, and Russia
1888	Emperor Frederick III reigns as German emperor for single year.
1888–1918	Reign of Emperor Wilhelm II
1890	Bismarck dismissed as German chancellor by Wilhelm II.
1914–1918	World War I
1918	Germany surrenders on November 11.
1919	Weimar Treaty signed and Weimar Constitution ratified.
1919–1925	Friedrich Ebert named first president of the Weimar Republic.
1924	Hitler writes *Mein Kampf,* "My Struggle," in prison.
1925	Paul von Hindenburg elected Weimar Republic's president.
1926	Germany admitted to League of Nations.
1929	Great Depression destabilizes German economy.
1930–1933	Germany is governed under emergency decree, Article 48.
1933	Adolf Hitler named chancellor on January 30, passes Enabling Act in March, granting right to suspend constitutional government for four years.

1934–1945	Third Reich: Hitler suspends Weimar Constitution and rules Germany as führer.
1935	Saar region returned to Germany; Hitler announces German rearmament; Jews subject to discriminatory "Nuremberg Laws."
1936	Hitler remilitarizes the Rhineland in March; Germany supports fascists in Spanish Civil War; Berlin Olympics.
1938	Germany absorbs Austria and seizes Sudetenland; Kristallnacht (Night of Broken Glass).
1939	German invasion of Czechoslovakia; Hitler's invasion of Poland after signing of secret pact with the Soviet Union
1939–1945	World War II and the Holocaust
1945	Hitler's suicide in Berlin and the surrender of Nazi Germany; occupation of Germany by U.S., British, French, and Soviet allies
1945–1946	International Military Tribunal meets in Nuremberg to try Nazi war criminals.
1948	American Marshall Plan helps rebuild Western Europe; Soviet Union responds with failed Berlin Blockade.
1949	Federal Republic of Germany founded on May 23 in West Germany; in the Soviet zone, the German Democratic Republic established on October 7.
1949–1963	Konrad Adenauer, Christian Democratic Union (CDU) head, serves as chancellor of the Federal Republic.
1953	Walter Ulbricht, head of the SED, the German Democratic Republic's ruling party, suppresses demonstrations in East Germany with Soviet troops.
1955	Federal Republic of Germany granted sovereignty and joins NATO, the North Atlantic Treaty Organization, with the ratification of the Treaty of Paris of May 1955; the Soviets found the Warsaw Pact, and East Germany joins in 1956.
1957	Saarland rejoins Federal Republic of Germany.
1958	On January 1, West Germany joins France, Italy, Belgium, Luxembourg, and the Netherlands in

	a common market known as the European Economic Community (EEC).
1961	Berlin Wall is erected in East Berlin to stop defections to the West.
1963	German Democratic Republic adopts "New Economic System."
1963–1966	Ludwig Erhard of the CDU/CSU serves as chancellor of West Germany.
1965	The European Community (EC) is formed.
1966	The former Nazi, Kurt Georg Kiesinger of the CDU/CSU, is named West German chancellor, with the support of the SPD.
1969–1974	SPD leader and former mayor of West Berlin, Willy Brandt, serves as chancellor of the Federal Republic of Germany.
1971	Walter Ulbricht replaced by Erich Honecker as leader in German Democratic Republic.
1972	The Federal Republic of Germany and the German Democratic Republic sign the Basic Treaty, regularizing their relations.
1973	The Federal Republic of Germany and the German Democratic Republic are admitted to the United Nations on September 18, 1973.
1974–1982	SPD leader Helmut Schmidt serves as chancellor of the Federal Republic of Germany.
1977	Red Army Faction terrorist attacks in West Germany during the "German Autumn."
1978	Green Party founded in West Germany.
1982	Helmut Kohl of the CDU/CSU elected West German chancellor.
1987	Erich Honecker becomes first GDR leader to visit West Germany.
1989	In September, Hungary opens its border crossings with Austria, and tens of thousands of East German defectors travel to the Federal Republic; mass demonstrations for reform erupt in Leipzig and other cities in the GDR in September, lasting until early November; on October 7 Soviet leader Mikhail Gorbachev visits East Germany and declares that USSR will not interfere in GDR's politics; Erich Honecker resigns

on October 18; Berlin Wall falls on November 9; on November 28, West German chancellor Helmut Kohl proposes plan for German unification; Kohl meets in Dresden with East German prime minister, Hans Modrow, regarding unification on December 19.

1990 East Germany holds its first free elections on March 18, and Modrow is ousted by a coalition led by East German CDU leader Lothar de Maizière, which favors German unification; on August 31, treaty signed in Berlin dissolving the German Democratic Republic and absorbing its territories into the Federal Republic on October 3, 1990; on September 12, Treaty on the Final Settlement with Respect to Germany officially ends the occupation of Germany by the allied powers, acknowledging the full sovereignty of Germany.

1993 The European Union (EU) is formed through the Maastricht Treaty, joining Germany, France, Italy, Belgium, Luxembourg, the Netherlands, Denmark, Ireland, the United Kingdom, Greece, Spain, and Portugal in an economic, political, and security partnership.

1995 German troops sent to Bosnia as part of a multinational NATO peacekeeping force enforcing the Dayton Peace Accords.

1998 SPD candidate Gerhard Schröder, the minister-president of Niedersachsen (Lower Saxony), elected chancellor.

1999 German aircraft participate in the NATO bombing of Yugoslavia during the Kosovo conflict.

2000 German citizenship laws liberalized to facilitate the naturalization of foreign residents in Germany.

2001 Bonn Agreement establishes a provisional Afghan government and mandates a new constitution and democratic elections; Germany provides troops for the NATO-led International Security Assistance Force to help stabilize the country.

2005	Angela Merkel elected chancellor by grand coalition of SPD-CDU.
2009	Angela Merkel reelected chancellor, governing center-right coalition of CDU-CSU-FDP; Chancellor Merkel hosts 20th anniversary commemoration of fall of Berlin Wall in Berlin.
2010	Germany reluctantly contributes to the EU/IMF bailout of Greece amid concerns over the Greek debt crisis and its effects on the eurozone economy; President Horst Koehler resigns in the midst of controversy over his remarks that link Germany's economic interests with continued overseas military deployments; in the second quarter, the German economy grows at its fastest pace since reunification; Thilo Sarrazin, a prominent banker, is forced to resign from the board of the Bundesbank after making derogatory remarks about Europe's Muslim and Jewish minorities.

APPENDIX 3

BIBLIOGRAPHY

Arnold, Benjamin. *Medieval Germany, 500–1300: A Political Interpretation.* Toronto and Buffalo, N.Y.: University of Toronto Press, 1997.

Asch, Ronald G. *The Thirty Years' War: The Holy Roman Empire and Europe, 1618–48.* New York: St. Martin's Press, 1997.

Bainton, Roland Herbert. *The Age of the Reformation.* Princeton, N.J.: Van Nostrand, 1956.

———. *Here I Stand: A Life of Martin Luther.* New York: Abingdon-Cokesbury Press, 1950.

Barclay, David E., and Eric D. Weitz, eds. *Between Reform and Revolution: German Socialism and Communism from 1840 to 1990.* New York: Berghahn Books, 1998.

Beiser, Frederick C. *Enlightenment, Revolution, and Romanticism: The Genesis of Modern German Political Thought, 1790–1800.* Cambridge, Mass.: Harvard University Press, 1992.

Benecke, Gerhard. *Society and Politics in Germany, 1500–1750.* London: Routledge and Kegan Paul, 1974.

Biess, Frank, Mark Roseman, and Hanna Schissler, eds. *Conflict, Catastrophe and Continuity: Essays on Modern German History.* New York: Berghahn Books. 2007.

Blackbourn, David. *The Long Nineteenth Century: A History of Germany, 1780–1918.* New York: Oxford University Press, 1998.

Blanning, T. C. W. *Joseph II and Enlightened Despotism.* New York: Harper & Row, 1970.

Brady, Thomas A., Jr. *German Histories in the Age of Reformations, 1400–1650.* Cambridge and New York: Cambridge University Press, 2009.

Breuilly, John. *Austria, Prussia and Germany, 1806–1871.* New York: Longman, 2002.

Caesar, Julius. *Caesar's Commentaries on the Gallic and Civil Wars.* Edited by William Alexandra M'Devitta. London: Henry G. Bohn, 1853.

————. *The Conquest of Gaul.* Translated by S. A. Handford. Revised with a new introduction by Jane F. Gardner. London and New York: Penguin Books, 1982.

Carr, William. *A History of Germany, 1815–1990.* 4th ed. New York: Routledge, Chapman, and Hall, 1991.

Carroll, Maureen. *Romans, Celts, and Germans: The German Provinces of Rome.* Stroud, U.K.: Tempus, 2001.

Carsten, F. L. *The Origins of Prussia.* London: Oxford University Press, 1958.

Clark, Christopher M. *Iron Kingdom: The Rise and Downfall of Prussia, 1600–1947.* Cambridge, Mass.: Belknap Press of Harvard University, 2006.

Conradt, David P. *The German Polity.* 5th ed. New York and London: Longman, 1993.

Coppard, George. *With a Machine Gun to Cambrai.* London: Imperial War Museum, 1980.

Craig, Gordon A. *Germany, 1866–1945.* New York: Oxford University Press, 1978.

Davis, William Stearns, ed. *Readings in Ancient History: Illustrative Extracts from the Sources.* 2 vols. Boston: Allyn and Bacon, 1912–1913.

Dennis, Mike, and Eva Kolinsky, eds. *United and Divided: Germany Since 1990.* New York: Berghahn Books, 2004.

Detwiler, Donald S. *Germany: A Short History.* Carbondale: Southern Illinois University Press, 1999.

Du Boulay, F. R. H. *Germany in the Later Middle Ages.* New York: St. Martin's Press, 1983.

Einhard and Notker the Stammerer. *Two Lives of Charlemagne.* Translated by Lewis Thorpe. Baltimore: Penguin Books, 1969.

Eley, Geoff, ed. *Society, Culture, and the State in Germany, 1870–1930.* Ann Arbor: University of Michigan Press, 1998.

Erasmus, Desiderius. *The Praise of Folly.* 2nd ed. Translated by Clarence H. Miller. New Haven, Conn.: Yale University Press, 2003.

Evans, Richard J. *The Coming of the Third Reich.* New York: Penguin Press, 2004.

————. *The Third Reich in Power, 1933–1939.* New York: Penguin Press, 2005.

Friedländer, Saul. *The Years of Extermination: Nazi Germany and the Jews, 1939–1945.* New York: HarperCollins Publishers, 2007.

Fuhrmann, Horst. *Germany in the High Middle Ages, ca. 1050–1200.* Cambridge and New York: Cambridge University Press, 1986.

Fulbrook, Mary. *Anatomy of a Dictatorship: Inside the GDR, 1949–1989.* Oxford: Oxford University Press, 1995.

————. *The Divided Nation: A History of Germany, 1918–1990.* Oxford and New York: Oxford University Press, 1992.

Füssel, Stephan. *Gutenburg and the Impact of Printing.* Aldershot, Hampshire, Burlington, Vt.: Ashgate, 2005.

Geary, Patrick J. *Before France and Germany: The Creation and Transformation of the Merovingian World.* New York: Oxford University Press, 1988.

Heiber, Helmut. *The Weimar Republic.* Oxford and Cambridge, Mass.: Blackwell, 1993.

Emperor Henry IV. "Response to Gregory's Admonition." In *Power and the Holy in the Age of Investiture Controversy,* edited by Maureen C. Miller. New York: Bedford/St. Martins, 2005.

Horne, Charles F., ed. *The Great Events of the Great War.* Vol. 4. n.p.: The National Alumni, 1920.

Hunter, James Davison. *To Change the World: The Irony, Tragedy, and Possibility of Christianity in the Late Modern World.* New York: Oxford University Press, 2010.

Jacobs, Henry Eyster, ed. *Works of Martin Luther with Introductions and Notes.* Vol. 1. Philadelphia: A. J. Holman Company, 1915.

James, Simon. *The World of the Celts.* London New York: Thames and Hudson, 1993.

Jones, Alun. *The New Germany: A Human Geography.* Chichester and New York: John Wiley, 1994.

Jordan, Paul. *Neanderthal: Neanderthal Man and the Story of Human Origins.* Phoenix Mill, U.K.: Sutton, 2001.

Kitchen, Martin. *The Cambridge Illustrated History of Germany.* Cambridge: Cambridge University Press, 1996.

————. *A History of Modern Germany, 1800–2000.* Malden, Mass.: Blackwell, 2006.

Kors, Alan Charles, and Edward Peters, eds. *Witchcraft in Europe, 400–1700: A Documentary History.* Philadelphia: University of Pennsylvania Press, 2001.

Lewis, Rand C. *The Neo-Nazis and German Unification.* Westport, Conn.: Praeger, 1996.

Lindberg, Carter. *The European Reformations.* 2d ed. Malden, Mass.: Blackwell, 2010.

Luther, Martin. *Works.* Jaroslav Pelikan and Hartmut Lehmann, eds. 55 vols. St. Louis, Mo.: Concordia Pub. House, 1955–1986.

Maier, Charles S. *Dissolution: The Crisis of Communism and the End of East Germany.* Princeton, N.J.: Princeton University Press, 1997.

Marsh, David. *The Germans: A People at the Crossroads.* New York: St. Martin's, 1990.

McAdams, A. James. *Germany Divided: From the Wall to Reunification.* Princeton, N.J.: Princeton University Press, 1993.

Merkl, Peter H. *German Unification in the European Context.* University Park: Pennsylvania State University Press, 1993.

Miller, Maureen C. *Power and the Holy in the Age of the Investiture Conflict: A Brief History with Documents.* New York: Bedford St. Martins, 2005.

Mommsen, Wolfgang J. *Imperial Germany, 1867–1918: Politics, Culture, and Society in an Authoritarian State.* London: Arnold, 1995.

Oberman, Heiko Augustinus. *Luther: Man between God and the Devil.* New Haven, Conn.: Yale University Press, 1989.

Ozment, Steven. *A Mighty Fortress: A New History of the German People.* New York: HarperCollins, 2004.

Parker, Geoffrey, and Simon Adams. *The Thirty Years' War.* 2nd ed. London, New York: Routledge, 1997.

Peukert, Detlev J. K. *The Weimar Republic: The Crisis of Classical Modernity.* New York: Hill & Wang, 1993.

Pulzer, Peter. *German Politics, 1945–1995.* Oxford: Oxford University Press, 1995.

———. *Jews and the German State: The Political History of a Minority, 1848–1933.* Detroit: Wayne State University Press, 2003.

Randers-Pehrson, Justine Davis. *Germans and the Revolution of 1848–1849.* New York: P. Lang, 1999.

Robinson, James Harvey, ed. *Readings in European History.* 2 vols. Boston and New York: Ginn and Company, 1906.

Schulze, Hagen. *The Course of German Nationalism: From Frederick the Great to Bismarck, 1763–1867.* 2d ed. Cambridge and New York: Cambridge University Press, 1991.

Schutz, Herbert. *The Germanic Realms in Pre-Carolingian Central Europe, 400–750.* New York: P. Lang, 2000.

Seward, Desmond. *Metternich: The First European.* New York: Viking, 1991.

Sheehan, James J. *German Liberalism in the Nineteenth Century.* Chicago: University of Chicago Press, 1978.

Simpson, William. *The Second Reich: Germany, 1871–1918.* Cambridge and New York: Cambridge University Press, 1995.

Sisa, Stephen. *The Spirit of Hungary: A Panorama of Hungarian History and Culture*. Morristown, N.J.: Vista Books, 1995.

Smith, Preserved, ed. *Age of the Reformation*. New York: Henry Holt and Company, 1920.

Smith, Woodruff D. *The German Colonial Empire*. Chapel Hill: University of North Carolina Press, 1978.

Snyder, Louis L. *Documents of German History*. New Brunswick, N.J.: Rutgers University Press, 1958.

Spaeth, Adolph, L. D. Reed, and Henry Eyster Jacobs, eds. *The Works of Martin Luther*. Vol. 1. Philadelphia: A. J. Holman Company, 1915.

Stern, Fritz. *Dreams and Delusions: The Drama of German History*. New Haven, Conn.: Yale University Press, 1999.

Synod, Roman. "Decrees against Lay Investiture." In *Power and the Holy in the Age of Investiture Controversy*, edited by Maureen C. Miller. New York: Bedford/St. Martins, 2005.

Tacitus. *Dialogus, Agricola, Germania*. Translated by William Peterson. London: William Heinemann, 1914.

———. *Germania*. Translated by J. B. Rives. Oxford and New York: Oxford University Press, 1999.

Tracy, James D. *Erasmus of the Low Countries*. Berkeley: University of California Press, 1996.

Turk, Eleanor L. *The History of Germany*. Westport, Conn.: Greenwood Press, 1999.

Turner, Henry Ashby, Jr. *Germany from Partition to Reunification*. New Haven, Conn.: Yale University Press, 1992.

Vierhaus, Rudolf. *Germany in the Age of Absolutism*. Cambridge and New York: Cambridge University Press, 1988.

Weinberg, Gerhard L. *A World at Arms: A Global History of World War II*. Cambridge: Cambridge University Press, 1994.

Wende, Peter. *A History of Germany*. New York: Palgrave Macmillan, 2005.

Wilson, Peter. *From Reich to Revolution: German History, 1558–1806*. Houndsmill, Basingstoke, U.K.: Palgrave Macmillan, 2004.

Appendix 4

Suggested Reading

General Works

Berghahn, Volker Rolf. *Modern Germany: Society, Economy, and Politics in the Twentieth Century*. 2d ed. New York: Cambridge University Press, 1987.

Blackbourn, David, and Richard J. Evans, eds. *The German Bourgeoisie: Essays on the Social History of the German Middle Class from the Late Eighteenth to the Early Twentieth Century*. New York: Routledge, 1993.

Detwiler, Donald S. *Germany: A Short History*. Carbondale: Southern Illinois University Press, 1999.

Eley, Geoff. *From Unification to Nazism: Reinterpreting the German Past*. Boston: Allen and Unwin, 1986.

Evans, Robert John Weston. *The Making of the Habsburg Monarchy, 1550–1700: An Interpretation*. New York: Oxford University Press, 1984.

Fuhrmann, Horst. *Germany in the High Middle Ages, ca. 1050–1200*. Cambridge and New York: Cambridge University Press, 1986.

Fulbrook, Mary. *A Concise History of Germany*. 2d ed. Cambridge and New York: Cambridge University Press, 2004.

———. *The Divided Nation: A History of Germany, 1918–1990*. Oxford: Oxford University Press, 1992.

Gagliardo, John G. *Germany under the Old Regime, 1600–1790*. London: Longman, 1991.

Haffner, Sebastian. *The Rise and Fall of Prussia*. London: Weidenfeld and Nicolson, 1980.

Hamerow, Theodore S. *Restoration, Revolution, Reaction: Economics and Politics in Germany, 1815–1871*. Princeton, N.J.: Princeton University Press, 1958.

Hoffmeister, Gerhart, and Frederic C. Tubach. *Germany: 2000 Years*. New York: Ungar, 1986.

Holborn, Hajo. *A History of Modern Germany.* 3 vols. New York: Knopf, 1959–1969.

Hughes, Michael. *Early Modern Germany, 1477–1806.* Philadelphia: University of Pennsylvania Press, 1992.

Ingrao, Charles. *The Habsburg Monarchy, 1618–1815.* Cambridge: Cambridge University Press, 1994.

Jelavich, Barbara. *Modern Austria: Empire and Republic, 1815–1986.* New York: Cambridge University Press, 1987.

Kann, Robert A. *A History of the Habsburg Empire, 1526–1918.* Berkeley: University of California Press, 1974.

Kitchen, Martin. *The Cambridge Illustrated History of Germany.* Cambridge: Cambridge University Press, 1996.

———. *A History of Modern Germany, 1800–2000.* Malden, Mass.: Blackwell, 2006.

Orlow, Dietrich. *A History of Modern Germany: 1871 to Present.* 3d ed. Englewood Cliffs, N.J.: Prentice Hall, 1995.

Ozment, Steven. *A Mighty Fortress: A New History of the German People.* New York: HarperCollins, 2004.

Ramm, Agatha. *Germany, 1789–1919: A Political History.* London: Methuen, 1981.

Rosenberg, Hans. *Bureaucracy, Aristocracy, and Autocracy: The Prussian Experience, 1660–1815.* Cambridge, Mass.: Harvard University Press, 1958.

Schulze, Hagen. *Germany: A New History.* Translated by Deborah Lucas Schneider. Cambridge, Mass.: Harvard University Press, 1998.

Sheehan, James J. *German History, 1770–1866.* New York: Oxford University Press, 1989.

Snyder, Louis L. *Documents of German History.* New Brunswick, N.J.: Rutgers University Press, 1958.

Taylor, A. J. P. *The Struggle for Mastery in Europe, 1848–1918.* New York: Oxford University Press, 1974.

Turk, Eleanor L. *The History of Germany.* Westport, Conn.: Greenwood Press, 1999.

Wende, Peter. *A History of Germany.* New York: Palgrave Macmillan, 2005.

Wilson, Peter. *From Reich to Revolution: German History, 1558–1806.* Houndsmill, Basingstoke, U.K.: Palgrave Macmillan, 2004.

Prehistoric Germany

Biel, Jörg, Peter Frankenstein, and Jörg Jordan. *Der Keltenfürst von Hochdorf.* Stuttgart: K. Theiss, 1985.

James, Simon. *The World of the Celts*. London and New York: Thames and Hudson, 1993.

Jordan, Paul. *Neanderthal: Neanderthal Man and the Story of Human Origins*. Phoenix Mill, U.K.: Sutton, 2001.

Orschiedt, Jörg, and Gerd-Christian Weniger. *Neanderthals and Modern Humans: Discussing the Transition: Central and Eastern Europe from 50,000–30,000 B.P.* Mettmann, Germany: Neanderthal Museum, 2000.

Germania: Barbarian Germany

Carroll, Maureen. *Romans, Celts, and Germans: The German Provinces of Rome*. Stroud, U.K.: Tempus, 2001.

Creighton, John, Roger John Anthony Wilson, and Dirk Krausse. *Roman Germany: Studies in Cultural Interaction*. International Roman Archaeology Series, no. 32. Portsmouth, R.I.: Journal of Roman Archaeology, 1999.

Geary, Patrick J. *Before France and Germany: The Creation and Transformation of the Merovingian World*. New York: Oxford University Press, 1988.

Luttwak, Edward N. *The Grand Strategy of the Roman Empire from the First Century A.D. to the Third*. Baltimore: Johns Hopkins University Press, 1976.

Murdoch, Brian, and Malcolm K. Read. *Early Germanic Literature and Culture*. Rochester, N.Y.: Camden House, 2004.

Schutz, Herbert. *The Germanic Realms in Pre-Carolingian Central Europe, 400–750*. New York: P. Lang, 2000.

Tacitus. *Germania*. Translated by J. B. Rives. Oxford and New York: Oxford University Press, 1999.

Medieval Germany

Abulafia, David. *Frederick II: A Medieval Emperor*. London: Penguin Press, 1988.

Arnold, Benjamin. *Medieval Germany, 500–1300: A Political Interpretation*. Toronto and Buffalo, N.Y.: University of Toronto Press, 1997.

Blumenthal, Uta-Renata. *The Investiture Controversy: Church and Monarchy from the Ninth to the Twelfth Century*. Philadelphia: University of Pennsylvania Press, 1988.

Du Boulay, F. R. H. *Germany in the Later Middle Ages*. New York: St. Martin's Press, 1983.

Duckett, Eleanor S. *Carolingian Portraits: A Study in the Ninth Century*. Ann Arbor: University of Michigan Press, 1962.

Einhard and Notker the Stammerer. *Two Lives of Charlemagne.* Translated by Lewis Thorpe. Baltimore: Penguin Books, 1969.

Fuhrmann, Horst. *Germany in the High Middle Ages, ca. 1050–1200.* 2d ed. Cambridge: Cambridge University Press, 1995.

Innes, Matthew. *An Introduction to Early Medieval Western Europe, 300–900: The Sword, the Plough, and the Book.* London: Routledge, 2007.

Kantorowicz, Ernst Hartwig. *Frederick the Second, 1194–1250.* New York: F. Ungar, 1957.

Leyser, Karl. *Communications and Power in Medieval Europe: The Carolingian and Ottonian Centuries.* Edited by Timothy Reuter. London and Rio Grande, Ohio: Hambledon Press, 1994.

Otto I, Bishop of Freising. *The Deeds of Frederick Barbarossa.* Translated by Charles Christopher Mierow. New York: Columbia University Press, 2004.

Munz, Peter. *Frederick Barbarossa: A Study in Medieval Politics.* Ithaca, N.Y.: Cornell University Press, 1969.

Reformation Germany

Blickle, Peter. *Communal Reformation: The Quest for Salvation in Sixteenth-Century Germany.* Atlantic Highlands, N.J.: Humanities Press, 1992.

Brady, Thomas A., Jr. *German Histories in the Age of Reformations, 1400–1650.* Cambridge and New York: Cambridge University Press, 2009.

Dixon, C. Scott. *The Reformation in Germany.* Oxford and Malden, Mass.: Blackwell, 2002.

Füssel, Stephan. *Gutenburg and the Impact of Printing.* Aldershot, Hampshire, and Burlington, Vt.: Ashgate, 2005.

Moeller, Bernd. *Imperial Cities and the Reformation.* Translated by H. C. Erik Midelfort and Mark U. Edwards, Jr. Philadelphia: Fortress Press, 1972.

Oberman, Heiko Augustinus. *Luther: Man between God and the Devil.* New Haven, Conn.: Yale University Press, 1989.

Roper, Lyndal. *The Holy Household: Women and Morals in Reformation Augsburg.* Oxford and New York: Oxford University Press, 1989.

Tracy, James D. *Erasmus of the Low Countries.* Berkeley: University of California Press, 1996.

Confessional Germany and the Thirty Years' War

Asch, Ronald G. *The Thirty Years' War: The Holy Roman Empire and Europe, 1618–48.* New York: St. Martin's Press, 1997.

Forster, Marc R. *The Counter-Reformation in the Villages: Religion and Reform in the Bishopric of Speyer, 1560–1720.* Ithaca, N.Y.: Cornell University Press, 1992.

Karant-Nunn, Susan C. *The Reformation of Ritual: An Interpretation of Early Modern Germany.* London and New York: Routledge, 1997.

Parker, Geoffrey, and Simon Adams. *The Thirty Years' War.* 2d ed. London and New York: Routledge, 1997.

Sabean, David Warren. *Power in the Blood: Popular Culture and Village Discourse in Early Modern Germany.* Cambridge: Cambridge University Press, 1984.

Soergel, Philip M. *Wondrous in His Saints: Counter-Reformation Propaganda in Bavaria.* Berkeley: University of California Press, 1993.

Vann, James Allen. *The Making of a State: Württemberg, 1593–1793.* Ithaca, N.Y.: Cornell University Press, 1984.

Absolutism and Enlightenment

Beiser, Frederick C. *Enlightenment, Revolution, and Romanticism: The Genesis of Modern German Political Thought, 1790–1800.* Cambridge, Mass.: Harvard University Press, 1992.

Blanning, T. C. W. *Joseph II and Enlightened Despotism.* New York: Harper & Row, 1970.

Browning, Reed. *The War of the Austrian Succession.* New York: St. Martin's Press, 1993.

Clark, Christopher M. *Iron Kingdom: The Rise and Downfall of Prussia, 1600–1947.* Cambridge, Mass.: Belknap Press of Harvard University, 2006.

Duffy, Christopher. *The Military Life of Frederick the Great.* New York: Atheneum, 1986.

Reill, Hans Peter. *The German Enlightenment and the Rise of Historicism.* Berkeley: University of California Press, 1975.

Robisheaux, Thomas. *Rural Society and the Search for Order in Early Modern Germany.* Cambridge: Cambridge University Press, 1989.

Sorkin, David Jan. *Moses Mendelssohn and the Religious Enlightenment.* Berkeley: University of California Press, 1996.

Vierhaus, Rudolf. *Germany in the Age of Absolutism.* Cambridge and New York: Cambridge University Press, 1988.

Napoleonic Germany and the Revolution of 1848

Blanning, T. C. W. *The French Revolution in Germany: Occupation and Resistance in the Rhineland, 1792–1802.* Oxford: Clarendon Press, 1983.

Eyck, Frank. *The Frankfurt Parliament, 1848–1849.* New York: St. Martin's, 1968.

Randers-Pehrson, Justine Davis. *Germans and the Revolution of 1848–1849.* New York: P. Lang, 1999.

Seward, Desmond. *Metternich: The First European.* New York: Viking, 1991.

Sperber, Jonathan. *Rhineland Radicals: The Democratic Movement and the Revolution of 1848–1849.* Princeton, N.J.: Princeton University Press, 1991.

Walker, Mack, ed. *Metternich's Europe.* New York: Harper & Row, 1968.

Unification and Empire

Berghahn, Volker Rolf. *Imperial Germany, 1871–1914: Economy, Society, Culture, and Politics.* Providence, R.I.: Berghahn Books, 1994.

Blackbourn, David. *The Long Nineteenth Century: A History of Germany, 1780–1918.* New York: Oxford University Press, 1998.

Chickering, Roger. *Imperial Germany: Historiographical Companion.* Westport, Conn.: Greenwood Press, 1996.

Eley, Geoff. *Society, Culture, and the State in Germany, 1870–1930.* Ann Arbor: University of Michigan Press, 1996.

Friedrichsmeyer, Sara, Sara Lennox, and Susanne Zantop. *The Imperialist Imagination: German Colonialism and Its Legacy.* Ann Arbor: University of Michigan Press, 1998.

Henderson, William O. *The Rise of German Industrial Power, 1834–1914.* Berkeley and Los Angeles: University of California Press, 1975.

Kent, George. *Bismarck and His Times.* Carbondale and Edwardsville: Southern Illinois University Press, 1978.

Maehl, William Harvey. *August Bebel: Shadow Emperor of the German Workers.* Philadelphia: American Philosophical Society, 1980.

Mommsen, Wolfgang J. *Imperial Germany, 1867–1918: Politics, Culture, and Society in an Authoritarian State.* London: Arnold, 1995.

Pflanze, Otto. *Bismarck and the Development of Germany.* 3 vols. 2d ed. Princeton, N.J.: Princeton University Press, 1990.

Röhl, John. *The Kaiser and His Court: Wilhelm II and the Government of Germany.* Cambridge and New York: Cambridge University Press, 1994.

Schulze, Hagen. *The Course of German Nationalism: From Frederick the Great to Bismarck, 1763–1867.* 2d ed. Cambridge and New York: Cambridge University Press, 1991.

Sheehan, James J. *German Liberalism in the Nineteenth Century.* Chicago: University of Chicago Press, 1978.

Simpson, William. *The Second Reich: Germany, 1871–1918.* Cambridge and New York: Cambridge University Press, 1995.

Smith, Woodruff D. *The German Colonial Empire.* Chapel Hill: University of North Carolina Press, 1978.

Stern, Fritz. *Gold and Iron: Bismarck, Bleichröder, and the Building of the German Empire.* New York: Knopf, 1977.

The Great War and Weimar Germany

Breitman, Richard. *German Socialism and Weimar Democracy.* Chapel Hill: University of North Carolina Press, 1981.

Evans, Richard J. *The Coming of the Third Reich.* New York: Penguin Press, 2004.

Gay, Peter. *Weimar Culture: The Outsider as Insider.* New York: Harper and Row, 1968.

Heiber, Helmut. *The Weimar Republic.* Oxford and Cambridge, Mass.: Blackwell, 1993.

Joll, James. *The Origins of the First World War.* New York: Longman, 1984.

Kolb, Eberhard. *The Weimar Republic.* London and Boston: Unwin Hyman, 1988.

Laqueur, Walter. *Weimar: A Cultural History, 1918–1933.* New York: Putnam, 1980.

Mosse, George L. *The Crisis of German Ideology: Intellectual Origins of the Third Reich.* New York: Grosset & Dunlap, 1964.

Peukert, Detlev J. K. *The Weimar Republic: The Crisis of Classical Modernity.* New York: Hill & Wang, 1993.

Nazism and World War II

Bracher, Karl Dietrich. *The German Dictatorship: The Origins, Structure, and Effects of National Socialism.* New York: Praeger, 1970.

Browning, Christopher R. *Ordinary Men: Reserve Police Battalion 101 and the Final Solution in Poland.* New York: HarperCollins, 1992.

Evans, Richard J. *The Third Reich in Power, 1933–1939.* New York: Penguin Press, 2005.

Fischer, Klaus P. *Nazi Germany: A New History.* New York: Continuum, 1995.

Friedländer, Saul. *The Years of Extermination: Nazi Germany and the Jews, 1939–1945.* New York: HarperCollins Publishers, 2007.

Haffner, Sebastian. *The Meaning of Hitler.* Cambridge, Mass.: Harvard University Press, 1983.

Hilberg, Raul. *The Destruction of the European Jews.* 3 vols. New York: Holmes and Meier, 1985.

Hoffmann, Peter. *German Resistance to Hitler.* Cambridge, Mass.: Harvard University Press, 1988.

Stern, Fritz. *Dreams and Delusions: National Socialism and the Drama of the German Past.* New York: Vintage, 1989.

Trevor-Roper, Hugh R. *The Last Days of Hitler.* Chicago: University of Chicago Press, 1992.

Turner, Henry Ashby, Jr. *German Big Business and the Rise of Hitler.* New York: Oxford University Press, 1985.

Watt, Donald Cameron. *How War Came: The Immediate Origins of the Second World War, 1938–1939.* New York: Pantheon Books, 1989.

Weinberg, Gerhard L. *Germany, Hitler, and World War II: Essays in Modern German and World History.* Cambridge: Cambridge University Press, 1995.

———. *A World at Arms: A Global History of World War II.* Cambridge: Cambridge University Press, 1994.

The Cold War: Division and Reunification

Carr, Jonathan. *Helmut Schmidt: Helmsman of Germany.* New York: St. Martin's, 1985.

Fulbrook, Mary. *Anatomy of a Dictatorship: Inside the GDR, 1949–1989.* Oxford: Oxford University Press, 1995.

Griffith, William E. *The Ostpolitik of the Federal Republic of Germany.* Cambridge, Mass.: MIT Press, 1978.

Jarausch, Konrad H. *The Rush to German Unity.* New York and Oxford: Oxford University Press, 1994.

Joppke, Christian. *East German Dissidents and the Revolution of 1989: Social Movement in a Leninist Régime.* New York: New York University Press, 1995.

Keithly, David M. *The Collapse of East German Communism: The Year the Wall Came Down, 1989.* Westport, Conn.: Praeger, 1992.

Lippmann, Heinz. *Honecker and the New Politics of Europe.* Translated by Helen Sebba. New York: Macmillan, 1972.

Maier, Charles S. *Dissolution: The Crisis of Communism and the End of East Germany.* Princeton, N.J.: Princeton University Press, 1997.

———. *The Unmasterable Past: History, Holocaust, and German National Identity.* Cambridge, Mass.: Harvard University Press, 1988.

McAdams, A. James. *Germany Divided: From the Wall to Reunification.* Princeton, N.J.: Princeton University Press, 1993.

McCauley, Martin. *The German Democratic Republic since 1945.* London: Macmillan, 1983.

Merkl, Peter H. *German Unification in the European Context.* University Park: Pennsylvania State University Press, 1993.

Prittie, Terence. *The Velvet Chancellors: A History of Post-War Germany.* London: Frederick Muller, 1979.

Shumaker, David H. *Gorbachev and the German Question: Soviet-West German Relations, 1985–1990.* Westport, Conn.: Praeger, 1995.

Smith, Bradley F. *The Road to Nuremberg.* New York: Basic Books, 1981.

Stern, Carola. *Ulbricht: A Political Biography.* Translated by Abe Farbstein. New York: Praeger, 1965.

Turner, Henry Ashby, Jr. *Germany from Partition to Reunification.* New Haven, Conn.: Yale University Press, 1992.

———. *The Two Germanies since 1945.* New Haven, Conn.: Yale University Press, 1987.

Contemporary Germany

Art, David. *The Politics of the Nazi Past in Germany and Austria.* Cambridge: Cambridge University Press, 2006.

Balfour, Michael. *Germany: The Tides of Power.* London: Routledge, 1992.

Conradt, David P. *The German Polity.* 5th ed. New York and London: Longman, 1993.

Dennis, Mike, and Eva Kolinsky, eds. *United and Divided: Germany Since 1990.* New York: Berghahn Books, 2004.

Glees, Anthony. *Reinventing Germany: German Political Development since 1945.* Oxford and Washington, D.C.: Berg, 1996.

Haussmann, Helmut, and Hermann Horstkotte, eds. *Europe Acquires New Dimensions: From Economic Community to European Union.* Bonn, Germany: Inter Nationes, 1997.

Jones, Alun. *The New Germany: A Human Geography.* Chichester and New York: John Wiley, 1994.

Lewis, Rand C. *The Neo-Nazis and German Unification.* Westport, Conn.: Praeger, 1996.

Marsh, David. *The Germans: A People at the Crossroads.* New York: St. Martin's, 1990.

———. *Germany and Europe: The Crisis of Unity.* 2d ed. London: Mandarin, 1995.

Pulzer, Peter. *German Politics, 1945–1995.* Oxford: Oxford University Press, 1995.

Smyser, W. R. *The German Economy: Colossus at the Crossroads.* 2d ed. New York: St. Martin's, 1993.

Watts, Meredith W. *Xenophobia in United Germany: Generations, Modernization, and Ideology.* New York: St. Martin's, 1997.

INDEX

Note: **Boldface** page numbers indicate primary discussion of a topic. Page numbers in *italic* indicate illustrations. The letters *c* and *m* indicate chronology and maps, respectively.